DOUGLAS N. MORGAN, Professor of Philosophy at The University of Texas, taught until 1960 at Northwestern University, where the ideas in this book were first presented. He has also taught at Illinois and at Michigan. Dr. Morgan has written in theory of art and art criticism, and in political theory. Lecturing widely in universities, he was Gillespie Lecturer at Chatham College during 1963.

L O V E

PLATO, THE BIBLE AND FREUD

LOVE

PLATO, THE BIBLE AND FREUD

Douglas N. Morgan

Prentice-Hall, Inc. A SPECTRUM BOOK *Englewood Cliffs, N.J.*

PREFACE

To his own professors, his colleagues and his students, every teacher owes inexpressible debts. The ideas in this book were first presented many years ago in Northwestern's University College; they have been set down at the original suggestion of my friend Professor William A. Earle of Northwestern University, and with the encouraging guidance of Prentice-Hall's personnel. Mrs. Faye Oatman and many others have helped importantly in editing and typing.

Permission to use copyrighted materials has been kindly granted by Ernest Benn, Ltd.; by George Allen & Unwin, Ltd.; by Routledge and Kegan Paul, Ltd.; by W. W. Norton & Co.; by Liveright, Publishers, N.Y.; and by Basic Books, Inc. *Judaism* originally published the discussion of Old Testament love, and I am grateful for the permission of the editors and The American Jewish Congress to reproduce it here.

For patient love and support, to my father, Neil H. Morgan of Clearwater Beach, Florida, to my wife's mother, Mrs. Ella Okerwall, to her daughter Greta and to my daughters Caroline and Merry, go loving gratitude.

D. N. M.

CONTENTS

II

BIBLICAL LOVE, 47

III

FREUDIAN LOVE, 129

L O V E

PLATO, THE BIBLE AND FREUD

INTRODUCTION

LOVE MAKES A DIFFERENCE IN HUMAN EXPERIENCE MORE PROFOUND THAN
any other truth about us. Life without love too often is vacuous. Our
spoken moral convictions and our unspoken metaphysical commitments
are deeply directed and stained, beautifully or hideously, by the ways
in which we love. We are what we are, and become what we become,
only as we love. It is out of these convictions that this book is written.

You will find in this book other convictions, too. Maudlin love—which
is ignorant, misdirected, and undisciplined love—is the vulgar root of
much personal and social disease. When sentimentality replaces senti-
ment, muddleheadedness replaces reason and we wallow. Much or even
most of what has been popularly written about love is nonsense. Finally,
a basic condition for genuine love is a desperate honesty with ourselves,
which is all but impossible to attain.

In a manner of speaking, this book is for beginners; certainly no reader
is presumed to bring to his reading any breadth or depth of philosophical
or psychological knowledge. Yet no one able to read this book is altogether a beginner, either, for he will certainly have loved, and almost
certainly he will have been beloved. Primarily, this book is for those
who, like its author, are puzzled by love. Here, for a first example, is a
puzzle.

Love is, among many other things, a fact. The simplest thing we can
say about love is that some occasions of physical sexuality are expressions
of it. But every eating of breakfast food might be said with hardly more
justification to be an expression of physical hunger, and every drinking
of water an expression of thirst, and every breath we draw an expression

of our need for air. If love's expression can be compared with these expressions of other needs, how then can we explain the importance men assign to love? Physiologically, we know that air and water and food and rest are essential to the survival of organisms like our bodies, while overt sexuality is not. But fully human men do not seriously and extensively dedicate themselves to breathing and drinking and eating and resting, any more than to trivial sexuality. Unless they frame their other needs within a context of love, and perhaps build a beautiful religious citadel around them, men at their most human do not talk or think or dance or sing or paint their bodily hungers or thirsts. Why all the bother about love? Why do we human beings single it out for the special attention of our painters and poets, our philosophers and religious teachers and psychologists?

Our first suspicion, naturally and properly, is of ourselves. Perhaps, we may sensibly suppose, we in this transient cultural moment disproportionately exalt to a place of nearly supreme importance what is really a simple natural phenomenon. Perhaps we can write off our concern for love as a romantic, unhealthy addiction, a passing foolishness to be outgrown in a wiser stage of cultural maturity.

But history shows us other ages no less absurd than our own in this singular addiction. A write-off of love would wrench out of every culture altogether too much that makes the deepest difference to man: too much beauty and too much ugliness, too much good and too much evil. A human culture without love, like a culture without religion or language or art, would really be no culture at all. Nowhere and never do men live, work, and play together over any period of time wholly without love.

How and why men have tried to understand the dimensions of love are matters for philosophy, in the broadest sense of that currently dishonored term. In this broadest sense, philosophy just means sense-making, or the analysis and assignment of meanings: the tracing out of presuppositions and implications, the unraveling of the logic of language, the construction of concepts. Traditionally, a philosopher of love tries to reduce the chaos of talk and feeling about love to some kind of cosmos of understanding: to trace out metaphysical and moral dimensions, to plot and map a human, infra-human and super-human economy of love.

I have chosen the Platonic, the Christian, and the Freudian interpretations for our study because these are among the basic, comprehensive positions that have, without our willing and often without our even knowing it, most deeply shaped our minds, and because in each of these ways of understanding man in his world, love is central. Platonically, the world would never have come into being except for love, and except for love, our world would now be no more than static, nonmoral nonsense.

As Jews and Christians, we are fully men only as we reflect God's love by loving our God and our fellow men. Psychoanalytically, we live in health only as we can love, and thereby work, in health.

To the Platonic scholar, my presentation of Plato's philosophy will inevitably seem loose and inconclusive; the strokes with which I sketch it seem far too broad even to me, and certainly they are broad enough to blur the fine points of subtle textual interpretation on which I, in any case, am incompetent to speak, since I do not even read Greek with ease. However much I must omit, and however broad my brushwork, I hope not to have said anything explicitly false or extravagantly misleading about Plato's thought.

Hebrew-Christian believers or scholars (or both, for these, despite occasional appearances, are not really exclusive designations) will certainly find my interpretations of love in our major Western religious traditions warped. There is, as everyone knows, no such thing as *a* Jewish or *a* Christian conception of love; I take some small spiritual comfort in the intellectually unhappy fact that there are so many Jewish and Christian persuasions that one can hardly ever say anything demonstrably outside every one. I cannot read Hebrew at all, and claim no extensive knowledge of theology. I do not defend any one creed or dogma; instead I candidly and respectfully select from the vast riches spread before us those Hebrew and Christian interpretations that, from my own limited, partial, and ignorant point of view, seem most interesting and most revelatory of our common human predicament.

To the professional Freudian, my observations may seem shallow, impertinent, and, from one aspect or another, seriously askew. This again I take to be inevitable, since psychoanalysis, like Christianity, has become so generously variant that, while one can easily remain vulnerable to attack from every quarter, one can hardly be accused of total infidelity to every Freudian and post-Freudian teaching.

For the dreary conventional borderlines between subject matters—this is philosophy, that is psychology, and that over there is literary history —I have no respect at all, and suffer no pangs of conscience for my trespasses.

It is finally in order here to disavow any intention of expounding the "real meaning" or the "essence" of love. There is no such thing. *Love* is, as the currently fashionable phrase has it, an "open" concept. If we are to be satisfied only with a unique, universally applicable, all-time definition of "love," we may as well not even enter upon our adventure. Interesting words don't usually work in ways that permit such precision. We are wiser to ask instead, "Under what conditions do we decide to describe a phenomenon by using the word 'love'?"

But this cautious counsel need by no means disbar us from the Platonic,

Biblical, or Freudian courts. For the insights in these traditions, however unhappily put for contemporary purposes, remain rich and rewarding. I am not interested in accusing Plato of the crime of "essentialism," because I am too much concerned to see whatever "family resemblances" he, by using his own beautiful language, can bring out. And so with our brothers in Hebrew-Christianity and psychoanalysis—how they talk is not, for present purposes, nearly so important as what they say. I am convinced that they say a very great deal, and that we stand to learn from what they say.

Here, then, we together meet three comparable but deeply different ways of conceiving our world. As we ask of Plato, of the Bible and of Freud, so we shall also ask of ourselves, these perennially puzzling questions: Who are we who love? Whom are we to love? Why do we love? What do we love? What does love mean—and how does love mean—in the lives we lead?

I

P L A T O N I C L O V E

BEFORE PLATO, NO CONCEPTION OF LOVE HAD EVER BEEN EVEN REMOTELY adequate to the depth and scope of human love. Since then, every philosopher and psychologist of love—and, indeed, every thoughtful human —has been in Plato's debt.

Platonic love is not what most people think it is. It is not a cold and sexless friendship, or a dreamy, rococo thinking of beautiful thoughts together. It is not inhibited chivalric sentimentality, nor is it an adolescent device for concealing gonadal agitation. Nor, finally, is it (in the neoclassical metaphor of Dorothy Parker) "the gun you didn't know was loaded." Platonic love is a disciplined, passionate commitment to all that is good and true and beautiful, and through these things, to the Goodness, Truth, and Beauty that make them so.

As a psychological genius, Plato was both sensitive and tough-minded. As a hard-boiled moralist, his mind was disciplined. As a poet, he sought vivid clarity of thought, feeling, and expression. As a philosopher, he dared to triangulate the universe.

Again and again throughout these writings (we shall not try to filter out Socratic from Platonic teachings, since our main interest is not historical) Socrates' and Plato's minds keep returning to love: wondering about it, marveling at it, building a myth or breaking one, puzzling how and why love should be as rich and all-embracing as it is.

In a word, Platonic love is motivation, but this word takes its meaning and color only within the architecture of Plato's entire thought, and we must at least survey that architecture in order to find love's place in it.

Yet there really is no Platonic "architecture" to study, for (as I read him; the issue has long been disputed among philosophers) Plato was not a system-builder in the Teutonic manner. He was rather, through and through, a level-headed Golden Greek, looking with clear and steady eyes at the ugliness and agony around him, calmly analyzing meanings and tracing implications. Profoundly discontented with every partial answer, he honestly tried to think things through.

PLATONIC DIALECTIC

His name for thinking things through was "dialectic," which is far closer to our "dialogue" than to the current post-Marxist misuse. By dialectic Plato meant a process of sustained intellectual analysis, a comparative, dynamic judgment-procedure exhibited in serious discourse at its best. An idea is taken by Plato as a point of departure for subsequent probing and intellectual experimentation.

The dialogue form in which Plato cast his writings became a superficial literary form only late in his life. Typically and at its healthiest, the dialogue does far more than merely entertain us, or keep our interests alive, as we follow conceptual complexities. It illustrates the very way we think when we think wisely and consecutively about humane and important issues.

In a dialogue we deliberate, going down tempting byways only to find them blind, returning to what we believe to be the main road only to discover a complex intersection, with no signs to direct us irresistibly toward any destination. Not that we really can or should, while we are deliberating, specify our destination; a key to the adventure is that we cannot do so. We are thinking-walking-talking along together, each of us exploring as much on behalf of the other as of himself. Each partial discovery along the way may be a clue, suggesting that this, rather than that, might lead to further clues.

Most frustrating of all, we may have to abandon the search. At the end of a Socratic dialogue the Sophist (or "wise man") whose views have been subjected to Socrates' pungent dissection often proves not nearly so much a wise man as a wise guy. His pomposity has been punctured, and his once persuasive arguments are now a shambles of self-contradictions.

"What," we very naturally demand, "*is* the answer? What *ought* the Sophist to have said when Socrates asked him what *good* means? What is Socrates' own belief? Where *is* the truth?" Sometimes we discover the explicit answer we seek; more often, we do not.

Yet usually, our answer lies there before us, waiting to be discovered. Typically, it is a higher-order answer. It teaches not really that this or that specific conceptual combination will open the safe and reveal the treasure. Instead, it teaches a more difficult lesson: that the very process of comparing combinations and of doing the intellectual work of discovering is itself the life of philosophy . . . that the ability to envisage alternatives and to deliberate judiciously among them is the stuff of the philosophical adventure. Plato's philosophy is misconstrued when we ask of it, "What are the answers to these explicit questions?" It is better understood when we ask, "How can I think for myself, analyze for myself, compare for myself alternative positions? What kinds of sense can I here take seriously? How can my mind grow?"

It is thus that I understand the Platonic dialectic: as the interchange of ideas among minds or within one mind, the ideas themselves (to invent a Platonic analogy) functioning as prisms. When each is turned to a fresh light, new radiance breaks out, shattering the easy, automatic pattern of expectation aroused by the previous idea; each new prism is clear and brilliant in its own right and light, and each sets new complex problems to be explored by the philosophical mind. We should not expect crystalline finality at any stage of the analysis, but rather relatively clearer, more nearly adequate, wider encompassing scope at every level.

However, Plato is not—as he has been taken to be—a nineteenth century Romantic. There is no muddy Goethean *ewig Weibliche* or "ever onward and upward" in the clear mind of Aristotle's teacher. There is, to be sure, a central dynamic of progress and growth and improvement; those who would paralyze Plato's philosophy into a monolithic and misunderstood "classicism" simply have not read him, and do not understand Greece. But this progress is thoroughly goal-oriented—not merely a going-somewhere-or-other-for-the-sake-of-going, but rather a going-where-we-belong, a going-where-we-ought-to-be. In short, Plato's progress is pointed, not aimless. Its point is perfection, nothing less. What lesser point could progress ever honestly have, and still make sense?

In the instrumental-utilitarian democracies of our present day, "progress" is a bravo-word and "goodness" is a boo-word. We suppose that we can intelligibly strive to make ourselves and our society better and better every day in every way, but we have no notion of what "better" could really mean; we evaporate any real meaning from the word by treating it as synonymous with "more comfortable" or "more luxurious," and then flaccidly refuse to face the Socratic-Platonic questions, "But is comfort good?" "Is luxury good?".

Plato faced questions like these. His traditions, like our own, were meeting corrosive challenges in such sophisticated questions as, "But moral principles are learned culturally. Are they not therefore merely customs or habits of social behavior, with no generally binding power?" and "But other peoples worship different gods and embody in their behavior different codes. Aren't your gods and codes therefore only idiosyncratic and local?"

But Plato had the courage to give the lie to specious arguments, and the dialectical skill to show them specious. He could and did argue that the fact that values are learned no more proves them false than the fact that mathematical truths are learned proves arithmetic false. He claimed that cultural differences in values prove no more than do cultural differences in scientific beliefs; one culture's beliefs may be more nearly correct in one field, another's in another, and differences are nothing to the point.

But his arguments, almost all the while, were dialectical rather than dogmatic. He usually did not preach, trying to persuade rhetorically. Instead, he liked to invite us to think things through for ourselves, to discover for ourselves the absurdities to which undisciplined opinion leads us, and to open up for our enlightened vision the ultimately unspeakable truth.

THE METAPHYSICAL-MORAL MILIEU

Suppose that we use the word "metaphysics" to mean simply a set of fairly general ordering categories or principles, within which whatever we know and believe, whatever we want and hope for and fear and love, can find some plausible sort of resting place for thought. "Plato's metaphysics" then will be taken to mean not any mechanical framework at all, but simply some comprehensive ways of conceiving what actually happens and what might possibly happen and, above all, what ought to happen.

Such ways were far from new, even in Plato's day. His two greatest teachers had already framed the universe in contradictory ways. Each of these ways had some plausibility and seemed to Plato to account admirably for certain aspects of the world. Yet neither could consistently account for those aspects that fit most neatly into the interpretation of the other.

One teacher, Parmenides, had been most deeply impressed by the inherent stability and continuity of the universe. However things may seem to us to change, they *are*. They continue to *be,* even when (apparently) transformed. Insofar as we know anything, we have pierced the deceptive veil of specious change, and struck home to a bedrock of being —to what genuinely and essentially *is* . . . for this is the very condition of truth itself, and hence of knowledge.

The structure of this bedrock of being, like the structure of a salt crystal or of a melting snowflake, is itself changeless: it is basically mathematical. Shapes and numbers are what they exactly and clearly are, eternally and changelessly. The cube has six faces and twelve edges, forever and ever—not a cube of this, or a cube of that, but the cube in and altogether of itself. Nothing any man can ever do or say or think can alter that cube.

This is not to deny the appearance of changes in all that is. It is merely to emphasize that whatever really is remains, and that the change we think we see and hear and feel is the sheerest of deception, as thin as the wind. The substance of knowledge and therefore of being, as Parmenides and his disciple Zeno taught, must of course be thinkable, and being thinkable, must be free from self-contradiction. But (as the famous paradoxes were intended to prove) we cannot consistently think about motion, or change of any kind, or their necessary condition, time; once we try to do so, we find ourselves inextricably entangled. For consistent thought and consistent understanding, there must be an underlying, stable unity essential to the universe, else the whole show evaporates before our bewildered eyes.

Conversely, and indeed contradictorily, Heraclitus and his disciples had embraced the vivid givenness of change as itself central in experience and essential in being. The one most general truth that can be held of everything we know or can conceive is simply this: It changes. Whatever "it" may be, it comes into being, endures a while as it changes, and passes away. Of living things, this is only too evidently true. But so also of the rocks being gradually worn away by the rushing, flowing river into which we not only cannot step twice, but not even once . . . for it is constantly rushing past us all the while. Life and death, things and ideas, are all like a fire kindling, blazing up, and dying away to embers and ultimate extinction.

This is not of course to deny that there seem to be permanencies in our changing world. Mathematical truths do indeed seem to have some enduring status. But (we are still with the Heracliteans) these very permanencies themselves are but relatively longer lived flowings and fluxions; they are the great, slow-moving rivers, in contrast to the rushing brooks of evidently transient experience. Yet rivers that flow slowly flow nonetheless, and literally nowhere shall we ever find the changelessness the Parmenideans sought in vain.

Not immediately or self-consciously, like a beginner in philosophy trying to paste together categorical incompatibles in order to "preserve the best of both"; nor deductively, like a mathematician trying to resolve a ready-set and clearly formulated problem; but rather humanly and in a rich moral context, Plato felt the force of each of these alternatives and sought a way in which each could receive its due. The moral context provided an evident parallel and, in our oversimplified exposition, a crucial clue.

The Athenian moral tradition (even then ancient), like ours today, was supernatural, religious, spiritual, and universal: The gods who had made the universe remained its masters and, though themselves bound by inexorable laws, required and deserved sacrifices and enjoined man's obedience. Immorality on earth meant the violation of these eternal, divinely enforced rules that prescribe propriety of human behavior. To the man who, for example, overstepped his limits and pretended in his boundless curiosity to be a god and to know more than is meet for man to know, went the inevitable punishment he had by the very laws of the universe brought upon himself . . . and upon his descendants as well. A man belonged to his city, and a city to its gods, who could and justly did punish wrongdoing. Ultimately, doing right meant doing what nature and nature's gods prescribe for man, whether man likes it or not. Duty included right action: disciplined education, civic participation, military service as required. Moreover, for Athenian citizens (though not of course for the metic and slave majority), duty included self-development; the humane enjoyment of the beauty of proportions, of skill, of ornamentation; proper pride in a public speech well thought and spoken; athletic expression in the palaestra; and pious fulfillment of religious-civil obligations.

Then came the challenge of the itinerant tutorial Sophists, who dared to teach a skeptical sophistication. They knew, and taught, that Athens was not all the world, and that the ways of other cities could seem, each after its own fashion, to be as well justified and as universally binding as those of Athens. Even more subversively, these Sophists could take the working practices of the people as identical with the underlying morality, and subtly substitute for the traditional question, "What ought man to do?" the apparently more practical one, "How can a man succeed?" One has only to substitute "success in society" for "morality" and "persuasiveness" for "truth" in order to transform "education" into "vocational training," and the undermining of the Athenian moral foundations was nearly complete.

Socrates and Plato never did, so far as we know, worship in the literal Homeric-Hesiodic tradition. Long before their time, this tradition had become the "old-time religion," honored still in ritual but rationalized and adapted in intellect to the needs of civic and personal morality. It is a mistake to think of Plato's moral contribution as essentially a conservative reversion to an earlier, more "absolutistic" pre-Sophistical age. It is truer to conceive him as a man who felt the force both of the tradition and of its challenge, and who honestly sought a way to reconcile them and thereby to preserve the intrinsic order, clarity, and discipline of the tradition, while accounting for the indisputable varieties of practice. This reconciliation Plato was to achieve exactly as he was achieving the reconciliation of the contradictory metaphysical positions that tempted him. And these were, in his clear eyes, not two reconciliations, but one, for his was not (as we today pretend ours to be) an uneasily married double world of value and fact, only accidentally and casually impinging upon each other. Plato's world, as he thought it through, became one in which every fact, simply in being factual, was saturated with value, and every value, in being embraced and pursued, was a fundamental fact.

Roughly speaking, the Greek words for love echoed our own, and for all the disparities in the objects of love, and despite differences in love's practices—like the passing fashion of homosexuality among some Athenian citizens—the Greeks loved many of the same kinds of things we do, and in many of the same ways. They enjoyed their sexuality, with perhaps more healthy candor and less shame than we do. Many of them loved their families devotedly. They enjoyed good food and wine and sport. They loved good talk. Most of them loved their city with a civic fervor that makes our latter-day patriotism seem childish by comparison. The opulence of visual display, the exquisite vigor of noble poetry, the luxury of lovely music and the inspiration of the music of war, the robust fun and the imaginative religious morality of the theater, the human and more-than-human exaltation of ceremonial worship in the Parthenon . . . all these loves, together with that love of wisdom they called "philosophy," made the human Athenians as fully civilized as any men our earth has ever known.

Plato was an Athenian among Athenians, walking about among them, talking humanly with them day by day, exhibiting in his person some of their weaknesses as well as many of their strengths. Pre-eminently, he was a thinking student and teacher of the meanings of everything Athenians held dear. What they held dear, he reasoned, they loved. And so, as his mind probed toward a tentative reinterpretation of the metaphysical problem and of the moral problem—and these were one problem, remember, not two—the concept of love began to grow in scope, in complexity, and in profundity.

The fundamental bent of his mind was mathematical, and Plato had learned his Pythagorean lessons well. He knew not merely as a conventional postulate but as a self-evident axiom that numerical and geometrical relationships (and these, too, were identical, for numbers then were thought of as shapes, rather like the numbers on our dice) were in themselves wholly objective, perfectly independent of every merely human concern or decision. Language aside (for language can, as Plato knew painfully well, deceive us), a dyad and a triad must make a pentad —or ˙ and ˙˙ must make ˙˙˙ —or two and three must make five. And they must make five for any people anywhere and at any time.

Not that people never make mistakes; of course they do. Children daily total two and three to four or six. But in recognizing a mistake as a mistake, we are not merely expressing a transient opinion of our own; we are claiming that the way the world really is, the way numbers really are, makes utterly impossible the claim that two plus three equals four or six. A mistake accepted and believed is no less a mistake than a mistake recognized and corrected, and no more a reflection of any casual or "relative" opinion, for the mistake consists not in belief or in practice, but in being. Of course we could juggle language and assign the name "two" to the number four and then "correctly" claim that "two" plus three equals seven. But to do this would be no more than to play a children's game with words, for what we now call "two" would stand in exactly the same relation to "three" and "five" as it always has and always will.

Here, then, we surely have a check on the pulsing change of the Heraclitean world. However much our world may change, however many or few twos or threes or fives there may ever be in mere actuality, the objective numerical relationships must inevitably and changelessly remain exactly what they are.

Furthermore, our genuine knowledge of the world—or so it seemed to Plato, as it has to many a physicist, mathematician, and philosopher since his day—always emulates the clarity, universality, and specificity of mathematics. The more mature a science, the more nearly its theory approaches pure mathematical deduction. We may idly watch things change or seem to change, and merely drift in dreams. But when we begin to measure as we watch, we are doing science. We are seeking to render explicit a changeless and general formula, a precise pattern of rate and direction of change.

Numbers, then, and shapes and principles and formulas or laws or objective rules: these are. They do not become. Of them we can never sensibly ask, "When did they come to be what they are?" or "How long will they last?" because they are the very conditions of sense-making. Without their secure and steady sense, the world we think we know would dissolve before our blinded eyes into a sea of unreality. All the outlines of everything we think we understand would blur, and their logical links, one with another, would be irreparably broken. We couldn't experience any thing as a thing, because there wouldn't be any principle to make that thing the thing it is, and to enable us to distinguish it from any other thing. Since we couldn't know any thing, we couldn't know anything. Without a clear, objective structure of principles, our world would become meaningless, homogeneous soup—and not even knowable soup, at that.

Nowadays, we are likely to pride ourselves on our reverence for what we call facts, and naïvely to take "fact" in only its most superficial sense. We suppose that what happens to us here and now, in this precious but fleeting instant of the temporal process, is "factual," and that this moment and all other specific moments are somehow the models to which science and mathematics must confess some ultimate responsibility. We flatter ourselves that our own experiences of and in and with the world are what science is about.

We could not be more wrong. What we ought to realize, Plato would counsel us, is that insofar as science really is science or knowledge, it must transcend this idiosyncratic moment of our passing consciousness, and every other such moment of every other such consciousness as well. What merely happens is but an exhibition, a showing-forth of what really is; the instant is but an instance of the law. The chemist is not really interested in these few zinc chips and these few drops of sulfuric acid; after all, what sensible man would bother his head with them, if they were all there were to science? That these chips dissolve in this acid and give off this gas, simply is not the point of chemistry. Nor is the point of chemistry the discovery that some other zinc chips will similarly dissolve in some other sulfuric acid. The point rather is that it is in the nature of zinc and of sulfuric acid to react, under appropriate circumstances, as the equation specifies. Not this zinc or that, not this sulfuric acid or that, but simply zinc and sulfuric acid.

The pattern expressed in the equation that characterizes the reaction of zinc and sulfuric acid is itself invisible to the human eye. When we write $Zn + H_2SO_4 \rightarrow ZnSO_4 + H_2 \uparrow$ " or "$v = 1/2gt^2$" or "$e = mc^2$," we make marks on paper, to be sure, but the marks on our paper are not what we are really concerned to say. We see things falling, but no man has ever seen the law of gravitation according to which (in limited realms) things fall. We hear harmonies and disharmonies in music, but no man has ever heard the laws of counterpoint. We may burn our fingers in a fire, but no man's fingers have ever touched the laws of thermodynamics. In all his quest for knowledge, man necessarily goes beyond the sensibly given, the merely-is, to approach the intellectually understood, the must-be.

It is we, caught up as we are in a world of kaleidoscopic and confused sensation, who pretentiously assign superiority to what we miscall "fact" and what we erroneously think of as "real" physical objects. We pretend that what we can see is therefore "genuine," and we conclude by a miracle of illogic that what we cannot see must therefore be specious or insubstantial. Plato shows us that insofar as we really know anything at all, both our knowledge and its object are beyond mere sensation, more than merely physical or transitory.

Try, for instance, to think of knowledge as physical, and you quickly enough recognize the absurdity. Knowledge is clearly an affair of conception. As conceptual, it is always extra-sensory, and whether "extra-sensory perception" involves a logical contradiction or not, extra-sensory conception clearly does not. Nothing is more familiar than for two men to have descriptively indistinguishable visible, auditory, or tactual experiences, while only one of them knows anything about what he sees or hears or touches. A child no more knows astronomy when he peers through a great telescope than the janitor in the Louvre "knows" the Mona Lisa whom he sees every day. We must always go beyond our organs of sense to know anything at all; we must, as we naturally say, use our minds. We must use our intelligence. We must *con*ceive, instead of merely *per*ceiving. We must think and comprehend, instead of merely feeling and apprehending.

So, too, with every object of knowledge. What we know is known. What we perceive are merely more percepts. What we conceive are concepts. These cannot be physical or sensible objects. We need only ask ourselves how much space the number fourteen takes up, or how long identity lasts, or how soft the binomial theorem is, or how much a circle weighs, to see the absurdity in which we involve ourselves by trying to think mathematics in any remotest analogy with the helter-skelter chaos of sense experience. Mathematical objects are, one and all, utterly invisible, inaudible, "untouchable" in the purest possible way.

And what is true of mathematical objects, Plato thought and taught, must be true of every other object of any possible knowledge. It sounds strange to our deaf ears, no doubt, to learn that *lead* has no weight, since we know that lead has weight. What can it mean to say that the lead we know is weightless and invisible like mathematical objects, while the lead we lift and put into the beaker has weight and can easily be seen?

Our chemical symbols can guide us in understanding this. Pb, after all (what it stands for, not the mark of ink) is weightless and invisible. And the heavy, visible lead chips are, for all science's interest—and for all possibility of knowledge—but an instance of Pb, an example, to coin an ugly word, of "plumbicity." If the physical lead is reasonably pure, one bit of it will do as well as another for experimental purposes, because we really aren't interested in the individuality or the peculiarity; we are interested in what it is that makes the individual that particular individual that it is; and what it is that makes this individual what it is, is not itself individual in the same way. It is what Plato called an *eidos*. It is the definition or basic scientific nature of the thing, and this lies surely and securely beyond sensation.

We can see this clearly even if we entertain the sentence "Lead is heavy" or "Lead has weight." For, as with *lead,* so also with weight: *weight,* as understood, has no weight at all. *Weight* is a concept, a mental object, a knowable and therefore unchanging thing. To say that lead has weight is not really to speak of any specific experience at all; it is not simply to say that this lead or that feels heavy when I lift it. It is rather to say that anything that is lead will feel heavy when lifted . . . and this proposition, a prototype of all we know or ever can know, has plainly no weight at all, and never can be lifted.

Seeing is sometimes believing, but believing is never knowing. What we see, we do not know. What we know, we do not see. This is the first and fundamental law of Plato's philosophy. It seems odd only to men whose understanding is beclouded by their senses, and who by habit close the eye of the mind to see only with the eye in the head.

Our act of coming to know, of course, is typically an act like any other. It occurs here and now, within a space-time context. It may be directed correctly or incorrectly, it may be right or wrong, correct or incorrect, true or false. But our mere act of knowing, like our mere symbolic formulation of our knowledge, never alters even the tiniest aspect of what is. It is for us to strive to bring our opinions and beliefs up to the level of knowledge, to remake our merely perspectival action in the light of our common focus. To borrow a later phrase, we may say that our knowing mission is to become adequate in our minds to what genuinely is, to see through the mists of shadow to the substantial and therefore invisible world of truth that lies behind sensation.

This is not to deny Heraclitean change, nor is it to construe quite all the world after the model of mathematics. Certainly it is not to deny that times are times and places are places. We in life are saturated with space and time, and so long as we merely *ap*prehend (fearing, or lacking the discipline, to *com*prehend), we all too easily rest content with our maybes and our probablies. And, as we exile the genuine truths of mathematics and mature science to a linguistically invented realm of tautology, we tread muddy water.

We should thus see these realms—of knowledge, of truth, of substance, on the one hand, and of mere opinion, of deceptive sensation, of shadow on the other—not as compartments into which the furniture of the entire universe must be neatly stacked, but as ways of making sense of ourselves: of what we are and have been and want to be, and of what we hope and fear. Thus far, they seem remotely disparate universes, the one of being and the other of becoming. And thus, unhappily, do beginners too often leave Plato. The bridge they miss is the intrinsic dynamic that makes the world a human unit once again. The name of that dynamic is love.

Even before we conceive our universe as set in loving motion, however, we can find a kind of logical correspondence between the partial, fuzzy pseudo-sense of sensation itself and the complete, clear, rational intelligibility of understanding. After all, even merely physical things can be crudely distinguished, one from another, and compared, one with another. They can respond in some vague measure, one to another. The grounds or principles of their distinctions and similarities and responses are, as we have already found, not themselves physical; they could not be so, for their very function is to be intelligible and to define. The logical correspondence between physical and intelligible, or between sense-able and sensible, cannot, however, be one-for-one, because the physical world is a world of multitudes of individuals, never really understood or known at all and never ultimately distinguishable, one from another.

The world of understanding, on the contrary, is disciplined, defined, discrete; here there are only so many forms, each definitively clear and determinate, perfectly distinguishable from every other. This latter realm, the Greek liked to think with a tone of approval, was finite, in contrast to the wanton, irregular "infinity" of the realm of sensation. (We today must remember our own inversion of this attitude. We have all but forgot the Hellenic preference for boundaries and clarity, definitions and finitude over boundlessness, obscurity, the indefinitely vague and merely infinite. When we boast about a thing or idea as "infinite," instead of apologizing for not yet having defined it clearly, we simply ache from a hangover resulting from an overdose of nineteenth century romanticism. Plato and his friends would have thought us still childishly drunk so long as we prefer fog and mystery over the crisp sunlight of precise understanding. "Infinite," to a Greek, meant vague, obscure, unintelligible, offensive, ugly; "finite" meant bright, precise, mathematical, admirable, brilliant, beautiful. How wanton it would have seemed to an Athenian, by the way, to hear one of us speak of worshiping an "infinite" god! As well willingly flounder about in the sticky mud of a bottomless swamp, in preference to the firm footing of clear understanding!).

In the Beginning . . .

Nobody knows, says Socrates, with modest candor, how it all began. So we speculate—not wantonly, but honestly seeking as clear a picture as disciplined responsibility to the facts permits. What needs explanation is how our interim world of history came to be—how and why it was created.

Plainly, the place to begin is with the uncreated. "What has always been and was never created?" Every device for evading the question is an absurd retreat into mysticism, as for example when the Oriental superstition speaks to us of "creation out of nothingness." To talk such a language is to flaunt reason and to play with words. If there is nothing to create with, and no creative force, then there is no creation, and that's the end of the matter. To suppose that the creative force was itself created is simply to push the inquiry one step further back. Equally, to

propose the formula "self-creator" is to substitute word-magic for understanding. If God created Himself, He must have existed before He existed
in order to have brought Himself into existence. It is (to an Athenian)
a monstrous affront against religion and human understanding to take
seriously any such nonsense as that.

It is just as plain that the defining principles themselves cannot have
been created because they are in their very nature eternal. It makes
no sense to ask when right triangles began to obey the Pythagorean
Theorem, or when the theorem itself was created. It couldn't ever have
been created. It is.

But the existence of a universe containing a creative force and some
defining, ordering principles will never alone suffice to explain the
making of this muddy, mundane realm in which you and I live. The
principles, transparently clear and precise as they are, occupy no place
in space and time; they aren't anywhere or anywhen. They not only
aren't physical things, but they also aren't mental events occurring in
the mind of any one man or of all men together; they are, we must
remember, rather the very intelligibility, the self-contained and autonomous structure of reason itself. No creative force, working with principles like these alone, could have come up with so insubstantial a guesswork world as this in which we live, and even if by some indescribable
(and, therefore, to a Greek almost inexplicable) miracle it could do so,
it plainly wouldn't.

So we need one more uncreated "element" to show how there can
have come to be the imperfect, individual things this world possesses in
abundance. This element is not to define anything, for the eternal principles do all of that. Nor is it to *do* anything in creation; our impersonal
creative force will do all that can be done. This last element is *to be
defined* rather than to define, *to be done to* rather than to do, to *receive*
rather than to give. When Plato calls this element by the misleading
name "receptacle" he means to designate the function of "receiving" the
definitions which are the ideal principles themselves. Naturally, we cannot say any more about the "receptacle," for if we are to say something
about anything we must always suppose that that something has some
characteristics or properties that our words can point to. But the "receptacle" doesn't yet have any properties at all. It just is; or, better, it
just isn't; it is so utterly unformed that it doesn't even exist yet. Plato
even calls it "nonbeing." We can best think of the receptacle simply as
a shapeless to-be-formed.

Now at last our catalog of the uncreated is complete. Before there
was any world at all, even before space and time could be, there must
eternally have been a dynamic force (translated as "God"—an unhappy
choice since this "demiurge" or "creative principle" of Plato's is to be

kept as free as possible from the limitations and weaknesses and mysteries to which all usual gods are heir). This force is definable only in dynamic terms, for there is no reason to endow it with any more properties than our explanation of creation will demand; to endow beyond explanatory necessity is for a fourth century Greek to retreat from philosophy to Homeric, Hesiodic (or, later, to Hebraic-Christian) superstition. There must also have been ideals (or models, shapes, forms, patterns), else the world-to-be could never achieve even the minimal clarity it so evidently has, but would always remain chaotic and, in principle, incomprehensible. Finally, there must also always have been the shapeless, unformed receptacle, perfectly indescribable in order that descriptions may by the creative force be imposed upon it, somewhat as the sand at the ocean's edge, washed smooth by the surf, receives a footprint far more cleanly than does the higher sand already shaped and trampled. Force, principles, material stand ready for creation.

But creation can never be, so long as we envisage our precreative eternal universe in this breathless, anticipatory, static suspension of to-be-createdness. Everything is there, but nothing happens; the stage is set, the curtain is up, the actors are present, but the show is frozen and cannot go on.

All we need now is the breath of life, the central, essential *movement,* and our "real" universe can spring into existence. This living breath, this very life itself, is love. Here, Plato speculates, is what might have happened. (He does not pretend to describe what actually did happen; he is too modest for this. He simply claims that this explanation, whether ultimately true or false, is at least consistent with all we know, even though because of our human limitations it must lamentably be phrased in spatio-temporal and psychological language.)

The forms, or models, for creation are radiant in their clarity and intelligible, disciplined perfection. The creative force cannot help, by its own inner nature, but be attracted to them. The creative force apprehends perfection.

Perfection itself (sometimes spoken of, almost always with apologies for the misleading weakness of language, as a form among forms, or as *the* Form of all Forms) is the only object in the universe of which it is literally true to say, "To know it is to love it." "Know" here means not merely "know about" from the outside, or "be able to describe with the use of categories." It means, better, "be really intimately acquainted with," "identify with," as when we say that we not merely know something about a person, but that we really *know* him. His very nature, we mean to claim, is somehow directly given to us and seizes us with its irresistible beauty. Its radiance is magnetic. We move toward it and into it by knowing it.

In this way, *app*rehending perfection and thereby *com*prehending perfection, the creative force itself is magnetized by perfection. It inclines toward the forms, reaches out to them, seeks to extend their brilliance even beyond their perfect selves.

When the creative force beholds the only other pre-creative element, the formless nonbeing or receptacle, it is repulsed by blankness, vacuum, absurdity. It realizes that this blankness could become more nearly coherent, the vacuum more nearly full, the absurd more nearly meaningful, only if the radiantly perfect forms could be brought to bear upon it. Therefore, because the creative force is magnetically drawn by the perfection of the forms—because it loves perfection and seeks to extend it as far as the stuff will permit—it brings into contact perfection and imperfection, being and nonbeing, clarity and chaos, meaning and absurdity. Because the creative force loves what is alone ultimately worthy of love, it creates.

We must remind ourselves that this is not the familiar Mosaic account of creation. It is *not* creation out of nothingness, which would be nonsense to a Greek. It is *not* creation by a person, which would be guesswork to a Greek. It is not "all-powerful" creation, whatever that might mean. (From a Greek point of view, the notion of omnipotence is, because rationally unintelligible, manifestly preposterous; a god, for example, could easily be thought of as more powerful than we are, but surely his power *must* be thought of as limited by reason and—as we shall soon see—by another factor as well.) Creation, for Plato, is the loving bringing into dynamic relationship of sense and nonsense, of ideal forms and chaotic matter.

Now, if this creative act had been perfectly successful (an impossible hypothesis), the world we live in would be perfect. All the things we see and touch would be ideal in their kind. We ourselves would, of course, perfectly understand everything, and we would always act with perfect knowledge of and obedience to justice and law. Our world would itself be perfection. The creative force, knowing perfection and therefore loving perfection, would have fulfilled its mission.

No honest, nonhallucinated man claims to be perfect or claims that this is a perfect world. He knows that, so long as this world remains even this *kind* of a world, it must forever remain imperfect, because its very "thisness" precludes the possibility of perfection (or, as Shelley was later to put it, "stains the white radiance of eternity"). We cannot seriously ask whether our created world is imperfect, but we cannot help but ask why it is so. There must be some reason somewhere.

Clearly, the reason cannot lie in the forms, for they are perfection, and they define perfection. Nor can the reason lie in the creative force itself. For the force loves perfection and seeks, as it were, with *all* its might, to create a perfect world. The ultimate reason for the imperfection of the world, even for the very possibility of imperfection, must therefore lie in the third uncreated element, the nonbeing material receptacle or "nurse of generation." We cannot, as Plato confesses, claim to understand this fully, but equally we cannot resist the force of our reasoning. Somehow there must be, right in the essential heart of the receptacle, an inherent resistance to the imposition of perfection. The receptacle must be recalcitrant, refusing to accept the ideal shapes offered in the creative act. Things are made in the image of perfection, but never quite exactly so. There is always some lack, however slight—some gap, some fuzziness. No particular *thing,* simply because it is particular and thus the mere embodiment of what genuinely *is,* can ever be what it "ought" to become and seeks to become. So long as it remains particular and unique, whether physical or psychological, it remains contaminated with the unwilling receptacle from which it once upon a time was made.

Analogies are always dangerous, as Plato (who used them so often, so brilliantly and so misleadingly) well knew. Crude and homely analogies were, however, favorites of Socrates. So, with apologies, let us consider a humble parallel with the creative act.

Suppose a pastry cook to find the most magnificent set of cookie cutters he had ever seen: a set of shapes dazzling in their brilliance, setting his culinary soul on fire. He cannot rest content merely to cherish the shapes of the cutters in all their purity; he naturally seeks to show them forth as actual cookies. He has at hand an unlimited quantity of dough, totally formless.

In order to express his attraction for and dedication to the beautiful shapes of his cookie cutters, the chef impresses the forms upon the dough, using all his skill to shape each cookie exactly to the cutter.

Do the cookies he bakes—however skillful he may be—exhibit exactly the perfect shapes with which the cook began? Of course not. The dough never quite precisely matches the shapes applied; there is always a tiny border not quite filled out, or ever so little spilling over the edge. The cookie can be recognized as a star or a triangle or a circle or a gingerbread boy. But it only approximates the shape imposed. The dough is the to-be-determined, not the determining rule itself. The resultant cookie is the only-partially-determined.

This is a poor analogy (if only because all actual cookie cutters are themselves physical and limited in perfection, while the forms to which they correspond are not), but it may do to make graphic the creative act we are here seeking to understand. It can serve to show us that imperfection must be attributed to that-which-is-to-be-shaped, and to teach us never to look in the world of individual things for that absolute perfection of shape which, they can only imperfectly exhibit.

Our chef, examining his finished creations, finds, alas, no single cookie that came out as well as he had hoped. His earnest attempt to embody perfection was doomed to fall short. Yet he finds that some of the cookies are far better shaped than others; some have more nearly accepted the impress of the forms imposed upon them; others "willfully" resisted the model cutters. The chef can now quite easily arrange the cookies according to their nearness to the ideal. Those approaching it closely he will call "good," those approaching it less closely he will call "fair," and those obviously misshapen he will have to call "poor." In grading his cookies, our chef is distinguishing those he likes best or most nearly approves of, from those he likes least and disapproves of. But notice—and this is the Platonically crucial point—the model cookie cutter itself is the only sensible standard for our chef to use in making his classification. His personal likes and dislikes, insofar as they are his alone, have nothing to do with the correctness of this grading. The chef, being an individual, may forget the perfect shape as he is judging his cookies. No matter; the value of a cookie is not determined by any subjective opinion or response of liking or pleasure; each cookie exhibits its model shape in some objectively determined degree. A mistake in grading reveals nothing about the cookies or the models after which they were made; it simply attests, once again, the fallibility of human judgment.

Out there beyond the chef, not *in* his mind *but* presented objectively *to* his mind, is a value-array. Some things are better than other things, whether we like it or not, and our choice is good if it approves what is good, bad if it approves what is bad. Objects are better as they more accurately mirror perfection, and this valuation is independent of the mind, independent of the eye, independent of the "taste," independent of the cultural environment, independent of space and time and everything else but perfection itself. To say "I like this better than that" is to engage in irrelevant autobiography. A discriminating value-judgment, instead, can and should be a clear, intelligent recognition of what really is.

Our analogy, if we now extend it one final step, can show us one more central dimension to our universe. Suppose our cookies to be animated, after the manner of the gingerbread boy in the children's fable. Let us, in fantasy, endow each cookie with a consciousness.

Some cookies, let us suppose, have no real notion at all of what it means to be a boy-shaped cookie, or even of what it means to be a cookie at all. They are so ignorant as to suppose that they really are nothing but dough (not realizing that if this were the case, they would never be able to realize it). As these foolish cookies act, they become doughier and doughier, instead of growing toward any significant fulfillment. These blind creatures are to be pitied and helped perhaps, but never to be admired. They know nothing at all; least of all do they know themselves.

Other cookies, instead, are astonished to learn that they are cookies, and indeed to discover that they can learn some other things as well. They open their eyes in wonder at the world around them. Even though imperfectly, they see their own shapes and the shapes of other cookies. They begin to recognize similarities and differences in shape, nearer and farther approximations to ideal shapes. Not that they can quite discern the cookie cutters themselves; that would be asking too much of a mere cookie. Yet these cookies' inner intelligence can illuminate their world and permit significant discriminations. At its best, this intelligent but partial understanding can inform action. And the action appropriate to a cookie is any action that will in a changing world enhance not his mere doughiness but his *cookiehood* or *boyhood* or *triangularity* or *circularity* or *humanity,* and thus bring him closer to what he inherently, objectively, and essentially ought to be. He must try his best to shape himself after the model, the ordering principle, the perfection which he only imperfectly embodies.

Of course we have been talking not about cookies, but about ourselves and our world and their meaning. The chef in our parable is the creative force, the cookie cutters are the beautiful formal guiding principles, the dough is the material receptacle. We, and every other thing in our world, are the cookies.

We can be known or understood, by ourselves or by anyone else, only in terms of ideals. Ideals are not fantasies, not dreams, not subjective preferential notions. They are ways of making intelligible what is, ways of understanding the world. What merely is, is imperfect, unclear, partial, changing, relative, cultural, historic, inadequate. We can know truths about ourselves, or any other truths, only because behind the mere "is's" there lie "oughts," real reasons for distinguishing what merely is from what ought to be—from what we and everything else are trying to become—and guides for our becoming.

Our understanding of these truths about ourselves (and, as we shall see, about our destinies as well) is, as our world views these things, a process or dynamic. It moves through time, and its movement may be straight or crooked. What motivates the movement is the same "active urge" within us that motivated the creative force when it made the world in the first place. We, too, envisaging through the eyes of our minds the truths implicit in our being what we are, find these truths irresistible—the more so, the more clearly we conceive them. They lure us with their perfection. Innately and naturally—according, that is, to our truly *human* human nature—we love them, through whatever embodiment they may appear to us. Not only you and I love, but every man loves: we are all lovers so long as we live, for living is loving.

And, broadly and deeply speaking, so too with all things that are and move: horses and sheep, flowers and trees—each implicitly and perhaps unconsciously seeks its *kind,* not merely an individual of its kind.

Finally, so it also is and must be for the very universe in which we live. The creative force, Plato tells us (without claiming any great certainty for his teaching here), may have cut the receptacle into spheres and shaped their orbits. The vast heavens may have stood still, motionlessly awaiting the call to motion, suspended in reflection of the eternal ideals. Then, with the first breath of life of the universe came its first breath of love, of longing to be what it can never quite wholly be but can and should always strive to become: perfection. The stars and planets moved. Time—the "moving image of eternity"—began. Love made the world go 'round.

And not only around, but *up* as well. Change may be simply monotonous and cyclical rehearsal of the same dull scenario. Plato is not entirely consistent here; he sometimes views historic change in this traditionally Hellenic manner. More often, however, he thinks of change as progress. Growing is always growing up, for if we are not growing up we are regressing. Growth and progress can make no sense except in terms of approaching norms; in terms of norms alone can we measure achievement.

This talk of goals rings oddly in contemporary ears, because genuine, specific, long-run goals are not in fashion today. We are taught to think and talk, not so much in terms of what should be achieved or what is to be achieved, as in terms of what makes us do what we do. The language of "cultural conditioning" and of "conditioned responses to stimuli" has become so habitual to us that we are likely to suppose it to be the only possible way of explaining personal or social change. Whenever a change occurs, we look backward and ask what brought it about—meaning, of course, to ask what antecedent circumstances were present when the change occurred. So well has this way of looking backward worked in physics that we have largely adapted our psychology and our social theory in its terms.

We shall never make any sense of Plato until we broaden this pattern of explanation. Plato does not deny that some events can, in limited manner, be partially explained in mechanical-causal terms. But he gives a central place to *purpose* in the dynamic of nature. Socrates tells us, as he sits in his cell awaiting the hemlock, that he had as a boy been strongly attracted by mechanical, backward-looking explanations of human actions in terms of muscles, nerves, and bones. But later he came to realize that truly important human concerns cannot be explained in this way. What have we really explained, he asks in effect, if we say that Socrates sits in his cell because his muscles contracted and his ligaments lifted his leg-bones to put him there? No, the real reason is instead a forward-looking one: Socrates is in his cell to carry out the commands of the Athenian citizens who condemned him.

Purposes, then, and purposes alone, will serve to make sense of our inmost selves; when men degenerate to mere responding organisms, they default their humanity. It is not the boot from behind that explains a man's truly human actions; it is the lure of the good beyond him. This is not to deny that men influence one another, or that men can live (for better or for worse) in social situations; Plato had at least as full an awareness of "social pressures" and of "social implications" as do most of us. Certainly it is not to deny that men learn. But it is explicitly to deny that education or any other human change can make any real sense at all, except in terms of what is truly to be learned.

Education, Plato believes, involves opening up the mind and heart to truth, learning to love what deserves our love and to hate what deserves our hatred. It is a long process of growth toward maturity through steady, progressive self-realization. *Discipline,* as a word and idea, is a cousin of *discern* and *discriminate;* it suggests "taking apart," isolating differing aspects in a complex so that they can be apprehended, then comprehended, learned. The educated man has been led out of himself into an apprehension of truths he can reach out for and grasp.

THE SYMPOSIUM

Plato's *Symposium* is a masterpiece of art as well as of philosophy, and the finest reading there is for a beginner in philosophy. The style is superb, and the literary structure is subtly and beautifully integrated with the development of the thought.

Ideally, the reader of this book will now lay it aside and read the *Symposium* with delight from beginning to end, letting his mind grow as he reasons in crescendo with each introductory speaker in turn, then following the climactic presentation Socrates makes in his speech, and finally coming to rest in the delightful coda. The *Symposium* is richly enjoyable to read, and Platonic love is presented there much more eloquently and accurately than it can ever be described here.

The *Symposium* is a complex dialogue (or polylogue), containing dialectical development within dialectic. Its setting is a party: a friendly evening of drink and talk. Its substance is a carefully analyzed presentation of the psychology, morality, and metaphysics of love. Throughout, the atmosphere of the discussion is perfectly tuned to the spirit of the talk; now warm, relaxed, informal; now calm and dignified; and sometimes rising in tension to sublimity.

The introductory pleasantries show us Apollodorus, one of Plato's fellow-disciples of Socrates, gladly agreeing to enliven a stroll by recounting to an unnamed companion the events that took place one evening long ago at Agathon's house in Athens. The companion is one of the "rich men and traders" who "run about the world, fancying themselves to be well employed," when they are really "most wretched beings." He and Apollodorus pity each other: the companion pitying the philosopher for being unhappy, the philosopher pitying the companion because he thinks he is doing something when in reality he is doing nothing.

But the spirit is friendly and light-hearted, chaffing and gay. Beneath this spirit we already find, as we so often do in Plato, revelation and anticipation, even before the dialogue begins. For already we have the genuine concerns of the philosopher (which appear so ludicrous to the man of the world) set in contrast with the trivial concerns of the man of this world alone. The golden realm of truth is already set against the brassy realm of pretense, sanity against neurosis. The *Symposium* is to show us how intimately related these worlds can become, if we but "learn to love aright."

Apollodorus then recounts the events of that wonderful evening in (so far as he can remember them) the exact words of Aristodemus, who had been present and who had told the story to him.

Socrates meets Aristodemus along the road, and invites Aristodemus to join him at Agathon's dinner. Teacher and pupil stroll along together. On reaching the house, Socrates drops behind in a fit of abstraction, asking Aristodemus to go on ahead. Agathon welcomes Aristodemus and sends a servant to escort Socrates in to dinner. But the servant, finding Socrates in the portico of a neighboring house, calls him in vain, for he is lost to this world, thinking out one of his problems. By way of contrast, the dinner inside proceeds abundantly, and is half over when Socrates finally appears, in good spirits. He congratulates Agathon upon the victory his tragedy won the day before—the occasion for the feast—and dines. Libations are offered, a hymn is sung to the gods, and the time comes for the group (following a pattern ancient even in those days) to settle down to some serious drinking.

Pausanias at once calls a halt, asking (since he and most of the other guests had been drinking heavily the evening before) how the drinking can be made the easiest. He is, Aristophanes agrees, quite correct; hangovers are the order of the day, and hard drinking is by no means desired. Agathon the host endorses the proposal for moderation, and so do Eryximachus, the foolish physician (who thinks drinking deep a bad practice, which he never follows "if he can help it") and Phaedrus. The motion carries, and Plato wryly remarks, "It was agreed that drinking was not to be the order of the day, but that they were all to drink only so much as they pleased." It has already been made plain that this is what Socrates does anyway; and, as we shall see, the very end of the dialogue has thus ingeniously been anticipated. Instead of heavy drinking there is to be conversation.

Our characters are thus introduced as equals in Athens' intellectual and artistic upper crust: all old friends, well fed and wined and ready for a feast of mind. The flute-girl is dismissed, and Eryximachus cites Phaedrus' earlier suggestion to the effect that Love, alone among the gods, has never been properly praised. To remedy this, he proposes that each of the guests make, extempore, a speech in honor of Love. Socrates (who professes to understand nothing but matters of love) speaks for the company in welcoming Eryximachus' suggestion.

The first speaker is Phaedrus, and his speech is a pleasant, polished model of rather flamboyant conventional rhetoric, replete (as a good speech was expected to be) with citations from the Homeric and Hesiodic traditions. It demonstrates, by the evidence of mythological heroes and heroines, that the gods approve true love. The speech presents one central insight: that love is an incentive to justice, to moral action. Phaedrus puts it this way:

> . . . the principle which ought to be the guide of men who would live nobly—that principle, I say, neither kindred, nor honor, nor wealth, nor any other motive is able to implant so well as love. Of what am I speaking? Of the sense of honor and dishonor, without which neither states nor individuals ever do any good or great work. And I say that a lover who is detected in doing any dishonorable act, or submitting through cowardice when any dishonor is done to him by another, will be more pained at being detected by his beloved than at being seen by his father, or by his companions, or by any one else . . . who would desert his beloved or fail him in the hour of danger? The veriest coward would become an inspired hero, equal to the bravest, at such a time; love would inspire him (178-9).[1]

Artistically, Plato is already weaving his dramatic texture: Phaedrus' speech is intentionally almost empty, but not entirely so. Shallow though he seems, Phaedrus is a man and represents a manner of human response. Philosophically, the truth he presents will later be developed in its proper context.

The turn comes to Pausanias, who mildly chastises Phaedrus for being too indiscriminate in praising all loves, but who also speaks almost too fluently and "prettily." He offers us a distinction in terms of a traditional myth, but it is simply a distinction between those occupations that are

well done and those that are ill done. Not all loves are equally to be
praised, he tells us:

> . . . actions vary according to the manner of their performance. Take,
> for example, that which we are now doing, drinking, singing and talk-
> ing—these actions are not in themselves either good or evil, but they turn
> out in this or that way according to the manner of performing them; and
> when they are well done they are good, and when wrongly done they are
> evil; so too, not every love, but only that which has a noble purpose, is
> noble and worthy of praise (181).

—and, after bemusedly reviewing Greek laws regulating the practice of
homosexuality, Pausanias sets forth the central teaching of his talk (which
alone, as before, Socrates is later to take up, leaving all the rest aside for
contrast):

> . . . whether such practices are honorable or dishonorable is not a simple
> question; they are honorable to him who follows them honorably, dis-
> honorable to him who follows them dishonorably. There is dishonor in
> yielding to the evil, or in an evil manner; but there is honor in yielding
> to the good, or in an honorable manner. Evil is the vulgar lover who loves
> the body rather than the soul, inasmuch as he is not even stable because
> he loves a thing which is in itself unstable, and therefore so soon as the
> bloom of youth which he was desiring begins to fade, he takes wing and
> flies away, in spite of all his words and promises; whereas the love of the
> noble disposition is life-long, for it becomes one with the everlast-
> ing . . . (183).[2]

> These two customs, one the love of youth, and the other the practice of
> philosophy and virtue in general, ought to meet in one, and then the be-
> loved may honorably indulge the lover . . . the one capable of com-
> municating wisdom and virtue, the other seeking to acquire them with a
> view to education and wisdom . . . (184).

Some loves, then, are objectively better than are other loves—some are
to be approved and encouraged, others to be disapproved and discour-
aged. Furthermore, and crucially, those that are to be encouraged are the
loves not of the blind flesh, but of the sighted, insightful wisdom.

Now the turn properly comes to Aristophanes, but Eryximachus (after
prescribing for Aristophanes' hiccoughs in a pleasant byplay) takes his
place. Eryximachus is, as we have said, a foolish physician, but even in
his foolishness (as Plato presents it) there is wisdom. The first mark of
this wisdom is an extension of Pausanias' good-bad distinction beyond
man to all that is: Love, as Eryximachus interprets it, is not merely a
human phenomenon, but a cosmic one; and this idea, too, Socrates will
appropriate in his climactic speech:

This double love is not merely an affection of the soul of man toward the fair, or toward anything, but is to be found in the bodies of all animals and in productions of the earth, and I may say in all that is; such is the conclusion which I seem to have gathered from my own art of medicine, whence I learn how great and wonderful and universal is the deity of love, whose empire extends over all things, divine as well as human. . . . There are in the human body these two kinds of love, which are confessedly different and unlike, and being unlike, they have desires and loves which are unlike; and the desire of the healthy is one, and the desire of the diseased is another . . . the best physician is he who is able to separate noble love from base love . . . and can reconcile the most hostile elements in the constitution and make them loving friends . . . (186). All sacrifices and the whole province of divination, which is the art of communion between gods and men—these, I say, are concerned only with the preservation of good love and the cure of evil love. . . . Such is the great and mighty, or rather omnipotent, force of all-encompassing love. . . . And the love, more especially, which is directed toward the good, and which is consummated in company with temperance and justice, whether among gods or men, has the greatest power and is the source of all our happiness and harmony, and makes us friends with the gods who are above us, and with one another (188).

By now we have had, for a time, our share of seriousness. With the sensitive ear and perfect timing of the artist, Plato introduces some comic relief, in the speech of Aristophanes. This is the same Aristophanes who wrote the *Frogs* and *Lysistrata,* and who parodied Socrates in the *Clouds.* Now, his hiccoughs happily cured, he launches into his preposterous presentation. Two things are remarkable about this tale: first, that for all its charming, deliberate idiocy, it contains a profoundly serious point; and second, that (despite the misrepresentations of some twentieth century readers) there is no evidence that Plato ever for an instant credited a syllable of it as history. On the contrary, Plato was a healthy, fun-loving genius. He could put lusty jokes in Aristophanes' mouth and laugh as he did so . . . all the time making sure that some genuine insight was being conveyed beneath the high-spirited fun. As with the very best humor of all ages, we are made to cry for our weaknesses as we laugh at them, and to see beyond our weaknesses to our potential strengths.

The tale Aristophanes tells us is absurd; it is a comical and profound myth of creation:

. . . the primeval man was round, his back and sides forming a circle; and he had four arms and four legs, one head with two identical faces, looking opposite ways, set on a cylindrical neck and precisely alike; also four ears, two sex organs, and everything else in proportion. He could walk upright as men now do, backward or forward as he pleased, and when he wanted to go fast, he could also roll over and over at a great

pace, turning on his four hands and four feet, eight in all, like tumblers
going over and over with their legs in the air (189-90).

Aristophanes tells us that these curious ancestors of ours were presumptu-
ous and disobedient toward the gods, even daring to scale heaven. Doubt
reigned in the celestial councils as to the appropriate punishment, Aristophanes says, when

> At last, after a good deal of reflection, Zeus discovered a way (190).

—and we should not miss the subtle Hellenic delight of the God of Gods
deciding upon a course of action "after a good deal of reflection." Can
anyone imagine the Hebrew-Christian God scratching his head, and deliberating on the best way to chastise rebellious man? The good Greeks
could and did dare this blasphemy, and laughed at it, and at themselves,
Here was Zeus's proposal:

> "Methinks I have a plan which will humble their pride and improve
> their manners; men shall continue to exist, but I will split them in two
> and then they will be diminished in strength and increased in numbers,
> . . . They shall walk about upright on two legs, and if they continue to
> be insolent and noisy, I will split them again and they shall hop about on
> a single leg" (190).

After the division, Aristophanes continues (and his underlying, serious
point becomes clear):

> . . . the two parts of man, each desiring his other half, came together, and
> throwing their arms around one another, entwined in mutual embraces,
> Longing to grow into one, they were on the point of dying from hunger
> and self-neglect because they did not like to do anything apart (191).

But these strange bisected creatures, with one further necessary adapta-
tion, became ourselves. And thus we naturally seek to complete ourselves
in each other:

> Thus ancient is the mutual love which is implanted in us, reuniting our
> original nature, making one of two and healing the state of man. Each of
> us when separated, having one side only, like a flat fish, is but half human,
> and he is always looking for his other half (191).[3] . . . the intense yearn-
> ing which [lovers] have toward each other does not appear to be the de-
> sire for sexual intercourse, but for something else which the soul of each
> desires and cannot tell, and of which he has only a dark and doubtful
> presentiment (192).

The reason, then, why we so urgently seek to become one with our be-
loveds is that

> . . . human nature was originally one and we were a whole, and the desire
> and pursuit of the whole is called love (193).

Just as this most serious point is made in the form of a myth, Aristophanes laughs and hilariously tops his own joke:

> . . . if we disobey the gods, there is a danger that we shall be split up again and go about in bas-relief, like the profile figures having only half a nose which are carved in outline on monuments, and that we may thus become like the flat, half-hearted discs that childish sweethearts wear (193).[4]

It is preposterous to suppose, as some have seriously done, that Plato really meant to set forth any such image as history. He was having good, healthy fun through Aristophanes, but his fun has its profound point: that each man, as an individual and apart from all other individuals, is desperately incomplete. He is not, and cannot be, a whole man, but he needs to become one. All the time, beneath the laughter, there is an undertone of sobriety. Plato's Aristophanes is not altogether a clown, for he is a dramatic character in a dialogue. He has a role to play, in advancing the dialectic, and this he does. For we now see, as we had not seen before, the poverty of individual man in his desperate search for fulfillment, and we have been given in the least likely place the important hint that, in loving, we desire something we cannot tell, but of which we have only "a dark and doubtful presentiment." Without endorsing Aristophanes' tale as it stands, Socrates will adopt its suggestions and turn them to the truth's advantage.

Only the greatest dramatic artists can make their devices seem so utterly natural as Plato does—at this moment, when Aristophanes has completed his ludicrously profound speech, Plato interjects some apparently casual byplay between Socrates and Agathon, *a propos* of Agathon's victory of the day before and of his forthcoming "trial" tonight. Socrates jibes Agathon for professing stage fright, on grounds that Agathon has faced the multitude only the day before. Agathon replies with wonderful wisdom:

> Do you think, Socrates, that my head is so full of the theater as to forget that a man of sense fears a few good judges more than many fools? (194).

And so Agathon, the poet, yesterday's winner of the tragic prize, undertakes his eulogy of love. A lesser poet than Plato might well have made of this penultimate speech a closer approximation to the speech of Socrates which is to follow, keeping his crescendo developing mechanically. Not so with Plato. By now, we are caught up in the dialogue; we hunger to hear what will happen next. And what Plato offers us is far from the most brilliant speech of the evening; or rather, it is the most brilliant of all, in terms alone of flamboyance. Agathon is indeed a master of superficial language. His sentences have a poetic ring, even in translation. No one could possibly speak more brilliantly of the glories of love . . . or more hollowly. What Plato shows us here is only the creative inspiration (or, in the Greek sense, the *poetry,* or making, doing) of love; love creates all forms of life and

> as to the artists, do we not know that he only of them whom love inspires has the light of fame?—he whom love touches not walks in darkness (197)

—and we hear the fundamental emptiness of mere talk. Agathon says of his own speech that it is

> half-playful, yet having a certain amount of seriousness (198)

—but the superficial beauty of the language cannot appease the hunger for truth which Plato the artist has all the while so skillfully been whetting.

And so—just as in our own day, when a rhetorically impressive speech has been concluded—there was a general cheer. It was indeed, as Socrates ironically says, "a wonderful oration."

And naturally, knowing Socrates' modesty, we expect to find, as we do, his hesitancy at following so brilliant an address with "mere truth." For, says Socrates,

> in my simplicity I imagined that we were expected to tell the truth and, assuming this, that out of the true the speaker was to choose the most beautiful things and set them forth as best he could. And I felt quite proud, thinking that I knew the nature of true praise and should speak well. Whereas I now see that the intention was to attribute to love every kind of greatness and glory, whether really belonging to him or not, without paying any attention to truth or falsehood . . . you attribute to love every imaginable form of praise which can be gathered anywhere; and you say "he is all this," and "the cause of all that . . ." (198)

—and so Socrates, claiming to have misunderstood the assignment, tries to beg off:

> I do not praise in that way; no, indeed, I cannot. But if you like to hear the mere truth about love, I am ready to speak it in my own way, though I will not make myself ridiculous by entering into any rivalry with you. Decide, then, Phaedrus, whether you would like to hear the truth about love, spoken in any words and in any order which may happen to come into my mind at the time. Will that be agreeable to you? (199).

Everyone, of course, gives him leave to continue, but continue he cannot, until some more ideas have been exchanged, some more clarifications developed.

We may now, at the brink of the climactic address, pause to observe that the development of the dialogue has been, through and through, *dialectical*. Each contribution has been foolish and empty and preliminary in its way—and each has had its own soundness, its own distinctive philosophical insights to offer. Each has been phrased in its own distinctive linguistic idiom: popular-pompous, technical, academic, comic, poetic-tragic. Artistically and philosophically, the stage has been perfectly set for Socrates' own interpretation.

Again, a lesser artist would now lay Socrates' speech forth directly. But Plato wants to develop his thought—or better, he wants us to develop *our* thought—dialectically, so he introduces still another sub-dialogue, in the prefatory interchange between Socrates and Agathon.

Here, with only a few carefully chosen questions (and answers), the entire stage is shifted, the plane of the entire discussion is elevated to insight. How, Socrates asks, can one seek that which he already possesses? He cannot, concedes Agathon. Is it not true, Socrates proposes, that a rich man desiring riches and a healthy man desiring health really desire only the continuation of their respective riches and health? So that whoever already possesses something cannot be said to pursue it?[5] Agathon must agree. Then, without torturing poor Agathon, Socrates calmly points out that love seeks beauty and goodness.

Agathon and the reader are left to draw the evident conclusion: that, in seeking beauty and goodness, love cannot itself be said to be beautiful and good. Love is a lack, a need, a longing, a want, rather than a fulfillment. In today's terms, love is a "drive" and a striving.

And so, taking leave at last of the pleasant byplay with his friends, the master undertakes the ultimate presentation of Platonic love. Yet even here he does not directly lecture us. Even here he thinks and discourses dialectically.

Socrates' device—and we know so little of Diotima of Mantineia, whom he introduces as his supposed instructor in love, that we cannot even say for sure that she was (as we suppose her to have been) simply a device—is presumably introduced simply because the direct-discourse alternative would have seemed immodest. She appears to us as a prophetess, who sets off the earlier earth-bound conceptions of love.

What she teaches Socrates, first, is that we (and all our colleagues at the Symposium) have all been mistaken in conceiving and praising love as a god. For, as we all know, the gods are good and beautiful. Diotima had shown Socrates, as Socrates has just shown Agathon, that love, in seeking goodness and beauty, cannot itself be good and beautiful. The conclusion—that love cannot be a god at all—follows inexorably.

Then, Socrates reveals himself as protesting naturally but a bit stupidly, if love is not beautiful, must it not be ugly? And if love is not a god, must it not be merely mortal? Not so extremely, Diotima assures Socrates: love may be a mean between beauty and ugliness, as true belief is a mean between reasoned understanding and ignorance. And so, too, love may be neither immortal and static-eternal like the gods nor mortal and transient like men, but somehow a mean between the two: a "demon" or force mediating between the gods and men.[6]

This mythical presentation sounds mysterious indeed to our twentieth century ears. The language of mortality and immortality, of gods and demons, has an archaic ring. But if we translate it into more familiar terms and remove the poetic personification we gain access to a clearer notion: that love is not a lover or loving person, nor yet is it a loved or beloved object; rather, love is the impelling relation moving lover toward beloved. Love is magnetism. In our impoverished vocabulary we may without too great a distortion call love a "goal-directed activity" or "drive," a search for satisfaction and fulfillment, or a "motivation." It will turn out to be not merely *a* drive but *the* drive, not one motivation among many, but motivation itself.

But first the myth must grow, and, in keeping with the tradition, love is supplied with a pedigree of poverty and plenty (or "resource"), and sensitively characterized as a creature whose mien and being are the very embodiment of paradoxical change: now flourishing, now decaying, now reviving again, always seeking the wisdom and beauty it possesses not—exactly, of course, as the earthly pursuer of wisdom or "philosopher" is always doing.

And now we are ready to broaden our dynamic concept. Agathon had already opened up the notion of "poetry" to its earlier, broader sense of creativity in general, and unconsciously anticipated Socrates-Diotima's bold stroke here. Just as we now speak of "poetry" only in the more restricted sense of the composition of verse and rhythmic language (while there are other compositions in music and painting that are also properly "poetic" in the earlier, truer sense), so also we tend today to use "love" more narrowly to designate only some restricted goal-seeking activities, while more fundamentally we can conceive every human pursuit as an evidence of love. Whenever, wherever, however men seek to possess goods and to be happy, they are in this generic sense "lovers." The good; the possession of the good; the everlasting possession of the good—of these things is love.

Here, with the notion of "foreverness," the argument advances another crucial step, and a dialectical one. The mortal lover cannot possess the beloved good forever because he himself is doomed to die, and he knows his own mortality. But since the underlying need is for the everlasting realization of the good and the beautiful, the lover's conscious desire is for a dynamic generation in, through, and of beauty. He feels a maturing fullness in him, a bringing-toward-birth. He seeks a beautiful mate to fulfill, with whom he can be fulfilled, and through whom immortality can be achieved by the generation of children. The man who loves, like other animals in this, lives and dies to live again through the children he begets. When we speak of a "race" of men or of the "culture" of a city through decades or centuries, we are not really referring to any single set of objects or things of any kind, for these all change; it is rather the continuous influx and outflow, the coming-into-being and passing-out-of-being in which a continuity can be discerned,[7] and through which the race or the city can be said to be immortal by comparison with the mortal individuals who make it up.

Yet, more profoundly, the same holds within the life of every single mortal man as well. For he, both in his body and in his mind, is never quite self-identical for any two years or days or seconds. Every cell in his body is continuously and simultaneously growing and decaying; every idea in his mind is flowing in and out. Yet we say of him that he is "a man" or "the man he was last year," despite all these changes, just as Athens was Athens before and after Plato.

The parallel is ingenious, and it grounds a greater one. For what Diotima now reveals to Socrates is the first of her two famous "ladders": the ladder of immortality. There are men, she teaches, who are pregnant in the body only, and whose pursuit of the immortality we all seek takes the sole direction of physical procreation. They leave behind them only physical offspring, who may well outlive them and thus permit the parents to defeat their own death. But other men—other lovers— are more pregnant in their minds or souls. They too seek immortality, but immortality of a higher order. These are our creators, artists, statesmen, lawgivers, educators: those who are remembered for the children, not of their loins, but of their brains and hearts. These are more fully men: they have embodied virtues and expressed them. As Diotima might have put it today, who remembers the twenty children the Frauen Bach bore to Johann Sebastian? But who can forget his *Art of the Fugue*?

And here Plato pauses at the gateway to the "inner mysteries" to follow. We have already incorporated the insights of the previous speakers into our enriched concept of love: its direction toward and inspiration of virtue, its drive toward the harmony of opposites and toward self-completion, its dynamic. We have found depth and breadth in love. And we are prepared for the second "ladder"—the ladder of love itself, which when understood will guide us up beyond the limited, insubstantial concerns we prematurely call love.

The path is presented as a course of education. The love proper to a beginner is of course appropriately and honestly sexual: it is the beautiful body that attracts him. This, however, is but the first step:

. . . soon he will of himself perceive that the beauty of one body is related to the beauty of another; and then if genuine beauty is what he
seeks, he would be foolish not to recognize that the beauty in every body
is one and the same. And when he learns this, he will love all beautiful
bodies, restraining the violence of his passion for one body, and condemning [this limited love].

Beginning from earthly beauties, the lover climbs for the sake of genuine beauty, loving one beautiful body, then two, then all, then advancing
from physically beautiful things to morally beautiful actions and from
morally beautiful actions to intellectually beautiful ideas, and ultimately
to the idea of beauty itself, until at last he knows the very essence of
beauty (210).

Here we reach a parting of the ways in an interpretation of Plato.
Plato's attitude toward sexuality can be read in either of two lights.
Those who emphasize the teaching of the *Phaedo* and of certain parts
of the *Republic* will, following an older tradition, consider Plato an
ascetic who condemns sexuality outright, and urges men to turn totally
away from the body and all earthly things in favor of the supermundane
forms. Those who, on the other hand, emphasize the *Symposium* and
the *Phaedrus* will concentrate upon the continuity of love's growth, and
claim some corresponding continuity between this imperfect world of
things and that other perfect world of forms.

In neither reading will sexuality be exalted. In the former, it will be
condemned outright; in the latter, it will be taken as a natural and
healthy first step in love, but only as a tiny first step.

The issue is basic, and as with so many other fundamental issues in
the history of thought, cannot be easily, definitively, and unequivocally
resolved. One must read many texts, try out alternative readings, and
tentatively decide where the preponderant weight seems to rest, without
finding or forcing any artificial consistency upon the author. Any decision
we make may be challenged.

In my own reading, Plato's teaching is that of a telic, disciplined, essential, proto-Aristotelian humanitarian, in no sense a "humanist," but
"essential" in urging that we live—and love—not merely in the light of
what we have been and are, but most importantly of what we may become. As I read Plato, he lives sanely in this world, but is as radically
discontent with it as any rational man must be. Genuine progress will
require that we rise above it, but progressively so, climbing the ladder
toward the good.

A consequence of this reading is that some of Plato—notably the
Phaedo—must either be interpreted as metaphorical exaggeration, or
set altogether aside, with a candid admission that there are two or more
Platos. This admission would be philosophically fatal only to a thinker

whose insights are bound up in a tight, systematic, formal structure. But Plato's is not this kind of mind. Plato's mind is broad, deep, and vivid. He focuses now on this kind of problem, now on that. He certainly can be fairly read as I here read him. That he can be fairly read in other ways as well, I gladly grant.

So, at last, we reach the intimately knowable but ultimately unspeakable goal of all our loving: beauty. It is beauty, radiating throughout creation, that we, all unconsciously, have been seeking as we have cherished physical things, admired and emulated noble acts, taken delight in understanding and teaching. Beauty is the final *why* of love. Of this beauty Diotima teaches that it

> . . . in the first place is everlasting, neither growing nor decaying, neither waxing nor waning; second, it is not beautiful from one point of view and ugly from another, or at one time or in one relation or at one place beautiful, at another time or in another relation or at another place ugly, as if beautiful to some and ugly to others, or through the image of a face or hands or any part of the body, or in any particular of speech or knowledge, or existing in any other being, as for example in an animal or in heaven or in earth or in any other place; but beauty absolute, separate, simple, and everlasting, which without diminution or increase or any change is imparted to the ever-growing and perishing beauties of all other things. [This is] the true beauty—the divine beauty, I mean, pure and clear and unalloyed, not clogged with the pollutions of mortality and all the colors and vanities of human life. [Imagine man as lover] conceiving, perceiving, identifying himself with true beauty simple and divine. Remember how in that communion only, beholding beauty with the eye of the mind, he will be able to bring forth, not images of beauty, but realities (for he has grasped not an image but a reality), and bringing forth and nourishing true virtue to become the friend of God and be immortal, if mortal man may (211).

To ask for "meanings" here is to misconstrue what has been achieved. Beauty cannot be "explained" in discursive terms because it is an ultimate category—or, better, *the* ultimate category. Without beauty, no beautiful thing would be beautiful, or knowable as beautiful, or lovable. Pure beauty explains impure beauties, but the explanatory process is not reversible. Precisely because beauty *is* pure and simple, everlasting and ultimate, it forms a principle for the explanation of everything else. All lesser, transient "becomings"—the things with which we aimlessly traffic every day—gain whatever meaning they have, and whatever attractiveness they have, only as they radiate or reflect the glory that is beauty.

When in chemistry we move from impurities toward purity, from compounds toward elements, we call the procedure "refining," and Plato's sense of intellectual and moral "refinement" is the human analogue of this process. The unrefined man is he who mistakes the obscure and merely immediate pseudo-beauties for genuine, who in closing the eye of his mind is blinded in physical vision by transience. He must touch the physical beloved, pretending that he can thus tangibly grasp what he loves. In opening the eyes of his mind, the man of refinement need not close those in his head, nor need he necessarily forgo the physical touch of the transient beloved. But he alone can come to realize with a vividness never available to his earlier self how and why his particular beloved attracts him: because the beloved embodies the beauty that his innermost soul seeks.

Thus the world of the man of refinement is imbued with intelligibility. He sees mere things clearly, knowing that insofar as they genuinely are, they exhibit the principles according to which they are what they are. And of all these principles, beauty is ultimate.

But this man is far from the soul-sick lover we refer to in the phrase "Platonic lover." The real Platonic lover is a well-balanced, vigorously active man. He does not spend most of his time devising new physical-erotic delights, but neither does any healthy man. He takes truth more seriously than do his myopic fellow-citizens. He is not ashamed of doing political work to improve the human community, for he remembers that *polis* is the same root word as *civis,* meaning city-society, and he knows that a truly *civilized* man is a *political* man. Most important of all, his loving work is intelligently passionate precisely because it is consciously directed toward intelligibility itself: the beauty we as humans, and with us all creation, inherently and naturally seek.

Most of our understanding of things in this world is properly discursive, reducible to systematic concepts which we can, even though imperfectly, render in language. Language is, in essence, a device for working with and through experience, and successful use of language is successful ordering of experience. On this level of everyday experiences, accurate definitions and clear deductions properly reflect precision of understanding.

But these frameworks of doing, and of talking about our doings, make sense only because they are conceived within limited ranges of being. Once those ranges are transcended, we are transported into a realm where words fail us because we have reached a level of insight more profound than language can encompass, a level toward which we and words have, as it were, all along been groping. It is (to borrow a famous metaphor from Plato's *Republic*) as if we were to describe the shadows here on earth in terms of thickness or density, and to read and measure these as degrees of brightness—and then to turn around and face the sun and move toward it, letting it fill our vision, blind us, and prove to us how inadequate the word "brightness" is, in comparison with light itself.

Even so, the ladder of love (as Plato implies also in his seventh letter) finally comes away. We who have so painfully climbed the rungs of self-discipline—which themselves are but the ideal reflections of stages along our own life's way—must now step out for ourselves into an air thinner than any our concepts can pave, but through which alone pure truth can radiate.

Plato the artist does far more than analytically and generically describe the true lover or man of refinement from afar. Instead, by way of contrast, he introduces into the company, perfectly naturally, the handsome, popular, proud, and very drunken young Alcibiades, who laughs and howls and reels, protests his love for the beautiful Agathon, and then suddenly sees Socrates, his old friend and teacher. Alcibiades, still further fortified, undertakes to present the "truth" that lies in wine, by regaling the company with a candidly confessional picture of Socrates himself, whom Alcibiades all but worships: We learn of Socrates' physical endurance, his moral courage, his gifts as a teacher, and the magic of his insight, even to the limit—all but incredible, to this company—of disdaining Alcibiades' erotic advances. As the stages along love's way had earlier been described in general terms, we see here in Socrates' own life and person their fulfillment: the man whom the world derides is far more a man than are those who deride him. He who seems least the lover—especially by contrast with Alcibiades—is really supreme in love, because he above all loves the truth which alone is genuinely worth loving.

This worshipful, rambling eulogy complete, the party disintegrates into a carouse only lightly and gracefully sketched by Plato. All the truth that can be told has been told, yet one last artistic revelation remains. We find, in the very wee hours, nearly everyone unconscious from drink, save only Socrates, sober as ever, and as intent as ever upon pursuing an idea (Are comedy and tragedy really the same?) with two drowsy companions. At length, they too collapse, and Socrates calmly arises and returns to his daily concerns. Thus, Plato shows, genuine love does triumph over the flesh.

The Phaedrus

Every word Plato ever wrote can be construed as relevant to love—indeed, one scholar says with no exaggeration that to Plato philosophy *is* love[8]—but in only one other important dialogue does the subject of love explicitly play a central role. This is the *Phaedrus*, and even here we find by no means as exclusive a treatment as we do in the *Symposium*.

In the *Phaedrus,* we have no convivial round-table discussion; our dialectic is compressed, transformed, and adapted to its location on the banks of a beautiful river. In idyllic surroundings, the young Phaedrus reads to Socrates a much-admired but shallowly rhetorical speech of Phaedrus' master Lysias, purporting to prove the improbable thesis that those who are not "in love" ought to be preferred as lovers over those who are. Socrates, unimpressed, manufactures a better ordered and generally more masterful piece of rhetorical argument, to a similar thesis. This confection contains hints of the doctrine to be developed, but is by no means conclusive or profoundly philosophical. The psychology here is frankly primitive and popular.

> . . . within each one of us there are two sorts of ruling or guiding principle that we follow: one is an innate desire for pleasure, the other an acquired judgment that aims at what is best. Sometimes these internal guides are in accord, sometimes at variance: now one gains the mastery, now the other. And when judgment guides us rationally towards what is best, and has the mastery, that mastery is called temperance; but when desire drags us irrationally towards pleasure, and has come to rule within us, the name given to that rule is wantonness (237D-238A).

Correspondingly, the definition of love is crude and preliminary;

> When irrational desire, pursuing the enjoyment of beauty, has gained the mastery over judgment that prompts to right conduct, and has acquired from other desires, akin to it, fresh strength to strain towards bodily beauty, that very strength provides it with its name: it is the strong passion called love (238B-C).

Though Phaedrus is impressed by Socrates' *tour de force,* Socrates himself is not, and soon recants, begging the gods' forgiveness for the "blasphemy" exhibited in each of these first two speeches. Under Phaedrus' insistent encouragement, Socrates at last undertakes his palinode, and builds one of the most brilliant poetic myths of all time. Both vividly and subtly, the philosophical life is at length set forth as the most genuinely loving life of all—and almost all of the setting forth is done through metaphor and allegory; consecutive, overt dialectic is rare. Rather the dialectic turns inward. Phaedrus nowhere seriously contradicts Socrates, until the loving life is all presented. The "contradictions" are instead laid bare by Socrates himself, within his speech, as he probes our souls. The resultant tension within the mono-dialogue thus also reflects the tensions within ourselves.

The first surprise is to find Socrates (who, following Lysias' poor example with malicious accuracy, has earlier praised the "sanity" of the nonlover over the "madness" or "mania" of the lover) here suddenly saying that

. . . the greatest blessings come by way of madness, indeed of madness that is heaven-sent (244A).

There are madnesses and madnesses, it seems, and he who appears mad to his sober-sided fellow citizens may be the man who is, in truth, too sane to be understood. Of Socrates himself we already know that this is often true. But Socrates is not here claiming any special insight on account of his own known eccentricity. He is distinguishing the unimaginative way of the workaday world from the incisive enlightenment of the creative man of genius, into whom the gods have entered. Such a man is, in Greek, en-thusiastic, the "thusiastic" part of this word being made of *theos,* God, and thus being a cousin of our "theology." The manic prophets of old, the poets who are divinely inspired, Saint Paul in *Second Corinthians*—these are all "en-thusiasts" in that the gods have "entered into" them.

Entered in, we may say, and taken possession. And here we have a second revelation. A manic man, we say in English, behaves like one "possessed." Possessed by whom, or by what? Why, by the gods or devils, of course. He no longer fully controls his every act. We call him "mad" and restrain him, but we should remember that poems are made by fools like him, and that without his madness we should all be vastly the poorer. Being "possessed" by the gods, this man (we may suppose, within our myth) has supernormal access to their secrets, and he may in some ways be able to reveal these secrets to us. He, in turn, may by the splendor of his music, his poetry, or his ideas "possess" the rest of us. Socrates repeatedly plays with this double sense of "possession," in comparing lover with beloved.

But Plato's Socrates, being himself in part the creation of a "mad" poet, is not always perfectly consistent in his characterization of divine mania. In Plato's clearest thinking moods—as in the climax of the *Symposium*—the mystical realization is epistemic; it is only by wholly transcending earth-bound concerns that we arise to the fullest vision of truth and beauty. This moment of vision is not merely an act of understanding; it is *the* act of understanding *par excellence.* We thus know best by sensing least, and our intelligence comes to rest in its proper object.

In Plato's poetic moods, however, the rapture prevails, even at the expense of understanding.[9] Or perhaps, stretching for the sake of consistency and confessing literal infidelity, we might even extend the text by saying rather "at the expense of limited understanding and in the interest of 'understanding' in some higher, mystical, and unspecifiable sense." Better, though, frankly to face the fact that Plato was sometimes more passionately concerned for clarity and persuasion than he was for architectural consistency.

The "proof" Socrates undertakes—which is to show that the "madness" of love is sent from the gods to both lover and beloved—will, he says, "convince the wise but not the learned." The proof of the soul's immortality is very brief. It stems from the idea of motion as essential to the soul. It leads back to love through one of Plato's magnificent images. Let the soul, Socrates says,

> . . . be likened to the union of powers in a team of winged steeds and their winged charioteer. Now all the gods' steeds and all their charioteers are good, and of good stock; but with other beings it is not wholly so. With us men, in the first place, it is a pair of steeds that the charioteer controls; moreover one of them is noble and good, and of good stock, while the other has the opposite character, and his stock is opposite. Hence the task of our charioteer is difficult and troublesome (246A-B).
>
> He that is on the more honourable side is upright and clean-limbed, carrying his neck high, with something of a hooked nose: in colour he is white, with black eyes: a lover of glory, but with temperance and modesty: one that consorts with genuine renown, and needs no whip, being driven by the word of command alone. The other is crooked of frame, a massive jumble of a creature, with thick short neck, snub nose, black skin, and grey eyes; hot-blooded, consorting with wantonness and vainglory; shaggy of ear, deaf, and hard to control with whip and goad.
>
> Now when the driver beholds the person of the beloved, and his whole soul is warmed by the sight, he begins to experience a tickling or pricking of desire; and the obedient steed, constrained now as always by modesty, refrains from leaping upon the beloved; but his fellow, heeding no more the driver's goad or whip, leaps and dashes on, sorely troubling his companion and his driver, and forcing them to approach the loved one and remind him of the delights of love's commerce. For a while they struggle, indignant that he should force them to a monstrous and forbidden act; but at last, finding no end to their evil plight, they yield and agree to do this bidding. And so he draws them on, and now they are quite close and behold the spectacle of the beloved flashing upon them. At that sight the driver's memory goes back to that form of Beauty, and he sees her once again enthroned by the side of Temperance upon her holy seat; then in awe and reverence he falls upon his back, and therewith is compelled to pull the reins so violently that he brings both steeds down upon their haunches, the good one willing and unresistant, but the wanton one sore against his will. Now that they are a little way off, the good horse in shame and horror drenches the whole soul with sweat, while the other, contriving to recover his wind after the pain of the bit and his fall, bursts into angry abuse, railing at the charioteer and his yoke-fellow as cowardly treacherous deserters. Once again he tries to force them to advance, and when they beg him to delay a while he grudgingly consents. But when the time appointed is come, and they feign to have forgotten, he reminds them of it, struggling and neighing and pulling until

he compels them a second time to approach the beloved and renew their offer; and when they have come close, with head down and tail stretched out, he takes the bit between his teeth and shamelessly plunges on. But the driver, with resentment even stronger than before, like a racer recoiling from the starting-rope, jerks back the bit in the mouth of the wanton horse with an even stronger pull, bespatters his railing tongue and his jaws with blood, and forcing him down on legs and haunches delivers him over to anguish.

And so it happens time and again, until the evil steed casts off his wantonness; humbled in the end, he obeys the counsel of his driver, and when he sees the fair beloved is like to die of fear. Wherefore at long last the soul of the lover follows after the beloved with reverence and awe (253D-254E).

The power of this language, and its intimate evocation of our own most personal struggles, intensifies the human moral message. Only a poet who had suffered deeply in learning to love could have set forth the agony of lust in such vivid contrast to the serenity of disciplined dedication.

A psychologist could quibble about the literal interpretation of the allegory, with its apparent division of the soul into the traditional faculties of reason, will, and desire. A scholar could patiently work through the comparison of this picture of the tripartite self with that in Plato's *Republic*. Our interest here is best served by reading the chariot image as a moral dynamic of love.

First, I do not believe that Plato seriously thinks of these elements as radically distinct or separable parts of the human personality. Nearly all of his psychological language rings true to a concept of selfhood as many-faceted but at least ideally capable of unification. We do, to be sure, sometimes behave as if we were brute animals, unbroken left-hand horses. So, if more rarely, do we sometimes behave rationally. So, too, do we sometimes discipline our entire selves. But this is not to suppose that the human being is a composite collection of independent faculties. It is still perfectly possible for us to think of ourselves, in contemporary terms, as complex systems of interrelated drives in varying stages of disequilibrium. When we act, for good or ill, it is all of us that acts.

Second, it is no accident that Plato conceives the personality in dynamic terms, and that the dynamism is total. It is not alone the lusty horse that moves us, restrained by the right-willed horse and the reasonable charioteer. On the contrary, the chariot-personality as a whole is forward-looking and forward-moving. The goal of the movement is that-which-is-sought; ultimately it is, of course, the ideal of the *Symposium*, beauty itself. Every aspect of man strives toward that one goal, but not every aspect does so with understanding discipline. The conflict between the horses is not—except rhetorically—"resolved" by the charioteer.

Rather, the charioteer and the right horse work together to master and restrain the rambunctious horse.[10]

Between the two presentations of the chariot allegory come Plato's pictures of the immortal soul: of reincarnation, and of moral regeneration. The reincarnation doctrine is itself moral, and exhibits the lover's state as the proper reward for the purest of souls. He will become a lover who has seen the most of beauty. The lower levels are reserved for those who have glimpsed less.

> . . . the soul that hath seen the most of Being shall enter into the human babe that shall grow into a seeker after wisdom or beauty, a follower of the Muses and a lover; the next, having seen less, shall dwell in a king that abides by law, or a warrior and ruler; the third in a statesman, a man of business or a trader; the fourth in an athlete, or physical trainer or physician; the fifth shall have the life of a prophet or a mystery-priest; to the sixth that of a poet or other imitative artist shall be fittingly given; the seventh shall live in an artisan or farmer, the eighth in a sophist or demagogue, the ninth in a tyrant (248D-E).

—and after enduring earth's tribulations, only the noblest souls are rewarded most nobly. The image here, once again, is that of soaring to the heights, this time not in a chariot, but with one's own wings. Wings are grown as they are earned.

> Therefore it is meet and right that the soul of the philosopher alone should recover her wings: for he, so far as may be, is ever near in memory to those things which cause a god, being near them, to be divine. If, then, a man remembers correctly, and comes closer and closer to initiation into the perfect mysteries, he and he alone becomes truly perfect. Standing aside from the busy doings of mankind, turning his attention to the divine, he is rebuked by the multitude who consider him mad and do not know that he is inspired (249C).

This man is

> . . . a lover. Such a one, as soon as he beholds the beauty of this world, is reminded of true beauty, and his wings begin to grow; then he longs to lift his wings and fly upward, but he lacks the power to do so. Since he gazes upward like a bird, and cares nothing for the world beneath, men accuse him of being demented (249E).

—and thus we return to "enthusiasm" or divine inspiration. True love is, as Hackforth says, the restoration of the soul's wings, the regaining of its divine purity.[11]

There remains the bringing together of the Platonic doctrines of recollection. As Plato presents the moral picture here, the soul does not really climb the ladder of love for the first time, but rather returns to the glory it once knew. Having once apprehended beauty and therefore appreciated it, the soul is filled with a deep and anguished longing to see and know it again. The true lover may see, through the earthly love of a beloved, that other beauty shining forth; yet here he truly sees nothing new, but the beauty he has seen before, reflected from within himself into his beloved. If, now, he but responds with discipline, he can grow and fly once again toward the truth whence he ultimately comes, for what men call "loving," says Plato, the gods call "winged."

There is in the *Phaedrus* no presentation of love contradicting that of the *Symposium,* but there is in the brilliant allegories an extension into realms poetic and divine, and a vivification of the persistent moral message: that love is pervasive, powerful, and perfect in its ideal fulfillment. We find an intimate identification of the act of love with acts of religious reverence and dedication; to find beauty in a beloved is conceived as finding holiness. Loving rightly is presented as living rightly, not in artificial or arbitrary repression of natural impulses—for, in the truest sense, genuine loving is natural to man's soul—so much as in the ordering of impulses appropriately to their object.

A NOTE ON HOMOSEXUALITY

When Plato refers to sexual love, he is usually thinking of what was taken by his companions in Athenian society to be the "normal" adult male manifestation of sexuality, namely pederasty, or the love of boys by men. By no means all Athenians practiced pederasty, and most of the men had wives and families. But gentlemen of the upper crust often preferred the company of fair youths over that of women, and loved their boys sexually. There is evidence (as in Alcibiades' confessional complaint, *Symposium* 217) that Socrates did not practice pederasty, and we have no convincing evidence that Plato did either, though he does in one place[12] seem to condemn heterosexual love even more strongly than (carnal) homosexual love.

The issue seems to me to interest only scholars of Athenian cultural history. Plato's philosophical interpretation of love stands wholly outside the problem of homosexuality and heterosexuality. Today, most men think of women as their "normal" sexual objects; in ancient Athens, some men thought of boys as their "normal" sexual objects, and relegated women to a generally inferior personal and social status. But everything Plato says about carnality can be taken without change as referring to any physical-sexual desire, however directed. The Greek word he usually uses is *pederastein,* which is formed from *paidos* or boy and *erastein* or love (in turn formed from *eran* with its noun *eros*). A lover is an *erasteis,* and Socrates who understood and practiced true love best was the greatest *erasteis* of them all. Were Plato living today, his language would presumably reflect our differing social customs, but would not require any fundamental revision on this account.

The point is of some importance for this reason: Today we sometimes associate (on psychological grounds) the overt practice of homosexuality with ill health or immaturity, and we retain in our laws and customs many curious and inhuman social-personal restrictions upon homosexual behavior. Far from considering homosexuality unhealthy or immature, the intellectual Athenian would have scoffed at a grown man who spent his time chasing after mere women.

But again, this is not the crucial distinction. In *either* cultural environment, the man who is consumed with merely carnal hungers and gratified in merely carnal manners is properly and identically condemned as bestial, foolish, childish, and infrahuman; Plato's presentation of love can stand as strong today as ever it stood.

NOTES ON PLATONIC LOVE

I have of course profited from the use of many standard commentaries on various aspects of Plato's thought, including those (by Robin and by Lagerborg) on his theory of love. One always begins with Jowett's translations, but I have freely emended them against the Greek. R. Hackforth's admirable *Plato's Phaedrus* (Cambridge: Cambridge University Press, 1952) has been the basis of my *Phaedrus;* minor emendations have been made at 253E, 254C, 249C and 249E. I have referred to Harold North Fowler's *Loeb Plato No. 36* (Cambridge, Mass. and London: Harvard University Press and William Heinemann, resp., 1950); and W. R. M. Lamb's *Loeb Plato No. 166,* ibid., 1953. In the end, therefore, the translations found in the text must be my own responsibility. In English, today's best Platonic buy is Hamilton and Cairns's one-volume *Collected Dialogues of Plato* (New York: Pantheon Press, 1961).

[1] These "Stephanos numbers" will be found in the margins of any decently edited text of Plato, and are the standard ways of referring to specific passages.

[2] See also *Alcibiades I,* 131.

[3] See also *Lysis* 222A.

[4] A *symbolon* was half a die, kept by each of a pair of lovers in confidence that his beloved's half alone could complement his own. Aristophanes laughingly threatens that we may become as thin as kings and queens of hearts and spades, even more helplessly incomplete than we now are. The "half-hearted" example cited in the text was during the mid-twentieth century a fashion among adolescent American sweethearts, each of whom wore on his chain about his neck a *symbolon* disc shaped as a broken heart thought uniquely to match the half "symbolically" worn by the beloved.

[5] See *Lysis* 221E.

[6] See *Lysis* 216D and 220D.

[7] My colleague Dean A. P. Brogan first pointed out to me the misleading gratuity of Jowett's reading of *meletan* and *meletei* at 208A as "recollection." Lamb's "conning" in the Loeb edition is not much more helpful. No English expression quite

suggests the flowing in and out of ideas; perhaps "continuous learning" does as well as any.

[8] See p. 10 of R. Hackforth's introduction to *Phaedrus,* in the Liberal Arts Press edition.

[9] See *Apology* 228C and *Ion* 534B, 536C.

[10] See Hackforth, *op. cit.,* p. 107.

[11] *Ibid.,* p. 93.

[12] See *Phaedrus* 250E and Hackforth, *op. cit.,* p. 98.

II

BIBLICAL LOVE

THE BIBLE IS A BOOK OF LOVE. IT IS A BOOK OF TORMENT AND POWER AND passion, too, but these are always tempered by a love of incredible breadth and depth: a love that truly does pass all human understanding.

These holy books of the Jews and Christians do not sing one unequivocal song. Written during a period of perhaps a thousand years, they reflect the yearnings of lonely wanderers in the desert and the dialectic of sophisticated Hellenists. They report historic events, trace genealogies, voice the hopes and fears of the human soul, prophesy, and preach. However, throughout, from Genesis through Revelation, no strain is more constantly sung than that of love.

There is no one Biblical interpretation of love. Nor is there even any one Jewish or Christian interpretation. It would be false to the texts and also foolish to force a set of categories upon materials so richly disparate. I shall therefore permit some books and chapters and verses to present their authors' insights, relating one to another as we go, and keeping to a minimum theoretical accretions from later centuries. My implicit claim throughout will be that love is the central and indispensable harmonizing theme, without which the Bible is as sounding brass. The discussion is divided into testaments for convenience alone; as we shall see, the consistency of Hebrew teaching with Christian teaching is, from love's point of view, at least as significant as the differences that may be found between them.

47

Love in the Old Time Religion

CREATION

> God made heaven and earth and all things in it. God made the fish
> and the birds and blessed them and told them to be fruitful and multiply
> and fill the skies and the waters in the seas. And he made the beasts and
> the cattle and everything that creeps upon the ground. And God saw that
> it was good.
>
> And God made man in his image, after his likeness, and blessed male
> and female, and told them to multiply and fill the earth and subdue it.
> And, after the sixth day, God saw everything that he had made, and be-
> hold, it was very good.[1]

Why God did all this, we are not told in Genesis. We are to know only
that he did, and the moral consequences of his having done so. He made
everything there is, in its natural and unspoiled state. He blessed everything he had made, including—we must presume—the male and the fe-
male, the fruitfulness, and the love.

Whence, then, the myth that some of creation—sexual-physical creation, for example—is evil and ugly, and to be suppressed or repressed?
Not, surely, from the oldest Jewish tradition in Genesis. Rather, we must
suppose, from traditions much later than and foreign to those of the
earliest Jews.

The creative act, as it has later been interpreted, is itself an act of
love. No perfect Platonic ideals outside God lured him to creation; no
receiving stuff stood there, eternally recalcitrant to the imposition of the
forms. Since God is and was and will be perfect and self-contained, only
a self-generated and spontaneous act of overflowing love, a supreme generosity and desire to create people to share the self-perfection already
enjoyed could account for there being a world at all.[2]

Immediately we meet a difficulty, one that anticipates complexities that
lie ahead. In a useful contemporary sense of "love," the verb is transitive:
one doesn't just love in general—one loves some*one* or some*thing*. Obviously this sense will not fit with the usual *ex nihilo* interpretation of
creation. For (it seems) the Lord cannot have created from love before
there was anything to love. It should logically follow that *love* and
creation are distinct: the Lord may (and does) love what he has created
after he has created it, but he can hardly be said to have created out of
love.

The answer most appropriately offered is that, while he cannot have
felt a love going out from himself to any object (there not yet being any
objects), the Lord did create lovingly, in that we must suppose him to
have been overflowing with spontaneous loving energy. In making heaven

and earth and all things in it, he was actively "going out" from his divine self.

Evidently, there are no close human parallels with this unconditioned spontaneity, for men are always conditioned. All true human love is differentiated and objectified. When we speak of a loving personality we do mean something specific, if only that its owner is open, constructive, and creative rather than closed and destructive. We may mean no more than a sentimental kind of general "good will toward men," but even this is a will *toward* something.

To the apparently simple question, then, "Why did God create?" there really is no serious answer: perhaps, indeed, the question is impossible even to ask. Or the question might be interpreted so that at least a verbal answer becomes possible. "God created," man was later to say, "just because God is creative," or "because God is creativity." "Why," man was similarly to ask, "does God love?" And all the fullness of Biblical wisdom can answer only, with John the Elder,[3] "because God *is* loving," "because God is love." Or, simply, because God is God.

A central difference between this account of creation and Plato's is evident at once: the creative love of *Timaeus* is (as we have interpreted it) already an outgoing love for an other, a co-eternal, intrinsically lovable principle of goodness, while the Hebrew creation is (in the text) unexplained and must remain an ultimate mystery, to be mystically filled out only by our inquiring minds.

It did not occur to the pre-philosophical Jews to inquire into a *reason* for the universe; our universe simply is, and we should thank God for it. Ours is not to reason why, but to live and die as good men. Genesis— and indeed the Bible as a whole—is a "how-book," not a "why-book." It is a story of how the world came to be, and of how you and I can live as we ought, rather than a discursive speculation on what might rationally be thought about any ultimate purposes of being.[4]

The Bible's very first love-teaching, then, is the act of creation itself: God our Father made this world and saw that everything in it was good, and blessed it, in an act of transcendent love for that which he had made. This was not, at first, a selective love for virtue as against vice, since everything was good.

Good, that is, so long as man accepted his place in the creative scheme, as God's own self-made copy. When man freely disobeyed God by trying to become God, committing the original and, from one plausible point of view, the only ultimate sin, he cast himself forever apart from perfect happiness here on earth, isolating himself from his divine origin and earning eternal condemnation and punishment.

God condemned and punished man, as in self-imposed justice he **had** to do; but God also pitied him. Always, God loved. The basic expression of that love was the Torah, or Law, which God laid down for man's guidance.

DEUTERONOMY AND THE TORAH

In the beginning may have been the Word, but the real beginning for the Jews was the Covenant. Here a Lord—very likely, at first, only one among other gods—chose a people. Among the many tribes of the earth, he selected not the richest nor the wisest nor the best, but rather the poorest, the meanest, the most hopeless. He needed them not, but they needed him desperately. And he loved them so much that he freely undertook to protect and guide them through their collective tribal life on earth.

With Abraham our ancestor (we are told), the Lord freely bound himself to us in a legal contract, promising us everything that we might justly want and need, and asking of us in return only that devoted love which is obedience to law. Fulfilling the obligation which he had placed upon himself

> the Lord your God bore you, as a man bears his son, in all the way that you went until you came to his place (Deut. 1:31).

And how does a man bear his son? Why, with sincere, intimate, personal love, and with protective guidance. And with abundantly generous rewards for doing well. And, too, with loving reproof for dereliction.

> for the Lord reproves him whom he loves, as a father the son in whom he delights (Prov. 3:12).

And how ought a son to be borne by his father? Why, with deep, loving gratitude, and willing obedience, and glad fulfillment of his duty.

> A fool despises his father's instruction, but he who heeds admonition is prudent (Prov. 15:5).

—and we have the first of the great pervasive metaphors of this great world religion: the fatherhood of God and the sonship of man, witnessing the complex, almost paradoxical relationship which is at once stern and yielding, formally objective and personal, legal and intimate. Men know these complexities in their own lives, in the knowledge of their own children. They know that, in punishment, they must "push away with the left hand and draw them near with the right hand." [5] Given this knowledge, we extend it to infinite limits, and know ourselves to be justly bound to "Our Father who art in heaven," as our children are justly bound to us who brought them into this life.

Children typically resent, hate, and hurt their punishing parents, even as they love them. Too often, they repent their resentment only after their parents are dead. In the Jewish and Christian faiths, the heavenly father will never die, but the children surely will. Their—and our— responsibility is to outgrow the resentment, the hate, and the hurt before it is too late.

But this loving father, unlike many an earthly one, is consistently committed to his beloved children. And he justly demands no less consistent a commitment of them. He *will* not fail us; we *must* not fail him, at pain of his jealousy.

> You shall not make yourself a graven image, or any likeness of anything that is in heaven above, or that is in the earth beneath, or that is in the water under the earth; you shall not bow down to them or serve them; for I the Lord your God am a jealous God, visiting the iniquity of the fathers upon the children to the third and fourth generation of those who hate me, but showing steadfast love to thousands of those who love me and keep my commandments (Exod. 20:4-6; see also Deut. 5:8-10 and 6:14-15).

Of course the Lord could not be jealous did he not love us, and, loving us, he could not but be jealous, in seeing us desert his fatherhood to follow after other gods. "He who loves without jealousy does not truly love," the Talmud teaches.[6] How natural, then, that we pride ourselves upon being faithful, thinking that because we fulfill the law and remain loyal to the Lord, we have thereby earned the love he feels toward us. And how desperately we err in such pride! [7]

Our Lord, unlike the gods of other tribes, protects us not merely out of duty, but out of genuine love. Most important of all, this love is unearned, given with complete freedom. The Lord does not love us because we are what we are; rather we are what we are because he loves us, and all that we have that we ought to have, we owe to him. The love he bears us is the primary category in terms of which all lesser loves are to be measured; the category itself can never be explained by man. All that we can say is that we are a humble and pitiable people. It may even be that our very humility inspires him to love us.

> God said to Israel, "I love you, but it is not because you are more than the Gentiles, and not because you do more commandments than they, for they magnify my name more than you do, and you are the smallest of nations. But because you make yourselves small before me, therefore I love you." [8]

Again, and again, we are reminded that we are preferred over others not because we are good, but because they are bad:

> Do not say in your heart, after the Lord your God has thrust them out before you, "It is because of my righteousness that the Lord has brought

me in to possess this land"; whereas it is because of the wickedness of
these nations that the Lord is driving them out before you. Not because
of your righteousness or the uprightness of your heart are you going in
to possess their land (Deut. 9:4-5).

The love he shows us is "steadfast," as our love for him should be but
—alas—is not. Yet we have the power to love the Lord, and we exercise
that power first and above all by fulfilling the commandments which he
laid upon us. His revelation of the law is itself an act of love for us. Our
fulfillment of his law is our love for him, for love is moral through and
through. "Hear, O Israel," Moses proclaims,

> the Lord our God is one Lord; and you shall love the Lord your God
> with all your heart and with all your soul, and with all your might
> (Deut. 6:4-5).

We are, therefore, commanded to love the Lord who made us. But
how can we be *commanded* to love anyone? Surely love, if it be love at
all, is freely given. The Jew, no less than the Christian—indeed, the
Christian *because* he is also a Jew—must resolve the problem.

We do not have to seek far for the solution. In the Torah, love is
identical with moral behavior. Love *means* fulfillment of the law.

Traditional moral obligation has been considered meaningless without a genuine, metaphysical freedom. We have been made free, and being free, are free to fall away from the law, as well as to fulfill it. We are
free to hate as well as to love. We *ought* to love, not to hate. Therefore,
the Lord's command that we love him is, in this first analysis, simply a
strong, personal restatement of our general obligation to fulfill the law.

> And now, Israel, what does the Lord your God require of you, but to
> fear the Lord your God, to walk in all his ways, to love him, to serve
> the Lord your God with all your heart and with all your soul, and to
> keep the commandments and statutes of the Lord, which I command you
> this day for your good? Behold, to the Lord your God belong heaven and
> the heaven of heavens, the earth with all that is in it; yet the Lord set
> his heart in love upon your fathers and chose their descendants after
> them, you above all peoples, as at this day (Deut. 10:12-15).

But the analysis must run deeper than this. For the word "love"
suggests to us, as it most certainly did to the passionate Jews of old, an
intimate dedication and intensely human commitment, as well as a
merely formal dedication to an impersonal duty. It is this intimate
dedication that seems so difficult to reconcile with the language of commandment.

This difficulty is merely apparent; it arises because the analogy between the love of man for man and the love of God for man is weak.
Truly, I cannot command the love of any man, for I have created no

man, much less created all men in my image. But the Lord is a Lord of love. He has created all men, and that very act is a personal commitment on his part. He has freely chosen his people—another free, personal commitment. He has revealed these truths to us—still further evidence of his love. And we who have been chosen are created in his image, as lovers, but lesser than he in love, as in all other things. He and we alike love essentially, but he alone loves necessarily, for he alone, by his own inner, self-imposed necessity, remains true to his essence. We, when we truly love, are truly ourselves, our own essential selves, as we were created to be. But, with freedom, we are also free to become less than ourselves, to lose our unique essence, and to degrade ourselves.

The fatherhood of God is synonymous with his love for the human family. Every creature is living proof that the father of all is a God of love. The classical expression of this idea is found in the aphorism of R. Akiba: "Beloved is man, for he was created in the image of God; but it was by a special love that it was made known to him that he was created in the image of God; as it is said, 'For in the image of God, made He man.' " [9]

Therefore, the *Shema,* "Thou shalt love the Lord thy God . . ." may be understood as a commandment that we truly *will*—and, since we have the power—that we truly *act* consistently with our own natural, essential selves, that we be men and Jews before God. But how can we who are tempted to sin, who feel attraction to other gods, *will* ourselves to the Lord? For, as we cannot will ourselves to fall in love with a likely young woman, so we seem not to be able to *will* our passionate, direct dedication to the Lord. And truly so: if it were merely in our feeble power, we could never resist temptation. But we are never alone.

> And the Lord your God will circumcise your heart and the heart of your offspring, so that you will love the Lord your God with all your heart and with all your soul, that you may live (Deut. 30:6)

—not forcing our love, but inviting it, opening us up so that if we do as we ought, we will come intimately into contact with him. We simply are created in such a way that love for the Lord comes naturally to us. But we willfully pretend to be what we are not, when we follow after false gods. The Lord gives us the power to direct our love truly and the law which shows us how to direct our love truly. The supreme example of love in action is the love he bears toward us.

It is not, of course, the Lord who benefits from our obedience, but we:

> the Lord commanded us to do all these statutes, to fear the Lord our God, for our good always, that he might preserve us alive, as at this day (Deut. 6:24)

—and these immediate benefits are naturally expressed in terms vivid to an agricultural people:

> And if you will obey my commandments which I command you this day, to love the Lord your God, and to serve him with all your heart and with all your soul, he will give the rain for your land in its season, the early rain and the later rain, that you may gather in your grain and your wine and your oil. And he will give grass in your fields for your cattle, and you shall eat and be full (Deut. 11:13-15).

There is a gratification, deeper than the material one depicted above, in store for the people if they truly love and honor and obey. This is the satisfaction that comes from belonging to one's fellow Jews as a community, and from belonging as a community to the Lord. This is a deep joy, and marks the genuine service, and is not, as some Christians have fondly misdeemed it, merely an ascetic, painful Pharisaism. The passionate Hasidic Besht, serving the Lord with a full and happy heart, naturally loves the world the Lord has made.

> It is the aim and essence of my pilgrimage on earth to show my brethren by living demonstration, how one may serve God with merriment and rejoicing. For he who is full of joy is full of love for men and all fellow-creatures.[10]

It reveals something of the rich and paradoxical complexity of the genuine Jew to set this full-hearted good cheer beside the deeply agonized breast-beating of the equally typical wailing at the wall.

In extending the love we rightly feel toward the Lord to a corresponding love for our fellow-men, the Besht was echoing in the eighteenth century of the Christian era the breadth of love prescribed even in the Torah. For we are there enjoined to love not merely the Lord—it being a manifest impossibility to love the Lord and to hate his creatures—and not merely our fellow Jews, but the entire creation. We are to love the sojourner within our gates, for we were sojourners in Egypt; we are to love women and slaves; we are to protect and preserve trees and birds and other animals (Deut. 20, 24, 25).

The ground for this is plain: We are all, Jews and non-Jews alike, the children of God, who "sorrows at the pain each one of us suffers." [11] The classic citation is, of course,

> You shall love your neighbor as yourself (Lev. 19:18).[12]

So too, again and again in the Old Testament the call to brotherly love rings forth. Isaiah sings:

> Open the gates, that the righteous (Gentile) nation which keeps faith may enter in (Isa. 26:2).[13]

Loving one's fellow man means, in traditional Judaism, not merely granting cold intellectual recognition to the obvious fact that the creator of all is the creator of the non-Jew as well as the Jew. It means, in moral practice, that one ought actively to help even—or even especially—one's enemies.

If two men claim thy help, and one is thy enemy, help him first.[14]

[Hillel's] maxim was: "Be of the disciples of Aaron, loving peace and pursuing peace, loving your fellow-creatures and drawing them near to the Torah" (Aboth I. 12). The story is told that a heathen came to Shammai with the request to be accepted as a convert on condition that he was taught the whole of the Torah while he stood on one foot. The Rabbi drove him away with the yard-stick which he was holding. He then went to Hillel with the same request; and he said to him: "What is hateful to yourself, do not to your fellow-man. That is the whole of the Torah and the remainder is but commentary. Go, learn it" (Shab. 31a).[15]

Alongside Hillel's "negative" formulation of the Golden Rule, one must place the positive Talmudic formulation of another rabbi:

"Thou shalt love thy neighbor as thyself." This is the great general rule in Torah.[16]

Loving our fellow man, we pray for him.

One must not only think of himself when praying; he should also be mindful of the needs of his fellows. "Whoever has it in his power to pray on behalf of his neighbour and fails to do so, is called a sinner; as it is said, 'Moreover, as for me, far be it from me that I should sin against the Lord in ceasing to pray for you'" (I Sam. XII, 23) (Ber. 12b). "Whoever prays on behalf of a fellowman, while himself being in need of the same thing, will be answered first." (Baba Quamma 92a).[17]

The centrality of brotherly love in Old Testament teaching, especially in the later books and in post-Biblical Jewish writings, is so well established and so widely known that it needs no extended documentation. The problem will not merely be to show that Christ's commandment "Love one another" (as in John 13:34) is typically Jewish; this is easy. It will rather be to distinguish in Christian love what is characteristically Christian, and these distinctions must wait.[18] In any case, and whatever the distinctions may be, not merely Jews, but

All flesh shall come to worship before me, says the Lord (Isa. 66:23).

In Deuteronomy's glorious twenty-eighth chapter, we have the great prophecy of Moses, every word of it in tune with his song of love. Do we but love and obey the Lord, we are promised in the first fourteen verses, all great and good things will come to us. But do we hate and disobey him, we are warned in the final fifty-three verses, every conceivable horror will be justly visited upon us. We meet, face to face, the most momentous option of all time: to live in love and happiness with our Lord, or to die in hate and suffering without him. The language in which the agony is pictured is stark, gripping, terrifying, as is our fate if we fall away.

We are shocked and sickened by the images employed, and this is certainly intended. For sin is shocking and sickening. Yet sin can always be avoided by living within the law of love. And the Lord, who loves us, shows us the way to love him.

In all this horror, it sometimes appears as if the good life were being preached on grounds of mere fear: We must obey, else we will be tortured. Doubtless this was a consistent, strong element in the preaching. But motivation counts in morality, too, and the wise old rabbis realized fully that the kind of obedience that means the most is not trembling, fear-ridden compliance with the law, but rather open, happy, loving fulfillment. A guiding principle of action was "Greater is he who acts from love than he who acts from fear." [19]

THE WISDOM LITERATURE

Proverbs. The first great proverbial lesson in love is that its proper object is wisdom:

> Get wisdom; get insight. Do not forsake her, and she will keep you; love her, and she will guard you (4:5-6).

> Say to wisdom, "You are my sister," and call insight your intimate friend; (7:4)

> "I, wisdom, dwell in prudence, and I find knowledge and discretion. The fear of the Lord is hatred of evil . . . I love those who love me, and those who seek me diligently find me (8:12-17). For he who finds me finds life and obtains favor from the Lord; but he who misses me injures himself; all who hate me love death." (8:35-36).

These paeans to wisdom do not merely present the old refrain that man should pursue knowledge for the sake of knowledge itself, or because it is intrinsically good to have insight. To praise science or philosophy for science's or philosophy's sake would be to belie every important direction of Old Testament teaching.

"Salvation is attained not by subscription to metaphysical dogmas, but solely by love of God that fulfills itself in action. This is a cardinal truth in Judaism," [20] says the medieval Rabbi Chasdai Crescas, complementing the scriptural

> For I desire steadfast love and not sacrifice, the knowledge of God, rather than burnt offerings (Hos. 6:6).

An important underlying element in the Jewish tradition is that all science, all philosophy, all wisdom, all insight is interested, not disinterested. And it is interested in God and man. It is *moral* through and through, and passionately moral at that.

The wisdom here praised is, therefore, *moral* wisdom. Moral behavior naturally arises out of serious study and earnest understanding of the source of all morality, God's will, as revealed in the Torah. This is why the Jewish boy studies the Torah. This is why the rabbi, the teacher, explains the Torah and applies it to the problems of daily living. The immediate aim is the intelligent understanding of the Law, and hence love for the Lord and fulfillment of the covenant. "Wisdom," in a word, means *Torah,* revealed law.[21]

In the early days man was not seen as a system of segregated machines, thinking and willing and feeling. Instead, man was seen as a creature of God, organically a part of his social-cultural-religious community.

It would have seemed absurd to the early Jew—as it did to Plato—to suppose that an intelligent man could genuinely understand the truth, and at the same time deliberately act in an immoral manner. The will is not isolated from the reason and from the emotion, to be dedicated to or withheld from the service of the Lord. On the contrary, a man is a man thinking, feeling, and desiring. The Lord wants the whole man.

The praise of wisdom in Proverbs must therefore be considered as a praise of right-thinking-and-right-acting, all in one. The wise man is not the man who knows the law but does not follow it, for no such person is wise. The wise man is the man who, as a total being, gives himself gladly and equally to the study of the Torah and to its enactment.

> The way of the wicked is an abomination to the Lord, but he loves him who pursues righteousness (15:9).

As we met the father-son metaphor in Deuteronomy, so here in Proverbs we meet the other magnificent metaphor of love; that of husband and wife. The husband is to cling to his wife faithfully, and not to stray longingly after harlots; and the wife is to cling to her husband, and not to wander after other lovers. So, too—and this is the focus of the metaphor, interpreted from the point of view of either sex—we Jews are to cling to our beloved Lord faithfully, and not to make love to other, lesser gods.

> Let your fountain be blessed, and rejoice in the wife of your youth, a lovely hind, a graceful doe.
> Let her affection fill you at all times with delight, be infatuated always with her love.
> Why should you be infatuated, my son, with a loose woman and embrace the bosom of an adventuress? (5:18-20)

Do not desire her beauty in your heart, and do not let her capture you with her eyelashes; for a harlot may be hired for a loaf of bread, but an adulteress stalks a man's very life.

Can a man carry fire in his bosom and his clothes not be burned?

Or can one walk upon hot coals and his feet not be scorched?

So is he who goes in to his neighbor's wife; none who touches her will go unpunished (6:25-29).

It is interesting to note, here and often through the Old Testament, the pervasive spiritual dimension that underlies the teaching of sexual morality. The early Jews had important practical problems of sex, and the preachers had to remind their flocks of their special obligations. But the double meaning, the spiritual lesson, was being taught at the same time. Necessarily so, for the immorality of an act of adultery, or of any other crime, can be known only in terms of the fundamental spiritual principle of morality itself. The physical act of copulation cannot be a sin in merely physical terms; no beast can commit adultery. Only from the spiritual love commitment can we derive the immorality of the adulterous act. So it is perfectly appropriate to use sexual examples and sexual language to convey the lesson of the spirit. The spirit is the ground of all obligation, and this ground is interpreted to us in physical terms.

But since, as we have already seen, a man's mind is not to be segregated into faculties, so too he is not to be cut apart, Paul-wise, into mind and body, with either fighting against the other. Thus, the adulterer is one physically, mentally, and spiritually, and he truly falls away from the path prescribed by the Lord. The union is assumed in the admirable lines

He who loves wisdom makes his father glad, but one who keeps company with harlots squanders his substance (29:3).

Remembering that the Hebrew word *yoda* means "to perform the sexual act" and also "to know"—witness Adam "knowing" Eve after eating from the fruit of the tree of "knowledge"—we find that the idea of sexual wisdom falls naturally into place in the tradition.

A man who holds to the path of righteousness, and truly loves, finds superabundant rewards, for he partakes of a creative strength that the Proverbialist identifies with the strength of peace.

Hatred stirs up strife, but love covers all offenses (10:12).

As love brings peace, so love brings life, and as love is knowledge, so hate is ignorance. And we find whole patterns of concepts interweaving around the poles of love and hate. With love are associated creativity and understanding and moral uprightness and open, peaceful living.

With hate are associated destruction and ignorance and sin and war.

The growth of the concept of love from Deuteronomy to Proverbs must by now be plain. The Lord's love in the Mosaic book is usually taken to be a love for a people, taken as a unified group, a love for that tribal community which, alone among the peoples of the earth, accepted the law when it was offered to them; Jews as a community loved the Lord or hated him. With the oft-remarked "individualization" of moral responsibility in the wisdom literature and in the prophetic books, and considering the moral nature of the concept of love, we should expect an individualization of love, of Jews for the Lord, and of the love of the Lord for the Jews.

This is exactly what we find. Evidence for this has already been cited—

> The Lord reproves him whom he loves (Proverbs 3:12)

—in which we meet the clear distinction among Jews: at a given time, some are loved by the Lord, and some are not. Correspondingly, some Jews love the Lord, and some do not. Love, therefore, has become at least in part an individual relationship between a man and the Lord; no longer is it exclusively a Jewish communal responsibility to love the Lord, nor is it exclusively a Jewish communal privilege to be beloved by him.

Even as early as Exodus we find a text that seems to reveal the discriminating individual love relationship, so expressed that only some men love the Lord and are beloved by him. The Lord says that he is a jealous God, visiting the iniquity of the fathers upon their children

> but showing steadfast love to thousands of those who love me and keep my commandments (Exodus 20:6).

We are told that the Lord loved Solomon,[22] and sent Gabriel to the praying Daniel to give him wisdom and understanding because Daniel was greatly beloved.[23]

This individualization does not, however, abrogate the Jewish community in any sense. A man is still born a Jew, and still owes, even as an individual, a debt to his ancestors and to his descendants. He still lives under the covenant. He now must love as an individual, to be sure, but he still must love as an individual Jew.

The very fact that the Lord punishes those who fail him is taken by the rabbis, as it had been by Job, as evidence of his love for us as men. If he did not deeply love us, he would not trouble to chastise us; hence we speak of the "chastisements of love," and express our gratitude for them.

> A man should rejoice in chastisements more than in good fortune; for if a man lives in good fortune all his days his sin is not remitted. How is it remitted? Through chastisements.[24]

Jeremiah. Here, the scholars tell us, we have a political tract, with profound moral overtones. Whatever be the historical facts—whether Jeremiah was, as some claim, merely debating the southern cause against the northern one, and urging a "no compromise" position with respect to the nations round about Judah and Israel—it seems plain that we have a genuinely prophetic, post-Exilic plea in the name of the eternal covenant of righteousness.

And the plea is made in the name of moral love. The prevailing figure is that of Israel as the bride of God.

> Thus says the Lord, I remember the devotion of your youth, your love as a bride, how you followed me in the wilderness, in a land not sown. Israel was holy to the Lord, the first fruit of his harvest. All who ate of it became guilty; evil came upon them, says the Lord (2:1-3).

> And I brought you into a plentiful land to enjoy its fruits and its good things. but when you came in you defiled my land, and made my heritage an abomination (2:7).

From East to West, no other God has loved his people as I have loved you, says the Lord. Yet, in return for the infinite gift of my love and protection, you have played me vilely false. You have turned yourself into a beast in heat:

> know what you have done—a restive young camel interlacing her tracks, a wild ass used to the wilderness, in her heat sniffing the wind! Who can restrain her lust? None who seek her need weary themselves; in her month they will find her (2:23-24).

> If a man divorces his wife and [or] she goes from him and becomes another man's wife, will he return to her? Would not that land be greatly polluted? You have played the harlot with many lovers; and would you return to me? says the Lord (3:1).

Miserable we are, and utterly undeserving, and all but hopeless. Yet not quite utterly hopeless, for the Lord our God still rebukes us. And his rebuke, though it stings bitterly, also bespeaks an unearned forgiveness. The Lord tells us how we have sinned. Jeremiah writes to warn us of the just consequences of our sin, and to plead with us to mend our ways, and with the Lord to forgive us.

The essential point seems to be that we Israelites have actually falsified the love we rightly (and *naturally*) feel toward our God. By our own willful sin, we have turned our love into hate, and deserve only that the Lord hate us in return. In terms of the covenant, we have lost every right we were given through Abraham. A contract is breached by the failure of either party to fulfill its terms; and the other party is, in law, thereby released from his obligations. When, as in the case of the covenant, the Lord's obligations were self-imposed in the first place, so much the more clearly is he exempt from any further duty toward us. Yet, so great is the love he feels for us, he will yet (we may trust and hope, but not expectantly deserve) fulfill his service abundantly, and raise us once again from the slough of sin into which we have descended.

Ezekiel. Twenty-four chapters of doom and twenty-four chapters of utopia: the choice is our own and imperative and immediate. We must now live in love or die in hate. Thus far, we have lived as if we wanted to die. For we who owe everything to our lover the Lord have ungratefully and criminally deserted him.

> And as for your birth, on the day you were born your navel string was not cut, nor were you washed with water to cleanse you, nor rubbed with salt, nor swathed with bands. No eye pitied you, to do any of these things to you out of compassion for you; but you were cast out on the open field, for you were abhorred, on the day that you were born.
>
> And when I passed by you, and saw you weltering in your blood, I said to you in your blood, "Live, and grow up like a plant of the field." And you grew up and became tall and arrived at full maidenhood; your breasts were formed, and your hair had grown; yet you were naked and bare . . .
>
> I swathed you in fine linen and covered you with silk. And I decked you with ornaments, and put bracelets on your arms, and a chain on your neck . . . And your renown went forth among the nations, because of your beauty, for it was perfect through the splendor which I had bestowed upon you, says the Lord God.
>
> But you trusted in your beauty, and played the harlot because of your renown, and lavished your harlotries on any passer-by. . . . And in all your abominations and your harlotries you did not remember the days of your youth, when you were naked and bare, weltering in your blood (16:4-22).

Judah is of course the foundling girl-child. The "harlotries" against which Ezekiel speaks may be political alliances with Egypt and Chaldea; in any case, the lesson is there to be learned by the Jew today. For a harlot, in the prophet's eyes, is any woman who gives herself to a man illegitimately; certainly any woman who owes everything she is and has to a man, owes him also loyalty. It is at least as disloyal to follow other lesser gods as it is to enter into ill-advised political alliances. And it is unquestionable that the disloyalty persists.

There is even more in store: we, Ezekiel tells us, are not merely professional whores who sell themselves to any man who will pay. We are far worse: we are so lustful that we pay men to possess us. The result, naturally and justly, is punishment: nakedness before our lovers, poverty, stoning, and death by the sword. So, again and again and again the prophetic warning rolls out: we are miserable sinners, unnatural criminals, haters of all that should be loved. And we deserve only that we be struck to ruin instantly. "The love story of the Bible," says Hugh Thompson Kerr, Jr., "is the story of God's unrequited love." [25]

How can we explain the persistent, pervasive sexual imagery of the Old Testament literature? The Torah itself contains long series of sexual taboos, similar to many of those found in pre-literate cultures in different parts of the world. Not only is sexual loyalty to the marriage mate enjoined, and not only is homosexuality proscribed, but a whole system of detailed restrictions is placed upon the faithful, who must not commit incest even with distant relations, who must not appear naked before anyone but the spouse, who must not touch the sexual parts of the husband's enemy, who must not enter the Temple after nocturnal emissions until cleansed, or while menstruating, and so on and on. And from Deuteronomy on through Malachi[26] the theme is varied, every variation carrying its moral lesson of sin, commitment, duty, and passion.

Three answers suggest themselves: one easy, and two that are more profound.

The first is simply that sexual relations are intimate and vivid in the daily life of every man. He knows the agony of longing for the beloved, the ecstasy of passion, and the anguish of jealousy. Therefore, to make the spiritual lesson powerful and unmistakable, precisely to show the inescapably moral nature of every act, it is only natural to use the direct and powerful words of sexual love.

More profoundly, the sexual imagery may have been chosen because of a sure and subtle conviction that love, in all its manifestations, is the telling force in human nature. Love, even as biological, cannot be merely one biological function on a par with all others, else it would not disturb and excite us so deeply. Nor, psychologically, can love be merely one inclination among others. Nor can we radically dissect the need of man to love and to be beloved. Nor, finally, can love ever be utterly divorced from moral considerations. Realizing all this, the Hebrew poets and prophets thought and felt truly in teaching the lessons of the Lord in the language of love.

Even more profoundly, they may, as Kerr has proposed, have been speaking in sexual terms out of a full, acute consciousness of the power of God's love—not as an anthropomorphic way of coming to the knowledge of God, but out of a deep conviction that human love derives from God's love. The imagery, Kerr suggests, is "not simply a human way of speaking about God, but a divine way of speaking about human relationships." [27]

Hosea. Here at last, in the warmest and most human of all the prophets, we find the ultimate and loving reconciliation, the greatest gift of all. The metaphor is the metaphor of marriage, and the drama is played out in terms which, for all their touching, homely intimacy, are nothing less than epic and eternal in their scope.

Obedient to the Lord, Hosea married a harlot named Gomer. He loved her, and she bore him three children. Then Gomer returned to her early ways. Thinking to enjoy life more with her lovers than she did with her husband, she said: "I will go after my lovers, who give me my bread and my water, my wool and my flax, my oil and my drink" (2:5).

But, alas for Gomer, she found no horde of ardent lovers eager to come to her as before. She slipped down the rungs of the ladder, until she became a common whore in the marketplace, deserting the good life of free and honest love for the miserable life of its mockery.

Hosea himself had every right in justice to denounce and divorce Gomer, and to condemn her to the ugly life she had earned for herself. He would indeed act with perfect justice, for he had given the full measure of his love in taking to his bosom a harlot, making a wife of her, honoring her with his seed, and sharing his roof with her in decency.

Yet this Hosea did not do, for he had not yet given the full measure of his love. Hosea loved Gomer. Gomer was his wife. Hosea went down into the marketplace.

> So I bought her for fifteen shekels of silver and a homer and a lethech of barley. And I said to her, "You must dwell as mine for many days; you shall not play the harlot, or belong to another man; so will I also be to you" (3:2-3).

Hosea did not buy Gomer back because this was his duty, for it was not. Nor did he buy her back because he was generous, willing to forgive and forget. Hosea was a sober, righteous man of God, who really hated sin, and who must have suffered deeply as his wife betrayed him.[28] He bought her back simply because he loved her so deeply. Because he loved her so deeply, her actions had wounded him deeply. Yet this man could love beyond other men.

The story is old, the allegory clear and simple and persuasive. Even though the people of Israel have whored, and deserted all their heritage, and left the bed of bliss for beds of agony, yet still does the Lord have forgiveness in his heart. Despite all our sins, there is yet hope that we may be redeemed, not by our own good deeds, for we perform none, but by the overflowing love of God in heaven. The Lord's word here for "love," as in 6:6—"For I desire steadfast love and not sacrifice, the knowledge of God rather than burnt offerings"—we transliterate as "hesedh," literally meaning "dedication" or "covenant faithfulness," but carrying in this context a strong sense of confident, passionate courage.

In a beautiful parable, a father complained to the Besht that his son had forsaken God. "What, Rabbi, shall I do?" "Love him more than ever," was the Besht's reply.[29] In a beautiful confession of love, the Lord smiles

> How can I give you up, O Ephraim! . . . My heart recoils within me, my compassion grows warm and tender . . . I will heal their faithlessness; I will love them freely, for my anger has turned from them (Hos. 11:8, 14:4).

God's infinite love can transcend even his infinite justice. In mercy, we who transgress can yet be beloved. His loving justice rightly condemns those of us who fall away, and at the same time grounds our hope of redemption.

In the light of this love, we owe it to ourselves—and ultimately to the Lord—to love what the Lord has made. We love our fellow man gladly, and gladly serve the Lord with him. We love and respect and help the Gentile, the stranger, the orphan, natural creation itself. Love motivates our struggle to live better lives.

These our loves, like our very selves, are dependent. They but reflect the love our Lord bears toward us. The highest of all our human loves, in Old Testament terms as well as New, is that of sacrificial atonement, and the most holy lover is the man who prays to give himself up utterly, if only his people can be saved. That man is Moses pleading out of a greatly suffering heart

> Alas, this people have sinned a great sin; they have made for themselves gods of gold. But now, if those wilt forgive their sin—and if not, blot me, I pray thee, out of thy book which thou hast written (Exod. 32:31-32).

Why should we lead better lives? Why should we be good? Historically and legally and morally, because of the covenant. Prospectively, because we shall be rewarded materially and spiritually. Essentially, because we are Jews created in the divine image. As God is the ultimate source, so is he also the ultimate object of love.

As both source and object, he can guide us into free expressions of our love. No man, as the saying goes, is free to choose whether or not to love; he is free only to choose what he shall love.[30] On that choice depends the world.

The values by which we live, for better and for worse, cannot be measured in human terms alone. As man measures things, love becomes hate and peace becomes war and all *does* become vanity. Yet we can see,

even in this despairing gloom, the light of genuine value in the Lord.
To embrace him utterly is to give ourselves to God, and to live aright.
Serving him, we create in peace. Failing him, we destroy in war.

> He has showed you, O man, what is good;
> And what does the Lord require of you
> but to do justice, and to love kindness,
> and to walk humbly with your God? (Mic. 6:8)

Eros, Agape and the Dimensions of Biblical Love

With the rich tapestry of the Old Testament as a background, the
drama of the New Testament is played in equally loving terms. Before
entering its world, we need to define some terms and to set the stage.

THE BIBLICAL LANGUAGE OF LOVE

We have already met, as Hebrew words translated "love," *hesedh* and
(perhaps) *yoda*. These words are freely used to characterize the love the
Lord bears toward man, and the love man owes, in turn, toward the
Lord and toward his neighbor. Greek is more complex in its language of
love, and the peculiarities of New Testament Greek require that we indicate some broad meanings, even before considering the scriptural texts.

In Plato's day, the common word for love was *eros*. It meant, generally,
"need" or "desire," a reaching out for whatever one lacked. Originally
and characteristically, a man felt sexual *eros* toward another human being. Plato put an arresting paradox, in speaking of a heavenly *eros* toward the gods, or toward the good. As the term broadened, a man could
be said to *erei* money or music or sculpture or poetry; toward whatever
he yearned for, he felt *eros*. In addition, especially as Greece (and Greek)
declined, he could broadly and generally be said to *agapei* anything
toward which he felt *eros;* the words were not sharply distinguished, except that the noun for love was almost always *eros,* while the verb could
be either *eran* or *agapan*. Insofar as the verbs were differentiated at all,
a man might incline to save *agapan* for the love of an object he esteemed;
while he might confess *eros* for an unworthy object, he would hardly say
that he "agaped" it.

More specifically (and still speaking of the days before Jesus) a man
could feel friendship and love his friends with the verb *philein* and the
noun *philia*. When those friends were his brothers (or when he thought
of them as brothers), he could speak of his fraternal love for them as
philos-delphos or *phila-delphia*. *Philia* was affectionate and warm, but
hardly ever sexual, as was (usually, but not always) *eros*. God's love toward man was later (by Clement and Origen) to be called *philanthropy*.

Finally, there is still another word for affection or fondness, especially but not exclusively the mutual love between superior and inferior, as between one in authority and those over whom he holds it. The classical word here is *stergein*. A monarch may "stergei"-rule his people lovingly, as a father may his children; people may respond with love for their monarch, as children may for their father. The gods in Aeschylus' *Eumenides* love men. In all of these cases and more, *stergein* is appropriately used. *Stergein* passed out of usage after the fourth century, to be succeeded by *storgein* and then *philostorgein*, with meanings approximately as broad and about the same as those of *stergein*.

By New Testament times, *eros* had lost some of its currency, especially in its heavenly sense, and *stergein* (although it might have seemed eminently suitable for Christian purposes) was no longer at hand. So we find the authors of the gospels and Paul and John using *philein* and especially *agapan* to translate the ancient Hebrew words for love whenever they quoted scripture, and to convey the new Christian meanings for love as well.[31]

Words have a way of responding to men's insistent demands upon them, and *philein* and *agapan* naturally tended to shift in meaning as the Christian writers impressed them into the Lord's service, and *eran*—presumably because of its sexual sense—dropped out of the religious vocabulary. From the popular verb *agapan* Paul coined the noun *agape*, and invested it with the heart of Christian love.

The key distinction—one of emphasis—is between *agape* and *eros*. Some scholars (Bishop Nygren, for example[32]) stress or even exaggerate the difference between them. Others minimize or even underestimate it. We may understand erotic love as a reaching out to complete one's self, in expression of and response to a deep inner need, and agapic love as a transcendent act of self-sacrifice, a love more outgoing than outreaching, a love that gives with no thought of getting. *Eros* may be absorbing, and may in mutuality even ground the human community; but *eros* inescapably remains *self*-fulfilling, *self*-rewarding, *self*-possessive. Sacrificial love or *agape*, on the other hand, in Reinhold Niebuhr's words:[33]

> completes the incompleteness of mutual love (*eros*), for the latter is always arrested by reason of the fact that it seeks to relate love to life from the standpoint of the self and for the sake of the self's own happiness. But a self which seeks to measure the possible reciprocity which its love towards another may elicit is obviously not sufficiently free of preoccupation with self to lose itself in the life of the other.

The pre-Christian Jews and the pagans, in this view, are thought to have loved only erotically, with an eye to the utilitarian benefits to be enjoyed by the human lover. They are supposed by Christians to have loved the Lord and each other for the ulterior purpose of enjoying dominion over their enemies, or enjoying the bountiful harvests, or escaping the prophesied punishments; their Lord, in turn, had contractually bound himself to protect his people in return for their obedient love. In this interpretation, Jesus is said to have come precisely to show us that this self-seeking, self-fulfilling, self-protective, ultimately selfish love is incomplete and, in ultimate terms, meaningless. Jesus did not seek to fulfill himself, but to sacrifice himself. He sought us, not for his sake, but for ours. His love for us was thus more *agape* than *eros*.

Finitely reflecting this sacrificial glory, men may go "beyond *eros*," dedicating themselves in *agape* to the Lord and through him to all mankind. This is not to say that in every historic case men should do so, setting aside every claim of *eros* in favor of any claim of *agape;* after all, men do live in history. Every man acts in a complex context of needs, and were he wholly to sacrifice himself, he might (immorally) be sacrificing others' interests[34] as well. Men in fact mediate the demands upon them. But their present loving, in the light and shadow of the cross, can in some measure become sacrificial *agape* as well as enlightened *eros*.

Following Jesus' own example, we find this distinction even in our own human families. A child (however old) may exhibit (or feign) love for his parents, in order that more of his desires be gratified. A parent (if mature) may love his children givingly, even in some sense sacrificially, asking not that they do this or that in return, but lovingly, hoping that they may grow morally.[35] Jesus uses the parallel beautifully in Matthew 7:11—[36]

> If you then, who are evil, know how to give good gifts to your children, how much more will your Father who is in heaven give good things to those who ask him?

Christians believe that God loves all men. This love, called *agape* in its basic sense, is the ultimate source of all other, lesser loves. *Agape* itself, although describable, is ultimately inexplicable. Being God's inmost essence, it is more primitive than any other truth. *Agape* is never "proved" in any logistic sense; it is to the Christian rather the condition of there being any world at all, and hence the condition under which and within which all "proofs" operate. *Agape* is, in this logical sense, assumed—it is a "given."

St. Paul takes the Lord's *agape* as a "given." *Agape* is usually a premise of his reasoning, not a deductive conclusion from it. It is for him an immediate and intimate fact. And most crucially of all, *agape* has been freely given and is being freely given by God to all men.

From the primacy of *agape* follows its spontaneity. God loves because God is love, not because what God loves is inherently lovable. God's love simply overflows his being and radiates upon us all.

Being thus spontaneous, God's love for us is said to be "unconditional" or "unconditioned" or, in Bishop Nygren's special sense, "indifferent to value." [37] God's *agape* is creative, in that it is the source of the love we bear toward him and toward each other. Itself unmotivated, *agape* is the supreme motive.

These are the characteristics cited by Nygren[38] as defining the "fundamental motif" of (Pauline) *agape,* and set off sharply against what Nygren takes to be the opposite "fundamental motif" of *eros. Eros*—best exemplified by Plato—is, according to Nygren, acquisitive-possessive, conditioned, egocentric, and "man's way to the divine," [39] while *agape* is pre-eminently and repeatedly called "God's way to man." [40]

Deriving from God's *agape* toward men, and strictly dependent upon it, is man's love of God. In an extended sense,[41] this God-inspired, God-directed love may also be called *agape,* in order to distinguish it from *eros.*

> The word *agape* signifies moral love; there is a hint of austerity in it. It conveys the idea of good will, of brotherliness, of friendship. There is an element of reverence in it, as indicating what man's attitude toward God and his fellow men ought to be. The love of which the apostle writes has nothing whatever to do with the senses or the instincts; it is an intellectual, moral, and spiritual quality. . . .[42]

But man's love for God can also be called *philia,* and we should be pressing our language much too hard if we were to force a sharp distinction between *philia* and *agape.*

Again, man's love for his fellow men—the social-communal fellowship on earth reflecting the Christian fellowship with God—is appropriately called *agape* as well as *philia.* As time wore on and morality crumbled, *agape* even came to be used of lewd love-feasts of certain pseudo-Christians.

In his important book, *Agape and Eros,* cited above, Bishop Nygren portrays the structure and history of the Christian notion of love in terms of competition and compromise between *agape* and *eros,* and between *agape* and the Hebraic law. Augustine and medieval "charity" he takes to be an unhappy blending of *agape* and *eros.* Luther's reformation he considers a restoration of *agape,* with its corresponding theocentricity, and a corresponding renewal of Pauline-pure Christianity.

Analysts may and sometimes must artificially separate elements that are always found, whether in nature or in history, together. The test of the analysis lies not in its artificiality, or in whether it puts asunder what God has put together, but in its contribution to our enlightenment. We ought to ask not, "Are *eros* and *agape* ever found apart in their respectively pure states?" but rather, "Do these categories aid our understanding?" I believe that they do, and that Nygren's analysis of the structure and history of Christian love is, in certain respects, enlightening.

Nygren argues[43] correctly that the fact that our one word "love" is used to translate both *eros* and *agape* does not prove that the realities for which *eros* and *agape* stand are identical or even related; there may be a colossal, historic-accidental pun at stake. Nygren sets out to prove, in effect, that this is what has happened. He fails to observe, however, that one can argue at least equally well that the fact that Greek contains two distinct words for love does not prove that *eros* and *agape* are distinct and unrelated realities.

While gratefully recognizing the significance of Nygren's important contribution, some scholars have suggested that his analysis has resulted in overdrawn distinctions[44] and in occasional slantings of the evidence. Nygren rests much of his case, for example, upon the fact that Paul regularly uses *agape* to refer to God's love for man. His text makes little or nothing of the fact that Paul often and equally naturally uses *agape* to refer to man's upward-striving love toward God.[45]

A more serious distortion, in my judgment, is Nygren's exaggerated distinction between Christianity and Judaism. Naturally, a Christian is anxious (as Paul was) to sharpen this difference, just as the early Jews found it necessary to sharpen the differences between their own religion and its competitors. But when Nygren uncritically accepts Paul's interpretations of Judaism and repeats many of the later misguided Christian criticisms, he does his analytic cause no service.

For example, Nygren says that *agape* is a social idea. He cites as a unique contribution of Christianity to ethics the movement from individualism to society.[46] Surely Nygren can be thinking only (and fuzzily, at that) of the Hellenic fourth century; he cannot claim that historic Hebraism had based its ethics wholly upon goods to be attained individually.

Again, Nygren cites as Christianity's unique contribution to religion its movement from "egocentric" religion (What can God do for me? How can I get to God?) to "theocentric" religion (in which God has absolute authority over the ego).[47]

> It is in Christianity that we first find egocentric religion essentially superseded by theocentric religion.[48]

—and Nygren says that this revolution is intimately associated with the idea of *agape*. I cannot reconcile these claims with my understanding of either testament. As I read the Old Testament, God does have absolute authority over the ego (within limits, as Nygren must allow, which will preserve human freedom); ancient Judaism is thus, in Nygren's terms, "theocentric." As I read the New Testament, a central, burning question is "How can man get to God?" and Christianity is in this respect "egocentric." The claim that the individual-social and egocentric-theocentric changes are "chiefly due to Christianity" [49] is simply not made out.

Nygren is on firm ground (as against altogether too many Christian apologists, who ignore the evidence) when he points out that the "double commandment"—the Shema plus "love your neighbor"—is not uniquely Christian at all, but good sound Old Testament teaching.[50] Instead, he finds the uniqueness in Jesus' call to sinners: "I came not to call the righteous, but sinners" (Mark 2:17).

Of this text, Nygren says that it turns Jewish values upside down.[51] It does no such thing. Every prophet, beginning with Moses, had come to call not the righteous, but sinners. If not to call sinners, why would any prophet come, or be sent? *Of course* Jesus came to call sinners. Who else? Are we not all sinners? What is distinctively Christian in all this?

Nygren takes as his starting point Matthew 5:44: "Love your enemies and pray for those who persecute you." Again, in the light of the Old Testament texts cited earlier, the distinctiveness of Christianity remains obscure.

It becomes clearer, though only *en passant* and dangerously, when Nygren later compares Deuteronomy 7:6-10 (including ". . . it is because the Lord loves you . . . that the Lord has brought you out with a mighty hand . . .") with (Christian) *agape*,[52] and concludes that these loves are distinct, because in Deuteronomy "the principle of retribution is still maintained." I grant that Deuteronomy contains the notion of retribution. But if Christian *agape* does not also imply retribution, it certainly is both sentimental and un-Christian. Bishop Nygren should ask St. Paul how Christianity can do without retribution. What is the "wrath and fury" of God in Romans 2:5,8? What is the "cutting off" in Romans 11:22? If these are not instances of righteous, retributive Christian justice, what are they?

Finally, and perhaps most astonishingly, Nygren cuts Judaism off from Christianity with what I submit is a radical misreading of the Hebrew texts.

> *Agape* is the opposite of "Nomos," and therefore a denial of the foundation on which the entire Jewish scale of values rested.[53]

Of Jewish "legalism" Nygren says: "Nomos is the controlling idea, and love has its place within the legal framework." [54]

I have already argued that in Judaism the law is the law of love. The "foundation on which the entire Jewish scale of values rested," to use Nygren's own language, is the creative, warm, loving, giving, dedicated concern of the Lord for his people. The foundation is not a mechanical, legalistic literalism, any more than the foundation of Christian love is a perfect attendance record at Sunday school. To say that, in Judaism, "love has its place within the legal framework" is every bit as ridiculous as to say that, in Christianity, "love has its place within the Sermon on the Mount." The only way these statements could be given any sense would be by postscribing "—and that place is completely, explicitly, and centrally defining." Love defines the meaning of the Torah, exactly as it defines the meaning of the Sermon on the Mount.

LOVE IN THE NEW TESTAMENT

MATTHEW, MARK AND LUKE

And to Mary a child was born.

The interpretation of this event is the continental divide between Christians and non-Christians. For the former, history moves to and from this moment: the birth to Mary of Jesus of Nazareth, only begotten son of God, was the greatest miracle of them all, the second creative act through which alone man is ultimately redeemed from his sin by love and sacrificial agony. For the non-Christian, Jesus' birth is a natural historic event to which have been imputed miraculous myths. Neither Christian nor non-Christian can question the historic importance of that event. Both can, through an understanding of the second testament, see even richer dimensions of love.

Jesus was a Jew, and however we interpret his birth, life, and death, we must never forget that fact. He was born a Jew, he lived a Jew, and he died a Jew. However scornfully, he was crucified as I N R I, Jesus of Nazareth, King of the Jews. He conceived himself a Jew; he believed that his teaching was completely consistent with the teaching of his prophetic forebears. He knew the earlier teaching and he preached it, saving his bitterest condemnation for those who, in his judgment, had perverted it.

Jesus knew the Torah and lived it perfectly. He outwardly embodied its inner essence, and since the Torah's essence is love, Jesus loved perfectly.

In the Christian teaching, Jesus' birth eminently exemplified God's love for man, in fulfilling the ancient promise that a descendant of David, a savior-messiah-Christ would be sent to the Jews, to lead them out of sin into righteousness. The arrival of any prophet was evidence of God's love; the evidence provided by Jesus' birth was pre-eminent, because this prophet was more than a holy man; he was God himself, God incarnate, God become man.

There is and can be absolutely no explanation of this incarnation. Categories can only be tortured in a hopeless effort to render the contradictory consistent, or the impossible possible. As man's mind measures his world, God as god cannot become man as man, take on himself flesh, suffer genuine temptation, undergo agony, and die to rise again. The story cannot rationally be understood and believed.

Yet believed it is, absurd though it is—or, as an early father put it, it is believed precisely *because* it is so absurd. The ultimate absurdity is not simply the surd, the conceptual incongruity of God-become-man-while-remaining-God; men have long demonstrated their ability to live with conceptual contradictions. Ultimately, the absurdity lies in the love God freely gives to unworthy man: the incommensurability between his unbounded devotion and dedication to us and our poor service of him.

Paul's illumination as he walked along the Damascan road must have been far more than a repentance and resolution to live a better life. It must have been a starkly astonished, staggering realization: that God could know how black his sins had been, and yet overwhelmingly love him, Paul, and through Jesus' blood wash his sins white.

In Jesus, God entered history while remaining beyond it. Jesus defined perfection. His perfection lay not simply in his obedience to the written law, or his avoidance of sin. Nor did it lie in his embodying and exhibiting, successively, all the virtues of man. His perfection lay in his love, both transcendent and immanent. Through him, God loved us deeply during his life and completely at his death. As Jesus and the Spirit are persons mysteriously distinct from the Father, love is mutual among them. Yet, paradoxically, the beloved son is sacrificed in love.

> Christ as the norm of human nature defines the final perfection of man in history. This perfection is not so much a sum total of various virtues or an absence of transgression of various laws; it is the perfection of sacrificial love.
>
> The paradoxical relation of sacrificial to mutual love clarifies the Christian doctrine of the sinlessness of Christ. Furthermore, it makes the doctrine that Jesus was both human and divine religiously and morally meaningful and dispenses with the necessity of making the doctrine metaphysically plausible.[55]

The effect of this epochal sacrifice should have been the deepest revolution the world has ever known: a radical turning away from evil and hatred toward goodness and love, a total transformation of history, human society, and mankind itself. In some manner and measure, this revolution has come about. Many men and some few societies have been transformed. Many more, alas, have not. Seeing this, men have despaired and turned yet again to the worship of idols, not recognizing that the glory of divine love, radiant in heaven and pervading the lives of the faithful, remains super-historic. To expect or even to envisage the possibility of men's achievement of perfection on earth is to default man's permissive obligation to do what he can while he can, to make this world a somewhat less intolerable place to live.

> . . . the Christian faith in its profoundest versions has never believed that the Cross would so change the very nature of historical existence that a more and more universal achievement of sacrificial love would finally transmute sacrificial love into successful mutual love, perfectly validated and by historical social consequences.[56]

That the love God bears us is true *agape,* as we have defined it, is beyond question for the Christian. It is spontaneous, unconditioned, uncaused, and not subject to calculating human expectations. God "makes his sun rise on the evil and on the good, and sends rain on the just and on the unjust" (Matt. 5:45). The apostles received without pay, and must themselves give freely (Matt. 10:8). And the last shall receive his denarius, as well as the first (Matt. 20:1-16).

Jesus' life on earth was a life of service to his father and ours, God in heaven. The miracle-reports of the synoptic gospels, whether historically true or false, are presented for at least three distinct purposes:

(1) to prove that Jesus was an exceptional person because he could perform magic.[57]
(2) to exhibit Jesus' own love for men. His was never black magic, meant for show.
(3) to reveal, through a clear metaphor, the profound relations between God and man.

The blind man, to take a nonsynoptic example, could never regain his eyesight by any human agency, and Jesus showed superhuman power in restoring it. The man needed to see, and Jesus' gift of sight was, even in human terms alone, a great one. Most importantly, we see, by means of the miracle, how we too can recover from our own spiritual blindness through faith.

Again, Jairus' daughter was really and truly dead. No mere man could restore her to life, but Jesus did. The gift of life was a gift of love. And we who are dead in our hearts and minds, having fallen away from the truth, learn through her story that we can by faith be restored to everlasting life.

So, too, with the parables. Every one of them can, as Nygren[58] claims, be read simply as a love story. Consider the paradigms of forgiveness:

> One of the Pharisees asked him to eat with him, and he went into the Pharisee's house, and sat at table. And behold, a woman of the city, who was a sinner, when she learned that he was sitting at table in the Pharisee's house, brought an alabaster flask of ointment, and standing behind him at his feet, weeping, she began to wet his feet with her tears, and wiped them

with the hair of her head, and kissed his feet, and anointed them with the ointment. Now when the Pharisee who had invited him saw it, he said to himself, "If this man were a prophet, he would have known who and what sort of woman this is who is touching him, for she is a sinner." And Jesus answering said to him, "Simon, I have something to say to you." And he answered, "What is it, Teacher?" "A certain creditor had two debtors; one owed five hundred denarii, and the other fifty. When they could not pay, he forgave them both. Now which of them will love him more?" Simon answered, "The one, I suppose, to whom he forgave more." And he said to him, "You have judged rightly." Then turning toward the woman he said to Simon, "Do you see this woman? I entered your house, you gave me no water for my feet, but she has wet my feet with her tears and wiped them with her hair. You gave me no kiss, but from the time I came in she has not ceased to kiss my feet. You did not anoint my head with oil, but she has anointed my feet with ointment. Therefore I tell you, her sins, which are many, are forgiven, for she loved much; but he who is forgiven little, loves little." And he said to her, "Your sins are forgiven." Then those who were at table with him began to say among themselves, "Who is this, who even forgives sins?" And he said to the woman, "Your faith has saved you; go in peace" (Luke 7:36-50).

There are many mysteries here,[59] to be sure, and the text may be analytically divided into a "story" and a "parable." But more simply, we have a despised whore sincerely expressing love for God, and being greatly and lovingly forgiven. Her heart had turned wholly to Jesus and he—always looking inwardly, rather than to the outward act—wholly erases her stain of sin. She had not strictly "earned" his forgiveness by weeping while anointing his feet, nor even yet by loving him. She had rather accepted the pure love she felt radiating from him. That accepting faith saved her, and she went in peace, as did the adulterous woman, under the command to sin no more.[60] That she had sinned was unchallenged; but under Jesus' counterchallenge, the sins of her cowardly, self-appointed judges, none of whom dared openly accuse her, outweighed her own, in Jesus' loving reckoning, and she too was forgiven.

The concentration upon God's *agape* as love-giving-itself-freely-without-counting-the-costs always suggests sentimentality, and Christianity has often been accused of it.[61] But sentimentality is "unreasoned love" in a shallow sense. It is a wanton, wallowing love, blindly blanketing every object in its path. *Agape*, on the other hand, loves fully and with metaphysical reason. The "reason" however must be carefully understood, else *agape's* genius be lost. If we think for an instant of the beloved's worthiness to be loved, we have lost it; men are forever (so long, that is, as they remain men) unworthy sinners. The "reason" why God loves men is that God is God, and this is reason enough. *Agape*, properly understood, is a love that, like sentimentality, does not discriminate its object,[62] but that, unlike sentimentality, does genuinely will its beloved's good, even though that good be painful to him. *Agape* is thus rescued from sentimentality, because it can brook the chastening and sacrificial agony of the beloved for his own sake. Only thus can God's Christian righteousness, his wrath and his fury, be preserved. Without the right-eousness, the wrath, and the fury, Christianity becomes flabby, and Nietzsche is confirmed. With it, God's authoritarian *agape* is reasoned, not in the sense that men's souls are themselves infinitely valuable,[63] but in the deeper sense that, however ugly and sinful they may be, they are—by an all-loving God—lovable.

Jesus thus enacted and exemplified love, at least as much as he preached it, and he preached it far more than he deduced it. His life, as a life of love, was given to us, we are taught, as a perfect and definitive model of humanity. So, too, was his death given to us: that we might find ourselves and learn to love each other through the deliberate, pain-ful sacrifice of God, by God, to God—but for mankind.

A central theme, first sounded by the synoptists but recurring again and again through the New Testament, is the proclaimed contrast be-tween "law" and "love." The Sermon on the Mount[64] at Matthew 5-7 contains the famous series of distinctions "You have heard this. . . . But I say that . . . ," and woe is proclaimed to the lawyers (at Luke 11:45-52). As we shall see, Paul never tired of offering Jesus' love in place of the supposedly outworn and superseded law.

There is one plain, direct sense in which this contrast can be drawn, and we have already met it in our consideration of the Old Testament. If any man strips the love from the Torah, he leaves it a hollow shell of platitudinous moralisms. Some Jews had done this, and Jesus and the synoptists and Paul were properly concerned (as some earlier prophets like Hosea had been) to revivify the law, and show forth its heart of love. So, too, were Augustine and Savonarola and Luther to be con-cerned. All were reformers.

But reform is not revolution, or abrogation of the law. It is not per-fectly clear whether Jesus thought himself a revolutionist, though there is no doubt that Paul considered him one, and that most subsequent Christians have followed Paul in this. Almost immediately after pro-claiming the beatitudes, Jesus explicitly denies any revolutionary am-bitions:

> Think not that I have come to abolish the law and the prophets; I have come not to abolish them but to fulfil them. For truly, I say to you, till heaven and earth pass away, not an iota, not a dot, will pass from the law until all is accomplished. Whoever then relaxes one of the least of these commandments and teaches men so, shall be called least in the kingdom of heaven; but he who does them and teaches them shall be called great in

the kingdom of heaven. For I tell you, unless your righteousness exceeds that of the scribes and Pharisees, you will never enter the kingdom of heaven (Matt. 5:17-20).

I believe that Jesus considered himself to have come as the Messiah, in fulfillment of the Law. He came, as all the prophets before him had come, to preach righteousness, and righteousness within the law, not any kind of love that would abrogate the law. He came, as the prophets before him had come, to interpret the law. In doing good out of love on the Sabbath, Jesus was not "relaxing" a commandment; he was revealing its loving essence.

But Jesus came not only to preach and interpret, to promise and threaten, to ask that the people repent their sins and mend their ways. He came to reveal truth, to give love, and to save mankind.

Here we approach the only important difference between Christian love and Jewish law. To the Jews as to the Christians, God's love grounds morality. Only because he loves man does God care deeply enough to instruct him. The Torah was, in its day, the most precious gift God could give to his beloved people. It enjoins love and demands it of men. It comes from God, who at creation empowered men to love, and who lovingly sustains them despite their sins.

The true Jew, in Jesus' day and our own, holds that the Torah contains all ultimate moral truth, and that the later prophets (including Jesus of Nazareth) were sent to recall man to his loving duties under the law. The Jew does not believe that there ever was a God-in-man, or Lord incarnate. God sustains us continuously in his love.

The Christian, in Jesus' day and our own, will hold that, in addition to the Torah and in fulfillment of the prophecies, God miraculously overflowed into history and actively sought to save each sinful man with his divine love through Jesus Christ. God freely gave himself to us, in giving Jesus to us. As Jesus, being God, demands righteousness of us, his imperatives empower us: he enlivens us with his love, even as he commands of us our love. No earlier prophet made this claim. It is in this sense, and I believe only in this sense, that John Knox can say[65] that the law only asks, while love both asks and gives.

At the heart of every Christian moral lies the profoundly challenging text "Love your enemies." In context,

> If you love those who love you, what credit is that to you? For even sinners love those who love them. And if you do good to those who do good to you, what credit is that to you? For even sinners do the same. And if you lend to those from whom you hope to receive, what credit is that to you? Even sinners lend to sinners, to receive as much again. But love your enemies, and do good, and lend, expecting nothing in return; and

your reward will be great, and you will be sons of the Most High; for he is kind to the ungrateful and the selfish (Luke 6:32-35).

Or again,

> Love your enemies and pray for those who persecute you, so that you may be sons of your Father who is in heaven; for he makes his sun rise on the evil and on the good, and sends rain on the just and on the unjust. For if you love those who love you, what reward have you? Do not even the tax collectors do the same? And if you salute only your brethren, what more are you doing than others? Do not even the Gentiles do the same? You, therefore, must be perfect, as your heavenly Father is perfect (Matt. 5:44-48).

These are, as the saying goes, hard teachings. Jesus lays upon us, as members of the faithful—as Jews, that is—an impossible claim: that we, as men, should be perfect, as God is perfect.

We can never hope to understand these texts simply, and unless we read Jesus' words of love deeply, we shall instantly and sensibly despair. He cannot and must not mean merely that we should perform any specific actions, like lending to poor credit risks and praying for our persecutors; this direction is rather toward the inward will, and his concern is almost always with the motive rather than with the act.

Nor can Jesus have meant that we should approve our enemies, feel kindly toward them as people, or even like them; he himself disapproves of and presumably dislikes at least some of our enemies.[66] Any man who really did approve his every enemy and feel kindly toward him would, in any human society, be in a hospital or a cemetery. Jesus surely meant far more than this.

He must implicitly have been promising as well as preaching. "*Love your enemy*" is really a paradox, for if I genuinely love a man, I cannot genuinely conceive him to be my enemy at all. Instead, I become one with him in fulfillment and in frustration. His aims become my aims, his needs my needs.

On the level of human conflict, in historic human society, this has never fully come to pass, and never will. My personality is far from totally unified, and I know only too bitterly how violently some of my own needs conflict with others. I become a self only by working out and living out some kind of basic balance as a human being. And if I have only a precarious unity within my personal self, how much more precarious, in human terms, is any unity of aim and need among enemies.

While speaking to us in history, and preaching historic peacefulness, Jesus is also taking us beyond the level of human history. He is claiming that, just as each of us is, in fundamental metaphysical terms, capable of becoming *a* self, essentially loving, so also each man can achieve a realization that he is fundamentally human, or humankind. Insofar as I am a man, I cannot essentially hate any other man as man, because all men are made in God's image, and because God loves. In hating any man, I myself am less than man: I am beast. Jesus does not charge me to be suddenly, here and now, perfect as God is, nor does he threaten or condemn me for failure to be this; he knows me better than that. He charges me rather with perfecting myself, by identifying myself basically with every human being, even my enemy, and thus growing in love.

"Well," we incline to say in humble confession or boastful denial, "if we are beasts, why then we are beasts. What's the good of telling us to be loving?"

And, if we were left to our own resources, we should be correct in our renunciation. But Jesus implicitly promises that the love with which we are to love our enemies comes not alone from within us, but from God the Father through him who teaches us this lesson. Jesus lived to love us; to infuse love into our hearts so overflowingly that we really can, in growing measure, come up toward the Father's perfection, if we will; and to save us from failure.

"Love your enemies" thus means "Will honestly to be your inner, Godlike loving self. Open your being to God. He will empower you to find your own intimacy with all mankind, to belong to humanity in peace. Dedicate your self to God through Jesus and man. Respect the preciousness of every person. Live in love."

For a Christian, no authority can be higher than that of Jesus himself, and it was he who called the "second commandment" like the first, which is of course the *Shema*:

> You shall love the Lord your God with all your heart and with all your soul, and with all your mind. This is the great and first commandment. And a second is like it, You shall love your neighbor as yourself. On these two commandments depend all the law and the prophets. (Matt. 22:37-40).[67]

The word "like" poses a problem. Some scholars[68] minimize the distinguishing power, taking "like" to mean almost "identical with," and thus reading the "double commandment" as essentially single. Loving one's neighbor is, in this interpretation, but an application of the Shema. Other scholars[69] insist upon the distinction expressed by "like" and sharply cut the two commandments apart.

Those who, with Nygren, want to exaggerate the distinctness, concentrate upon the "universality" of the Christian doctrine and minimize that of Judaism. Therefore, they interpret Jesus as spreading love abroad, even beyond the Jewish people, to the "Gentile-Nations" and all mankind.[70] That Jesus did so intend his love to spread is by no means beyond question; whether the pre-Christian Hebrew prophets, especially since Isaiah, did not also intend universality, is at issue. I believe that they did, and, with Buttrick, take the "double commandment" as single and complex.[71]

It is the so-called "second commandment" that has occasioned so much anxiety, if only because of its hopelessness. Yet even before we face the challenge, we have the "as yourself" to assess.

It may of course be that the gospel author cites Jesus' words in unquestioning acceptance of the belief that every man does love himself utterly: that self-love simply goes without saying, and that we are here being commanded to extend this abundant and overflowing love outward. Doubtless some readers have thus understood the text.[72]

Such an assumption can hardly go unchallenged today, for we now know that an excess of self-love is perhaps even rarer than its deficiency; many patients find their ways to physicians not because they love themselves too much (and their neighbors too little), but rather because they love themselves too little (and their neighbors, consequently, hardly at all). The man who lacks a certain self-esteem and self-respect lacks self-integrity as well. He is ill, and tends to fritter himself away in petty frustrations. Until he can find a self within himself, and find that self in some minimal sense approvable and lovable, there is no point in moralizing to him as a person, for there really is no person there at all.

At this very basic level, active loving is not only a condition for health and wholeness, but a condition for there being any personality at all. We *are* ourselves only as we can in some degree love ourselves . . . and we thereby become able to love our neighbors.[73]

To the lawyer's question, "And who is my neighbor?" Jesus offers one of his most beautiful stories:

> A man was going down from Jerusalem to Jericho, and he fell among robbers, who stripped him and beat him, and departed, leaving him half-dead. Now by chance a priest was going down that road; and when he saw him he passed by on the other side. So likewise a Levite, when he came to the place and saw him, passed by on the other side. But a Samaritan, as he journeyed, came to where he was; and when he saw him, he had compassion, and went to him and bound up his wounds, pouring on oil and wine; then he set him on his own beast and brought him to an inn, and took care of him. And the next day he took out two denarii and gave them to the innkeeper, saying, "Take care of him; and whatever more you spend, I will repay you when I come back." Which of these three, do you think, proved neighbor to the man who fell among the robbers? He said, "The one who showed mercy on him." And Jesus said to him, "Go and do likewise" (Luke 10:30-37).

The answer to the lawyer's question, in merely mundane terms, is that everyone is your neighbor, especially the man who needs you most —and, of course, whom you need most. The Samaritan's neighborly, loving, aid is, like Hosea's love for Gomer, far more than a nominal token. It exhibits Jesus' own characteristic *agapic* "extravagance" or "superabundance." Surely the Samaritan would have shown much love —far more than most of us would do today—simply by binding the victim's wounds. But he went on from here the "second mile," "giving the cloak as well," "seventy times seven times." [74]

We are all each other's neighbors. We all suffer. We need each other, not merely in the easily specifiable terms of any nominal duty, but abundantly. And so we should love, in Jesus' name. So loving, we meet a miracle, for we find that the giving of love is not like dispensing some precious possession in which we alone have property rights. The earthly well from which water is continuously drawn will run dry; but love is a divine paradox, in that as we spread it abundantly, our own supply is continually renewed. The more we give, the more is given to us to give, and the more we have.

So much for the universal scope of the love commanded of us. We are asked to love not merely everywhere and everything, but also in infinite degree. "You, therefore," Jesus says, "must be perfect, as your heavenly Father is perfect." And, as he confided to his apostles shortly before the end, "A new commandment I give to you, that you love one another; even as I have loved you, that you also love one another." [75] This is the climax of Jesus' "Sermon in the Chamber." [76] Its first wonder is the claim of newness, since Jesus is here privately conveying the esoteric doctrine to his beloved apostles, who of all men knew him best. Jesus is here about to give up his life. He has worked with and enlightened these faithful disciples during his entire mission. Surely they have heard him say, "Love one another" and "Love your neighbor" and "Love your enemies" time and again. What is so new about these next-to-last words?

As Dr. Abbott points out,[77] the newness lies in the qualifying "even as I have loved you." It is this that renders Jesus' new commandment so overwhelming. Those interpreters are surely correct who confess man's helplessness here: as men alone, we simply cannot love each other as Jesus loved us, however much we may wish to do so. But, we are reminded once again, we are not merely men. The same Lord who imposes the impossible commandment gives us the power of grace which, granted the dedicated faith within our hearts, will make even this possible. We truly can become as God in love; if we love him, he will give us the power of perfectly loving each other.

The "newness," at last, is only the newness of Christ himself. Beloved on earth by his disciples, he will in their memory after his death inflame their hearts with a new power to love the world and transform it. The meaning of the text is, in Abbott's words,[78]

> that after the death of Jesus, the memory of His love, enhanced in His absence, would spring up as an entirely new power within their hearts, so that "love" would assume a new meaning, and the command to love— though as old as the first influence of the Word, and therefore as the creation of man—would become essentially a new commandment.

This very human yet more-than-human effect of Jesus upon men's hearts is, to Christians, the most astonishing thing in the world. It is the loving "imitation of God" that transforms the way the world seems, and the way men will to live. It is faith, and faith—in Kerr's apt phrase[79] —does not make new things, but makes things new. The world is not new, but it is to be renewed through mankind's reflection of Jesus' love.

And as Jesus has died to this earth and to history, so in Christian eschatology, this earth and history itself are dying. As John the Elder says,

> Beloved, I am writing you no new commandment, but an old commandment which you had from the beginning; the old commandment is the word which you have heard. Yet I am writing you a new commandment, which is true in him and in you, because the darkness is passing away and the true light is already shining (I John 2:7-8).

This light can shine already in our souls. It is the birth of Jesus, our heavenly Father's perfectly loving gift, that truly distinguishes Christianity. But it is equally Jesus' death. He rose to new life after his death. So also we, as individual men and as the world, shall rise—or fall—at the end of history, when meaning will complete itself in love.

PAUL[80]

Each in its own way, the three first (or "synoptic") gospels tell a similar story. The fourth is evidently the product of a very different mind: more worldly and sophisticated, more interested in metaphysical thought, perhaps more esthetically sensitive, yet surely no less sincere and devout.

Still another mind, wonderful and wondrous in its way, is that of stormy, agonizing, fanatical St. Paul. Paul is a man possessed and consumed by a passion for the faith and for saving men's souls. He is the first of the circuit-riding preachers, the first of the ecclesiastical executives, the first of the Christian philosopher-theologians. He can meditate sensitively and speculatively, and he can rave resentfully; he can whisper and then thunder jeremiads.

Those of Paul's letters that are preserved as a central part of our New Testament are sometimes taken as practically defining Christianity, sometimes as violently distorting it. Liberal Christians of the twentieth century, for example, tend to consider Paul a Hellenist and an Orientalist who made Jesus into a supernatural figure. They attribute to Paul a primary role in the deplorable transformation of "essential" Christianity into a mythical world-view of doubtful truth and misleading morality; they prefer instead to set aside the metaphysics and the mysteries, along with the miracles reported in all the gospels, and to concentrate upon the Sermon on the Mount and the examples of natural love in Jesus' life.

Other Christians try to minimize the differences between the gospel teaching and that of St. Paul, and to weave the diverse strands together into a more or less coherent whole. Out of these conflicts have arisen competing interpretations of Christianity, some complementary and others contradictory, and arid acres of theological controversy. Incompetent to resolve or even clearly to present all of these controversies, I simply invite a sympathetic reading of the texts, with occasional observations on some of the issues. Our focus, as always, will be on the teaching of love.

Romans. Who were the Romans to whom Paul addressed his letter? No one knows; we may suppose that they were, for the most part, Gentile converts to Christianity, threatened with further conversion by conservative Jews to more literal obedience to the Mosaic law, and we may suppose that Paul wrote to these Romans, in advance of his pastoral visit, to forestall a suspected tendency toward Pharisaism.

In any case, this letter makes Paul's sharp distinction between the earlier law and the new dispensation through Jesus. It exemplifies his mission to the "uncircumcised" rather than the "circumcised." And it sets, for the centuries, the old, old problem of salvation (or "justification") through faith rather than through works. I shall suggest that the concept of Christian love is a way—I believe it to be the only way—of resolving these conflicts.

Some of the Christians of the mid-first century had been Jews before their conversion. These men had, of course, been circumcised. Circumcision was a part of the law, and a mark that then distinguished Jews from other men; very early, it became also a symbol for the faith of the Jews and membership in the Jewish community; the circumcised were not merely those whose penises had been cut back, but those who belonged morally and historically to the people chosen by the Lord; the uncircumcised were the "Gentiles" or "nations," those outside the law.

Paul, born a Jew, was proud of being among the circumcised. Some of his early preaching may have been among Jews, to convert them to the new faith whose followers he himself had persecuted, and to inspire in these converts the new vision of Jesus. But Paul saw his major work in the service of those who came to Christianity from the various pagan religions, or from none at all. It may even be that Paul took special pride in ministering to—and thus loving—those beyond the Jewish pale. After all, God, as Paul says here at 2:11, "shows no partiality." And David's blessing, "Blessed are those whose iniquities are forgiven, and whose sins are covered; blessed is the man against whom the Lord will not reckon his sin," Paul quotes as expressly intended not alone for the Jews, but for all men (4:7-13).

The law is, as always, basically the Torah. More fully, the word is used by Paul to stand for the way of life of those—typically, the too much maligned Pharisees whom Jesus had castigated—who believe that they discharge their entire religious obligation by "doing and not doing" . . . that is, simply by performing all the acts prescribed and abstaining from all the acts proscribed.

In teaching that this mechanical ritualistic correctness was not enough, Paul believed himself simply to be following Jesus' own teaching, just as Jesus, in his turn, had been following the teaching of some earlier prophets. But Paul's message was to go much further, and his claim was to be far more radical than this. It is not possible to state this message unequivocally, partly because Paul was a practical man, adapting his teaching to his audience as he went, convincing and clarifying as he exhorted. Naturally, he emphasized now one aspect of the gospel, now another. Equally naturally, theologians must torture his texts if they seek to render them meticulously consistent.

The problem of how salvation was to be achieved had not arisen before or during the Jewish exile; the problem then was not how, but whether. Having estranged themselves from the Lord, the Jews had wantonly fallen away into evil lives, worshipping—and loving—false Gods. The prophets preached a return to law-love, to the fulfillment of the ancestral love-contract. The distinction between faith and works simply had not come up.[81] When, during post-Exilic days, it did arise, it was resolved in ways not unlike those that Jesus taught later: that the faithful will naturally and lovingly fulfill the law, remembering that the law is made by the Lord for men.

With Jesus' birth, however, as Paul interpreted that event, the picture changes. No longer does the old law suffice for salvation, not merely because mechanical, outward obedience to the law may omit the essential dedication of the heart (for this was by now an old story), but even more importantly because that law has been infinitely extended or even superseded, now that the world has been transformed through God's dwelling among mankind. Jesus was not merely one more prophet, recalling men to the old-time truth and religion; he was very God himself, calling men forward to the new truths of Christian love. He dwelt here amongst us, Paul reminds us, asking only that we trust him, believe in him, love him, accept him as our only savior, yield up our sins to him, and allow him to transform us as he is transforming the world, so that we can be born again.

Ultimately, we have (so ran the general tenor of Paul's teaching, as he contradicted the literalistic Jews) only to give Jesus what he asked of us. He plainly commanded that we love God the Father and ourselves, that we freely and gladly give our most intimate selves up to God's love. We are to welcome the love God offers us through Jesus, and thereby to become empowered to serve him with the deepest faith we have within us—with what Tillich has called "ultimate concern." [82]

This I take to be Paul's sense of faith. This sense of faith means more (to borrow Philo's so-called "degrees") than simply believing what we see or hear; it means more than admitting the inevitability of a deductive inference to which we have been persuaded on rational grounds; certainly it is deeper and richer than the popular sense of faith that we employ when we speak foolishly of believing something "on faith" instead of "on reason," and mean no more than that we believe something irrationally and groundlessly. For Paul, and for most of the genius of historic Christianity since his time, faith means total *dedication* or Tillich's *ultimate concern,* an absorbing permeation of our total humanity by the new, loving light of Christ Jesus.

It is, Paul tells us, only through this total dedication that we are "justified" or "saved." The word "justify" is a peculiarly interesting and happy translator's choice, for it plainly carries its latin root *jus,* which means "law." Paul teaches that the new law takes the place of the old, and *justifies* us as Christians; he might as well have said "legitimizes" us, making us (morally) legitimate sons of God the Father. Thereby, in this life we live as we ought, in love. Thereby, too, we are promised, we shall enjoy life eternal with Jesus and the Father.

The polemic texts in which Paul urges faith in Jesus as the way to salvation are plentiful. Paul says, for example, that God justifies him who has faith in Jesus.

> Then what becomes of our boasting? It is excluded. On what principle? On the principle of works? No, but on the principle of faith. For we hold that a man is justified by faith apart from works of law (3:27-28).

> In [the gospel] the righteousness of God is revealed through faith for faith; as it is written, "He who through faith is righteous shall live" (1:17).

> . . . no human being will be justified in [God's] sight by works of the law since through the law comes knowledge of sin (3:20).

> The promise to Abraham and his descendants, that they should inherit the world, did not come through the law but through the righteousness

of faith. . . . That is why it depends on faith, in order that the promise may rest on grace and be guaranteed to all his descendants . . . his faith was "reckoned to him as righteousness." But the words, "it was reckoned to him," were written not for his sake alone, but for ours also. It will be reckoned to us who believe in him that raised from the dead Jesus our Lord, who was put to death for our trespasses and raised for our justification (4:13-25).

Let it be known to you therefore, brethren, that through this man forgiveness of sins is proclaimed to you, and by him every one that believes is freed from everything from which you could not be freed by the law of Moses (Acts 13:38-39).

. . . if you confess with your lips that Jesus is Lord and believe in your heart that God raised him from the dead, you will be saved. For a man believes with his heart and so is justified, and he confesses with his lips and so is saved (Rom. 10:9-10).

. . . a man is not justified by works of the law but through faith in Jesus Christ, even we have believed in Christ Jesus, in order to be justified by faith in Christ, . . . because by works of the law shall no one be justified (Gal. 2:16).

. . . no man is justified before God by the law; for "He who through faith is righteous shall live"; but the law does not rest on faith, for "He who does them shall live by them" (Gal. 3:11-12).

. . . by grace you have been saved through faith; and this is not your own doing, it is the gift of God—not because of works, lest any man should boast (Eph. 2:8-9).

For his sake I have suffered the loss of all things, and count them as refuse, in order that I may gain Christ and be found in him, not having a righteousness of my own, based on law, but that which is through faith in Christ, the righteousness from God that depends on faith (Phil. 3:8-9).

Therefore, finally,

since we are justified by faith, we have peace with God through our Lord Jesus Christ (Rom. 5:1).

Thus the classic foundation of Paul's preaching: faith, as utter, ultimate dedication in love, is the only way to justification and salvation. Upon this foundation (and others as well) the Reformers built their challenge to the Church of the fifteenth century: that the Church emphasized the doing of works, while the Holy Scripture in Paul's letters plainly dictates the primacy of the act of faith. Martin Luther, harking back through St. Augustine to St. Paul, set the epigram: "Love God and do as you please."

Our way would be clear if the case could be set to rest here, and the

Pauline picture of love, while complex and mystical, could be called complete. But the texts, both Pauline and extra-Pauline, seem also strongly to support an interpretation of the role of faith that, if not literally contradicting the classical Pauline presentation, at the very least requires us to explain it. In Paul's own words, for example,

> For [God] will render to every man according to his works: to those who by patience in well-doing seek for glory and honor and immortality, he will give eternal life; but for those who are factious and do not obey the truth, but obey wickedness, there will be wrath and fury (Rom. 2:6-8).

> All who have sinned without the law will also perish without the law, and all who have sinned under the law will be judged by the law. For it is not the hearers of the law who are righteous before God, but the doers of the law who will be justified (Rom. 2:12-13).

> . . . rendering service with a good will as to the Lord and not to men, knowing that whatever good any one does, he will receive the same again from the Lord, whether he is a slave or free (Eph. 6:7-8).

> Whatever your task, work heartily, as serving the Lord and not men, knowing that from the Lord you will receive the inheritance as your reward; you are serving the Lord Christ. For the wrongdoer will be paid back for the wrong he has done, and there is no partiality (Col. 3:23-25).

> For we must all appear before the judgment seat of Christ, so that each one may receive good or evil, according to what he has done in the body (II Cor. 5:10).

And outside Paul, but still well inside the New Testament, we find

> For the Son of man is to come with his angels in the glory of his Father, and then he will repay every man for what he has done (Matt. 16:27).

> He who has my commandments and keeps them, he it is who loves me; and he who loves me will be loved by my Father, and I will love him and manifest myself to him (John 14:21).

> I will give to each of you as your works deserve (Rev. 2:23).

> . . . the dead were judged by what was written in the books, by what they had done (Rev. 20:12).

> Behold, I am coming soon, bringing my recompense, to repay everyone for what he has done (Rev. 22:12).

. . . and finally, and most difficult of all, we find James 2:14-26, which is a sustained argument for works as indispensable to salvation:

> What does it profit, my brethren, if a man says he has faith but has not works? Can his faith save him? If a brother or sister is ill-clad and in lack

of daily food, and one of you says to them, "Go in peace, be warmed and filled," without giving them the things needed for the body, what does it profit? So faith by itself, if it has no works, is dead.

But some one will say, "You have faith and I have works." Show me your faith apart from your works, and I by my works will show you my faith. You believe that God is one; and you do well. Even the demons believe—and shudder. Do you want to be shown, you foolish fellow, that faith apart from works is barren? Was not Abraham our father justified by works, when he offered his son Isaac upon the altar? You see that faith was active along with his works, and faith was completed by works, and the scripture was fulfilled which says, "Abraham believed God, and it was reckoned to him as righteousness"; and he was called the friend of God. You see that a man is justified by works and not by faith alone. And in the same way was not also Rahab the harlot justified by works when she received the messengers and sent them out another way? For as the body apart from the spirit is dead, so faith apart from works is dead.

—and this *seems,* at least, to be a strong scriptural case for the primacy of doing, or works, over faith alone.

The history of Christian theology is rich with attempts to overcome this duality. We want to believe that good works alone are not enough to gain salvation—that faith in Jesus is essential. But we want also to believe that faith alone is not enough either, and that a man must behave as a Christian, as well as believe as a Christian, in order to be justified or saved. We want, in short, to be able to hold that both faith and works are necessary. But we cannot hold this and accept all the texts at face value.

Men seek salvation and naturally hope for success in their search. Each man asks himself whether he is seeking God correctly, whether he is doing all he can to achieve eternity. Therefore he approaches the faith-works problem by asking: "How can I earn salvation?" And once this question is asked, every answer becomes, for a Christian, Biblically impossible.

Can salvation be earned by faith without works? No, says James.

Can salvation be earned by works without faith? No, says Paul.

Can salvation be earned by both works and faith? No, say both Paul and James and Jesus too. It is not for us, even by unlimited faith and unlimited works, to place God under any obligation to save us.

Our faith prepares the way for what only God can do; by itself it is as powerless as any other good work is to win us acceptance, but it opens the door so that God may do for us what his grace designs.[83]

The easy way out is to devise a gnostic-scholastic redefinition that will turn faith into a work, or works into acts of faith.

The Christian answer to the question, "How can I earn salvation?" is

that the question itself is logically defective, and can no more be answered than, "How can I trisect an angle?" The one question assumes
in its asking that the angle can be trisected, the other that men can
somehow earn salvation. The correct answer to both rejects the question
and says flatly, "You can't." Faith is not a stratagem by which we win
the game of eternal life, nor are works a tactic.[84] God gives the game
away, because he loves us.

As I read my Bible, Jesus' message comes to nothing if heaven can be
earned at all.

> . . . if it is by grace, it is no longer on the basis of works; otherwise
> grace would no longer be grace (Rom. 11:6).

It is not we who put ourselves into heaven by achieving anything,
even faith; it is God who puts us there. The grace of God carries no
price tag. His love is perfectly free.

> It depends not upon man's will or exertion, but upon God's mercy
> (Rom. 9:16).

It is God alone who "gets us into heaven," if we are to get there at
all, and he does it wholly through love. In the wise old words of a
nineteenth century preacher, nobody ever got to heaven by trying to get
himself there, but only by trying to get somebody else there—by freely
accepting, that is, the love God freely offers us, and expressing that love
freely toward his fellow men.

And this, it seems to me, is as near as we can come to a resolution of
the faith versus works controversy. Active love is the key to faith; James
is correct. Informed and disciplined faith or concern inevitably reveals
itself in loving action.

> The immediate expression of love is action. Theologians have discussed
> the question of how faith can result in action. The answer is: because it
> implies love and because the expression of love is action . . . Faith im-
> plies love, love lives in works: in this sense, faith is actual in works. Where
> there is ultimate concern there is the passionate desire to actualize the
> content of one's concern. "Concern" in its very definition includes the de-
> sire for action.[85]

My proposal is far from new, and may conceivably require extension
of one text or another.[86] It is simply this: that neither faith nor works has
any Christian relevance at all, and hence any relevance to salvation or
justification, except in terms of love. Love is the central concept that
informs both faith and works, and makes them truly Christian. Given
love and love alone, the disunity between faith and works, and hence
the apparent dichotomy between Paul and James, becomes a unity once
again.

Abraham's test (in Gen. 22:9-14) is the classic case in point. Paul cites him as a typical example of the primacy of faith over works; because Abraham so devoutly trusted the Lord that he was willing even to sacrifice his only son Isaac, the angel was sent to stay his hand, and the ram was accepted as a sacrificial substitute. The faith that Abraham showed when the word of the Lord promised him as many descendants as there are stars in the heavens (Gen. 15:5-6) was "reckoned to him as righteousness." [87]

But Abraham is equally cited by James (2:21) as a typical example of the primacy of works over faith. It was not merely what Abraham believed, but what he did—namely, to bind Isaac to the altar and raise his knife—that counted.

Love withdraws the sting from the contradiction. Abraham was surely not justified in the eyes of the Lord simply because he assented intellectually to any proposition. Nor was he justified simply because he set about killing his son Isaac. Abraham was justified because he loved the Lord above all else, even his son's life. Paul is correct in disallowing the obedient act as itself sufficient to warrant Abraham's righteousness, and in insisting on Abraham's dedication to the Lord. But James is equally correct in disallowing the unexpressed (and hence unknown and unproved) inclination of the will as sufficient. Why did the Lord exact so terrible a test of Abraham? Not, surely, to discover whether Abraham believed in the Lord; for the Lord presumably knew that in advance. It must rather have been to show Abraham and his people forever after him how overwhelming God's love for man is, and how crucial man's love for God is—the love that abides in the heart and is expressed in action. So the ultimacy of Abraham's justification, that which is really reckoned to him as righteousness, is his human love for the Lord. That love was his faith and his work alike.

If we read our Bible in this way,[88] we shall find Paul assuring us with reasonable consistency that, on the one side, mere good works, unenlightened by love, and unmotivated by love, are meaningless in Christian terms; they cannot possibly assure us salvation. James will be assuring us, on the other side, that mere conscientiousness and sincerity, unexpressed in loving action, equally fail.

The magnitude and power of the love God bears toward undeserving man are exemplified in Paul's splendid fifth chapter in Romans. Here too the Old Testament theme is modulated into a Christian harmony. The wonder is, as Paul sees and feels God's love, that it can transmute tribulation and agony into confidence and hope, so that we can even rejoice in our sufferings,

> knowing that suffering produces endurance, and endurance produces character, and character produces hope, and hope does not disappoint us, be-

cause God's love has been poured into our hearts through the Holy Spirit which has been given to us (5:3-5).

What we as Christians undergo, we undergo bathed in the radiance of God's love, which is all the more miraculous, considering our selfish and sinful unworthiness. As the older prophets invariably did, and as Jesus often did, Paul takes his parallel from crises in human experience. It is rare enough that we would be willing to give up our lives for a beloved person whom we deem really worthy of our love. How miraculous, then, that Jesus could give his life lovingly, knowing that we who sin do not deserve the sacrifice. We "hardly" die for the lovable; he gladly dies for the unlovable.

> Why, one will hardly die for a righteous man—though perhaps for a good man one will dare even to die. But God shows his love for us in that while we were yet sinners Christ died for us (5:7-8).

Repeatedly[89] Paul reminds us that God's love is a gift or "free gift" or *charisma;* we may compare but not derive the Latin languages' *caro, cara*—"dear" or "beloved"—and the English "charity." It is this intimate sense of agape-love which we shall meet in the thirteenth chapter of I Corinthians.

The grand metaphor of life-death-rebirth is a favorite of Paul's. We have "died" to sin in our baptism and in Jesus' death; in his resurrection we have been "born again," becoming "new men." [90] The lesson we learn, we are to take to heart: that as death no longer has any dominion over Christ crucified and arisen, so the sin in which we were born no longer has any dominion over us, and we are morally freed. In Paul's curious words, we are now "not under law, but under grace" (Rom. 6:14).

This lesson, mysterious, heretical, and surely almost blasphemous in its day, must have shocked Paul's Roman readers. For a Jew, even a converted Jew like Paul, to tell us that we "are not under law" is amazing. I suspect that Paul frankly intended to shock and amaze his readers. Certainly he recognized the inference a naïve reader would immediately draw: that, if the law is abrogated, we are set totally free to do anything we like.

So Paul at once corrects this notion, with a concise analysis of "freedom," and an exhortation to righteousness in life, as against sin and death:

> What then? Are we to sin because we are not under law but under grace? By no means! Do you not know that if you yield yourselves to any one as obedient slaves, you are slaves of the one whom you obey, either of sin, which leads to death, or of obedience, which leads to righteousness? But thanks be to God, that you who were once slaves of sin have become

obedient from the heart to the standard of teaching to which you were committed, and having been set free from sin, have become slaves of righteousness . . . . When you were slaves of sin, you were free in regard to righteousness. But then what return did you get from the things of which you are now ashamed? The end of those things is death. But now that you have been set free from sin and have become slaves of God, the return you get is sanctification and its end, eternal life. For the wages of sin is death, but the free gift of God is eternal life in Christ Jesus our Lord (Rom. 6:15-18, 20-23).[91]

Freedom is thus inverted in its acceptation: far from being freedom from the law, so that we now enjoy freedom to sin, we have been freed by Jesus' sacrifice from the sin to which we had been slaves. I take "freedom" here in Paul [92] to mean more than the absence of restrictions. Freedom is a condition of fulfillment; the free man alone can fulfill his humanity. It is only Jesus' truth that sets men free, by making possible that fulfillment. "Where the Spirit of the Lord is, there is freedom" (II Cor. 3:17) and, in Cragg's words,[93] "Freedom is not the right to do whatever we wish, but the power to become what we were intended to be."

In context, it is plain that Paul has specifically in mind sexual sins, and the word translated below as "members" refers to the sexual organs themselves:

Let not sin therefore reign in your mortal bodies, to make you obey their passions. Do not yield your members to sin as instruments of wickedness, but yield yourselves to God as men who have been brought from death to life, and your members to God as instruments of righteousness. . . . I am speaking in human terms, because of your natural limitations. For just as you once yielded your members to impurity and to greater and greater iniquity, so now yield your members to righteousness for sanctification (6:12-13, 19).

While we were living in the flesh, our sinful passions, aroused by the law, were at work in our members to bear fruit for death. But now we are discharged from the law, dead to that which held us captive, so that we serve not under the old written code but in the new life of the Spirit (7:5-6).

Paul himself felt sexual temptation keenly, and suffered strong feelings of guilt because of his "lustful" desires. He tells us how powerfully his own body strains in the direction of sexual delight.

Here, as elsewhere, Paul's texts can be read in different ways. Years ago, he could be read directly, ascetically, and perhaps ungenerously as condemning sexuality. Then it was thought that Paul taught men to concentrate their attention on the imminent second coming, and to relegate sexual expression to a minor place.

Today, theologians (disenchanted, for the most part, about the imminence of the world's end, and somewhat sophisticated as lay psychologists) are attempting to fit Paul into the Old Testament spirit, recognizing the essential goodness of all creation, including human sexual fertility. To do this, the Pauline texts must be understood in exceedingly generous and extended senses. Bruce M. Metzger, for example, seeks to rescue Paul from the charge of condemning sexuality as such:[94]

> Paul nowhere intends to identify the physical nature of man as such with sin; rather he includes in the term "flesh" everything in man—his will and mind (Rom. 8:7; Eph. 2:3; Col. 2:18; see I Cor. 3:1-3) as well as his body—which is not led by the Spirit of God (Rom. 8:9-14).

Although Paul cannot literally be convicted of total asceticism on the strength of the texts alone, I do judge that Metzger (together with many others who wish to preserve Paul from the accusation) is ignoring many texts and extending the meanings of the texts he himself cites. Romans 8:7-8, for example, reads:

> For the mind that is set on the flesh is hostile to God; it does not submit to God's law, indeed it cannot; and those who are in the flesh cannot please God.

This at least appears to be a clear condemnation of the flesh-directed mind. In Ephesians 2:3, Paul says:

> Among these we all once lived in the passions of our flesh, following the desires of body and mind, and so we were by nature children of wrath, like the rest of mankind.

—but here too "the desires of body and mind" seem to be put ascetically.

These and many other passages seem to me to make a clear case for traditional mind-over-body moral dualism. Any text can, by a sufficiently extravagant two-way stretch, be made to mean anything we like, and I suppose that Paul's letters can be turned into psychologically sophisticated praises of the glory of all of God's creation, including human sexuality. Theologians who read Paul's *sarx,* flesh, as a synonym for any desire not divinely directed are engaged in a scholarly whitewash. For whatever the reason, Paul was the first Jewish Puritan, and we may as well admit the fact.

Almost consistently, Paul treats sexual desire as sinful outright, or at best a weakness. He is ashamed of feeling sexual urges in himself, and he considers them weak and evil-tending wherever they occur. He considers chastity superior to marriage—though if the faithful feel their sexual desires too strongly, Paul advises them to marry, lest they fall into the sin of fornication.

We have here another of Paul's sharp distinctions. Human sexuality is set off against and contrasted with human aspirations for eternal life. Essential and moral human love is only agapic yearning for God and filial-friendly encouragement of fellow Christians in God's service; erotic-sexual love is different in kind, weaker, sin-inclined. The framework within which this distinction is set is that Orientally exaggerated Platonism which sees things of "this world" or "this life" (or the "former life," before rebirth in Jesus) as of a different metaphysical order from things of the "other world" or "other life" of eternity with God.

We do not know much about Paul's own education, but it seems almost certain that he knew at least the popular philosophies of his day. His "other world" is inevitably reminiscent of Plato's realm of ideal forms, as his moralizing is reminiscent of the teaching of the *Phaedo*.

How Christian (or Biblical) Paul is in all this is a matter for judgment and dispute. The puritanical and ascetic traditions in Christianity take Paul at his words and implications: human flesh as such is weak and likely to lead us toward sin; this life on earth is to be endured; sexual behavior is a distasteful reproductive duty rather than a human pleasure; all or nearly all fleshly temptations are to be repressed for the sake of the greater glory of the spirit. Joy of any earthly kind, especially bodily joy in sexual love, is always suspicious and usually condemned as pernicious.

I have already claimed that this perennial historic attitude of other-worldliness, together with its radical metaphysical dualism, is not to be found at the center of Platonic teaching. I do not find it central (or, for that matter, even peripheral) in pre-Exilic Old Testament teaching. I do not believe it to be typical of Jesus' own teaching in the synoptic gospels. I certainly do not believe that every Christian must echo Paul's preoccupation with sexuality, or his attitude toward it.

Comparing Paul's puritanism with the Hebraic open acceptance of sexuality, we have a most interesting example of how the force of love is set to the service of religion. The prophets, from Moses to Hosea, although sternly forbidding sexual immorality—adultery, sodomy, incest—do not ever directly or indirectly condemn sexual activity itself as immoral. On the contrary, they themselves are lusty men. They love life and they love love-making. They feel the force of desire keenly, and treat it naturally as healthy human evidence of the Lord's love. So powerful is sexual love in human experience that they use it as a basis for teaching the intimate morality of our duty to Jehovah. Human sexual love, in its moral manifestations, is welcomed and approved and extended in the direction of God himself.

Paul, on the other hand, realizing equally the power of love in the human body, uses this power in his religious teaching by turning it about, instead of by extending it. As we feel longing in our "members," he says in effect, we discover how strong is our temptation to sin. So much the more strongly must we rise above this temptation, in loving and serving our Lord Jesus! In order to give our essential selves wholly to God, we must deny our "lower" selves so far as we can. Paul, in other words, contrasts men's proper love for God with men's sexual desires; the traditional Hebrews unify them.

The root of this difference lies in a metaphysical conception of the self and its world. Those who, with most of traditional Catholicism and with liberal Protestants, conceive the human self as a complex unity living in a complex but essentially unified cosmos, can welcome sexuality almost as honestly as their Jewish ancestors did.[95] For all these, God's genetic joy in creation includes his joy in sexuality, and his blessing upon everything he made is comprehensive. God knew no shame for having made Adam and Eve sexual creatures. No more need their descendants feel shame at being sexual, or even at enjoying their sexuality.

Those, who, with much of Calvinist Christianity, many Baptists, and some Methodists—presumably including all members of a sect founded in Tennessee in 1806 as the Old Two-Seed-in-the-Spirit Predestinarian Baptists—hold man's personality to be a precarious combination of forces, some evil-directed (or, which comes to the same thing, devil-directed) and the others good- (or God-) directed, locate all pleasures of the flesh in the former category. They conceive the holiest life to be that in which the least indulgence is suffered.[96] Their universe is really a polyverse, with an abyss between the world of temporality and that of eternity.[97]

The classic expression of the psychological dualism lies in Paul's seventh chapter. Here he overflows with his own surging confession. He feels (sexual) temptation powerfully, yet in recognizing it as temptation, his "inmost self" has already transcended it.

> I am carnal, sold under sin. I do not understand my own actions. For I do not do what I want, but I do the very thing I hate. Now if I do what I do not want, I agree that the law is good. So then it is no longer I that do it, but sin which dwells within me. For I know that nothing good dwells within me, that is, in my flesh. I can will what is right, but I cannot do it. For I do not do the good I want, but the evil I do not want is what I do. Now if I do what I do not want, it is no longer I that do it, but sin which dwells within me.
>
> So I find it to be a law that when I want to do right, evil lies close at hand. For I delight in the law of God, in my inmost self, but I see in my members another law at war with the law of my mind and making me captive to the law of sin which dwells in my members. Wretched man that I am! Who will deliver me from this body of death? Thanks be to God through Jesus Christ our Lord! So then, I of myself serve the law of God with my mind, but with my flesh I serve the law of sin (7:14-25).[98]

Whatever our metaphysical interpretation of the personality, we must respect the essential sincerity and outspoken, sensitive honesty of Paul's confession. He did not pretend to be wholly pure, even in his own terms; only too vividly, he felt the pangs of a sexual need.

We can read this confession as a candid recognition of the complexity and paradoxicality of the human mind, even without endorsing Paul's condemnation of his own desires. He is certainly correct, and profoundly correct, in showing that he and we deeply, urgently need conflicting and even sometimes incompatible gratifications. Any picture of the human personality that shows it as a simple machine responding in predictable ways to successive stimuli, like any picture that shows the personality as totally motivated by any one clear, direct, specifiable need, is too simple to be taken seriously. Whatever we humans may be, we are not just phototropic parameciae. We want and need to have what we do not and cannot have. We want and need to be what we are not and never shall be. We feel frustrated in our inevitable failures, and anguished at our evident inadequacies. In showing us his own inner torment, Paul shows us ourselves.

The bride-husband figure, so brilliantly set forth and developed in the Old Testament, becomes baptized into Christianity as Paul develops an ingenious bit of brotherly-loving legalism to show that Christians are now free of the old law, since they have been reborn:

> Do you not know, brethren—for I am speaking to those who know the law—that the law is binding on a person only during his life? Thus a married woman is bound by law to her husband as long as he lives; but if her husband dies she is discharged from the law concerning the husband. Accordingly, she will be called an adulteress if she lives with another man while her husband is alive. But if her husband dies she is free from that law, and if she marries another man she is not an adulteress.
>
> Likewise, my brethren, you have died to the law through the body of Christ, so that you may belong to another, to him who has been raised from the dead in order that we may bear fruit for God (7:1-4).

The climax of Romans comes in the eighth chapter, with Paul's sublime picture of the power of God's love. Secure in that love, we Christians become serene, for love has transcended the law by fulfilling it, and he who has by God's grace been enabled to love now unconsciously obeys the commandments.

> We know that in everything God works for good with those who love him, who are called according to his purpose . . . we are more than conquerors through him who loved us. For I am sure that neither death, nor life, nor angels, nor principalities, nor things present, nor things to come, nor powers, nor height, nor depth, nor anything else in all cre-

ation, will be able to separate us from the love of God in Christ Jesus our Lord (8:28, 37-39).

The remainder of Paul's letter, setting aside the description of his itinerary (15:22-29) and the greetings of the sixteenth chapter (which may belong in Ephesians anyway), consists less of explanation, analysis, and argument than of straightforward exhortation. Naturally, the exhortations to Christian love are central:

> Let love be genuine; hate what is evil, hold fast to what is good; love one another with brotherly affection . . . (12:9-10)

> Owe no one anything, except to love one another; for he who loves his neighbor has fulfilled the law. The commandments, "You shall not commit adultery, You shall not kill, You shall not steal, You shall not covet," and any other commandment, are summed up in this sentence, "You shall love your neighbor as yourself." Love does no wrong to a neighbor; therefore love is the fulfilling of the law (13:8-10).[99]

What Paul has achieved in Romans is nothing less than the full development of traditional Jewish love into Christian love. The older Jews had concentrated on loving as an active doing, a relationship between men and God. Paul makes of loving a fact as well as an act: of the verb *agapan* he makes the noun *agape,* to stand for a state of being. And then he returns to prophetic days by citing Jesus' admonition as a dynamic command. From *Loving* to *Love* to *Love!*: Paul has here explored, expressed, exhibited, and exposed Christianity as, above all, a religion of love.[100]

Corinthians. The urban, sophisticated, luxurious, and perhaps licentious Corinthians may have deserved Paul's most subtle and intellectual letters; they received his most lyrical and passionate ones. I Corinthians 13—called "the Beatitudes set to music" and "the Canticle of the New Testament"—is as lyrical a paean as has ever been sung to love.

Written in the first person, this poem is both a prayer and a sermon. Paul is personal and speaks for himself, out of his own heart; yet he is also transpersonal, and speaks both to and on behalf of all Christians. Not merely Corinthians, and not merely Christians and Jews, but all men esteem many different kinds of things. Paul preaches nothing less than the intrinsic, unlimited, and indispensable value of love as imparting to every object of every man's esteem any value it can claim. Christian love is not only good in itself; it infuses with goodness everything it informs, and unless so informed, nothing else has any goodness in it.

The key to an understanding of the poem is its situation. Paul was preaching neither to illiterate slaves nor only to Oriental Jews, but to a "knowledgeable" church, one inclined to substitute intellectual understanding for the dedication of the heart. The Corinthians' "gnosticism" tended toward Stoicism, and toward pride in the speculative philosophical disciplines. They felt superior to the disciples of the mystery-religions, and their Christianity moved more in the directions of Athens and Rome than in those of Jerusalem and Galilee.

Paul faces their knowledge claims boldly, confronting "knowledge" with "love." He denies the moral-religious relevance and even—at length —the very possibility of loveless knowledge, urging the faithful to return to the faith, to love God as God loves them.

> "Knowledge" puffs up, but love builds up. If any one imagines that he knows something, he does not yet know as he ought to know. But if one loves God, one is known by him (8:1-3).

Reminding the Corinthians that "it takes all kinds" to make a Christian community, Paul promises to show them a "still more excellent way" than they have known (12:31) and then fulfills his promise with his poem. The way, of course, is love.

"Inspired preaching," for example—the transport or rapture of the glib mystic who can amaze the throngs as he "speaks in tongues" or, in Old Testament language, "prophesies"—is wondrous to hear. Paul himself, physically unprepossessing and, we are told, as poor a speaker as he is brilliant a writer,[101] knows the popular magnetic power of these men. He also knows their shallowness, unless their hearts are truly inflamed with love. Their "speaking in tongues" is not inherently evil; but it is neutral and valueless.

> If I speak in the tongues of men and of angels, but have not love, I am a noisy gong or a clanging cymbal (13:1).

Nor are scholarship, knowledge, and wisdom evil; but neither are they, without love's blessing, good. So too with "faith"—used here atypically, to stand for a psychological attitude of confident assertion or of conviction, rather than (as in Romans) for the loving dedication—and also with charity and with self-sacrifice.[102] These too, if love be lacking, are meaningless.

> And if I have prophetic powers, and understand all mysteries and all knowledge, and if I have all faith, so as to remove mountains, but have not love, I am nothing. If I give away all I have, and if I deliver my body to be burned, but have not love, I gain nothing (13:2-3).

When our souls are transformed by God's love, we ourselves become loving, in kind but not in degree like him, and our lives can become transformed into our hearts' desires. This Paul expresses in a figure, by attributing the essential characters of God's *agape* and the supreme goods of a genuinely loving life to love itself.

Love is patient and kind; love is not jealous or boastful; it is not arrogant or rude. Love does not insist on its own way; it is not irritable or resentful; it does not rejoice at wrong, but rejoices in the right (13:4-6).

In his admirable study of New Testament love, Moffatt here translates "Love is never glad when others go wrong and always eager to believe the best." [103]

Love bears all things, believes all things, hopes all things, endures all things (13:7-8).

We can hardly read these lines without finding in them far more than a figure for the loving human life. We remember I John 4:8—"God is love"—and attribute the Johannine insight to Paul. In saying that love conquers all, Paul should surely be read as saying not only "Love enables us to endure all" and "We who truly love can endure all," but "God, who is the very essence of love, endures all." Granted the special Pauline meaning for "believe," we can consistently substitute "God" for "Love" in verses 4-8, without falsifying Christian doctrine. God-love forgives and understands human weakness, as we lovingly should do. Dramatically and traumatically, God-love bears all as we should do, in the self-sacrificial love of the Cross.

The endurance of love is handsomely presented in John Donne's pun on "end":

One of the most convenient Hieroglyphicks of God is a Circle, and a Circle is endlesse; whom God loves, hee loves to the end: and not onely to their own end, to their death, but to his end, and his end is, that he might love them still.[104]

The Christian transformation is far more than a "change of mind" on the part of the new believer. It is a radical "change of heart" or "change of life." In accepting Jesus, we leap out of temporality into eternity, out of partiality, relativity, and imperfection into essential wholeness, absoluteness, and perfection.

Love never ends; as for prophecy, it will pass away; as for tongues, they will cease; as for knowledge, it will pass away. For our knowledge is imperfect and our prophecy is imperfect; but when the perfect comes, the imperfect will pass away (13:8-10).[105]

—and this is real "maturity." Our pre-Christian lives were childish:

When I was a child, I spoke like a child, I thought like a child, I reasoned like a child; when I became a man, I gave up childish ways (13:11).

Our Christian lives, no longer childish, remain child-like.[106]

Yet even now, as we reach toward immortality, we are limited. We now know (as we had not earlier known) that our knowledge is limited, and this knowledge is already an infinite improvement over our earlier confident ignorance. We now realize that, although we can see some things, there is much more to be seen; our light is only beginning to dawn.

> For now we see in a mirror dimly, but then face to face. Now I know in part; then I shall understand fully, even as I have been fully understood (13:12).

"Faith," still used in the atypical psychological sense, is good, so far as it goes. "Hope" we cherish and enjoy. And these, with love, are ours forever. They abide. But the inner human and divine meaning of faith and hope alike is love. Love is the greatest of all.

> So faith, hope, love abide, these three; but the greatest of these is love (13:13).

—and this love, above all, is the love God bears toward man.[107] As always, we reflect this love in loving God and each other.

Still addressing the Corinthians, Paul extends his dualism in a remarkably Platonic passage—the "looking to things that are unseen" being, of course, not merely a contemplation, but an active yearning-loving:

> So we do not lose heart. Though our outer nature is wasting away, our inner nature is being renewed every day. For this slight momentary affliction is preparing for us an eternal weight of glory beyond all comparison, because we look not to the things that are seen but to the things that are seen but to the things that are seen are transient, but the things that are unseen are eternal (II Cor. 4:16-18).[108]

Once more, in II Corinthians, Paul transforms an Old Testament metaphor into Christian terms. The earlier Jews had been promised to the Lord as a maiden is promised to a man, and then, most typically, as she had whored, so the people strayed to false gods. Here (in II Cor. 11:2-3) Paul himself claims to have betrothed his Corinthian church to Christ, to present it to him "as a pure bride to her . . . husband." [109] And here, too, he fears lest serpentine evil seduce the bride and cause her to give up her purity. What she must do, Paul makes plain, is to abide by his own pure version of the gospel, denouncing competitive ministers in the name of "the God of love and peace."

Paul presents the reflexivity of love in intimate human terms, but surely he means this human picture to display the larger cosmic relationship:

> I will most gladly spend and be spent for your souls. If I love you the more, am I to be loved the less (II Cor. 12:15)?

Remembering Romans 5:5, we see the structure clearly shining forth: love is a mutual dynamic. Paul has loved his people the more; shall they, in turn, love him the less? Even so, and in infinitely greater degree, God, through his Holy Spirit, has loved us all the more, and all the more we ought to love him, and live in love as men.

The Later Letters. Whether or not it be truly Pauline—a technical point we leave to the scholars—Ephesians is a sustained case for the full Christian communion of Gentile and Jew alike. Love is of course the ground of that communion, and its "root" as well, and the only way by which we can come to understand the central Christian truths.[110] The relationship is complex: God, loving us, has mercifully and graciously inflamed our hearts with love. This love we feel (and which Paul bespeaks on our behalf) in turn permits us to "comprehend" and to "know" the love of Christ which surpasses knowledge.

> . . . (I pray) that Christ may dwell in your hearts through faith; that you, being rooted and grounded in love, may have power to comprehend with all the saints what is the breadth and length and height and depth, and to know the love of Christ which surpasses knowledge, that you may be filled with all the fullness of God (Eph. 3:17-19).

Having ourselves been thus "filled with all the fullness of God," we become (as Paul uses the organic metaphor) part of the body of the Church, still through love.

> . . . speaking the truth in love, we are to grow up in every way into him who is the head, into Christ, from whom the whole body, joined and knit together by every joint with which it is supplied, when each part is working properly, makes bodily growth and upbuilds itself in love (Eph. 4:15-17).

Ephesians' twin letter, Colossians, expresses the harmonizing function of love, complementing the comparative role shown in I Corinthians 13.

> Put on then, as God's chosen ones, holy and beloved, compassion, kindness, lowliness, meekness and patience, forbearing one another and, if one has a complaint against another, forgiving each other; as the Lord has forgiven you, so you also must forgive. And above all these put on love, which binds everything together in perfect harmony (Col. 3:12-14).

The love God bears toward us is perfect and infinite in degree, but man's love is a matter of degree, and may grow. As Paul wishes on behalf of the faithful:

> it is my prayer that your love may abound more and more, with knowledge and all discernment, so that you may approve what is excellent, and may be pure and blameless for the day of Christ, filled with the

fruits of righteousness which come through Jesus Christ, to the glory and praise of God (Phil. 1:9-11).[111]

Still without having to assume Pauline authenticity, we find in the so-called "pastoral epistles" indisputable new evidence of the Pauline teaching of love. The false teachers at Ephesus are condemned for distorting the gospel:

> whereas the aim of our charge is love that issues from a pure heart and a good conscience and sincere faith (I Tim. 1:5).

At once Hebraic and apocalyptic in tone, the railing in II Timothy reminds us of the old identity between true love and morality on the one hand, false love and immorality on the other.

> . . . in the last days there will come times of stress. For men will be lovers of self, lovers of money, proud, arrogant, abusive, disobedient to their parents, ungrateful, unholy, inhuman, implacable, slanderers, profligates, fierce, haters of good, treacherous, reckless, swollen with conceit, lovers of pleasure rather than lovers of God, holding the form of religion but denying the power of it. Avoid such people (II Tim. 3:1-5).[112]

Not yet have we met—in human terms at least—the notion that love can "cover" our sins, as if there were available to us a kind of natural penance or atonement, although we have repeatedly learned that Jesus' love can do so supernaturally. In I Peter, we find the apocalyptic warning:

> The end of all things is at hand; therefore keep sane and sober for your prayers. Above all hold unfailing your love for one another, since love covers a multitude of sins (4:7-8).[113]

The problem is the meaning of "cover." The text permits at least these very different interpretations:

(1) When we love each other unfailingly, as we ought, many of our own sins are forgiven us, presumably as a reward.

(2) When we love each other unfailingly, we become less critical of each other, more inclined to find each other lovable.

The first, "atonement" interpretation appears to make of our love a work, and thus again to violate Paul's notion of salvation by faith alone. Those scholars especially sensitive to this threat[114] prefer the second reading.

But the "atonement" reading avoids the notion of works if we remember that our unfailing mutual love is itself not a spontaneous achievement on our part—and thus no strategic way of earning salvation—but only a reflection of God's *agape*. Only Christians who accept God's free grace can love each other unfailingly. So the reward is not really a reward at all, but simply the saving love of God.

These two interpretations are by no means incompatible. It is barely possible that the author had both in mind. I see no reason why we may not impute both to the text.

JOHN[115]

> Why, Elder John, do you forever say, "Little children, love one another"? Why do you not vary your testimony?
> —Because it is a commandment of the Lord, and if it be done, it suffices.[116]

The Fourth Gospel. Some forty years or so after Jesus died on Calvary, one or more men wrote the book that has been included in our canon as the Fourth Gospel. This book, together with John's first letter, is, I believe, the pre-eminent religious expression of love in our culture. Scholars may dispute its authorship, its legitimacy, and—with an eye to its Hellenistic undertones—even its Christianity. They cannot question its devotion, its poetic beauty, or its mystery.

As Paul had, so John too wrote for practical reasons, refuting some of the divergent views then prevalent. The strongest enemies of true Christianity, in John's view, were certain forms of late Greek thought we have met already and know collectively as gnosticism. Since we can hardly hope to understand Johannine love except in contrast to the "heresy" [117] against which the teaching was directed, we must sketch two of these divergent patterns of Christianity.

"Gnosticism" derives from the Greek word that we translate as "know" or "understand." In general, the Christian gnostics were those who believed that salvation could be attained, if at all, through "coming to know" or "coming to understand" the divine truths. For them, the mysteries of Christianity are intellectual and moral challenges; only as we penetrate these mysteries can we hope to achieve our immortal destiny. We must, therefore, exercise our intelligence in unraveling paradoxes and clarifying obscurities.

Some of the gnostics took literally, perhaps too literally, Paul's proclamation that the grace of God had superseded the older law, and inferred (reasonably enough) from Paul's comments about the elect and from Jesus' evident love for sinners, that we Christians are now "beyond the law." Their emphasis on grace led to an extreme de-emphasis of law, and hence they came to be called "anti-legalists" or, in Greek, "antinomians."

Others of these gnostics tried to work out on a clear, consistent basis some of the surds that both the Bible and tradition had presented to them. The greatest of these absurdities was the notion that God could or would become mortal flesh and suffer and die. These must, so the sensible gnostics of the first and second centuries believed (as do many Unitarians of the twentieth) be mere myths, or vivid ways of expressing for the illiterate the underlying truths. It must be that Jesus as Savior really did appear to men on earth, as it is reported in the Bible; that he really did seem to suffer and die on the Cross; but it is only a self-contradictory and irrational children's fable to pretend that God himself could be killed.

Certain gnostic teachings about love plainly follow. That intelligent men can and should love mathematically ideal goodness, growing in spirit above the limitations of this life, is evident to a Greek—far more evident than that this perfect principle could be a person at all, and infinitely more credible than that perfection could be tempted by imperfection, or die in agony.

Against these divergencies and many others, the authors of scripture sought to defend what they conceived to be the true faith. They recognized honestly that Christianity was and is a mystery-religion, that many of its critical articles of faith seem paradoxical and nonsensical when measured against human standards of evidence, consistency, and truth. Paul and John showed, in my judgment, far more wisdom than some of their rationalistic successors, when they candidly confessed and proclaimed the mysteries, instead of trying dialectically to torture them out of existence.

John, for example, wrote for people anxious to believe, but unable (or unwilling) to do so. The heretical enemy within the Christian camp had already won some souls away from Johannine Christianity by the use of dialectical reasoning. So, instead of marshalling counterarguments, John the Jew[118] boldly sets forth his gospel of love as an impassioned moral metaphysic. He flings Christian paradoxes at us in all their naked power, and dares us to believe in Jesus. Jesus, he says, has always been and is and always will be, and was born and lived and died. Jesus really is God, and he really is God's son. Jesus is completely divine, and was at the same time completely human.

The Word in 1:1-5 was Jesus himself, co-eternal with God the Father. His light—the ancient metaphor again—is our light, and shines despite our darkness, to illuminate it.

Jesus' light of love is distinguished from its anticipation in John the Baptist (1:6-8, 15), and is said to have been unwelcome to the Jews (1:11), but to carry to all who believe the infinite power of becoming children of God.

> But to all who received him, who believed in his name, he gave power
> to become children of God; who were born not of blood nor of the will
> of the flesh nor of the will of man, but of God . . . Jesus answered

Nicodemus, "Truly, truly, I say to you, unless one is born anew, he cannot see the kingdom of God." Nicodemus said to him, "How can a man
be born when he is old? Can he enter a second time into his mother's
womb and be born?" Jesus answered, "Truly, truly, I say to you, unless
one is born of water and the Spirit, he cannot enter the kingdom of
God. That which is born of the flesh is flesh, and that which is born of
the Spirit is spirit" (1:12-13 and 3:3-6).[119]

Shall we take this notion of "rebirth" as another of the great metaphors of love, to be set beside those of the husband-wife and father-son?
The devout may want to insist that the rebirth is not metaphorical but
genuine: conversion transforms the personality, and we are spiritually
born again in the spirit of God, once we accept Jesus as our personal
savior. The validity of this metaphysical, psychological, and moral claim
need not be assessed; surely nothing less than this claim is made in the
present gospel.

The climax of this prologue comes in verses 14-18, with Jesus' entrance
into history, bringing "grace and truth" to the world, which had hitherto
known only the law through Moses. No doubt it was necessary for these
early Christians to distinguish themselves from other Jews, especially
since Jesus himself had explicitly taught them to confess their Judaism
proudly, and to cling to their ancient heritage. However, there are, as the
discussion thus far will have made clear, many fundamental and important similarities—and even identities—between Christian-Jewish and pre-
Christian-Jewish interpretations of love. There are also some important
differences.

First, as we have already seen, is the fact of Jesus' person. The Christian
who reads his Old Testament generously warms to and wonders at the
richness of God's love for man, and he shares the Jews' sense of suffering
from sin. He too, with his Jewish ancestors, has known what it means
to feel himself apart from God, to be cosmically and desperately alone.
The sin of Adam and Eve is—or so Paul Tillich has understood it[120]—
that of renunciation, of having cut oneself away from God. We have
made ourselves separate from God, and we need him to remake us, to
reconcile us with him—in theological terms, to redeem us.[121]

Nonetheless, to the Christian, Jehovah's overpowering love, superabundant and undeserved though it is, may seem somehow too distant, too
remote from our human concerns. Even though he made us in his image,
he remains way off there, knowable only through an all-too-occasional
prophet. He seems utterly infinite, while we know ourselves to be only
too finite. How can our human concerns be of any real interest to him?
We can believe that he loves us in spite of our sins, and we can read
his laws and know ourselves to be bound by them, and we can even

realize the (post-Exilic) individual need for total commitment to the Lord. Yet still we lack the most intimate touch of all: the humanity of a man like ourselves in feeling pain and gladness, in hoping and struggling, in undergoing genuine pangs of temptation to sin. God incarnate makes love incarnate, as it could hardly have become in the strictly Jewish canon.

Second is the shift in the overt focus of morality. Until Jesus' time, man's doing had for the most part been taken as direct and unquestioned evidence of his willing. The man who thoroughly fulfilled the Torah in life was understood to be thoroughly dedicated to the Lord in his soul. Even in ancient days, of course, the distinction had been made between mere ritual fulfillment and genuine, heartfelt, loving service. Jesus' condemnation of Pharisaic legalism was by no means new among the prophets; nor, we must regretfully add, has historic Christendom ever been without its Pharisees. Yet, granting this, we do find in Jesus' message a consistent (but not exclusive)[122] emphasis upon the orientation of the heart, and upon the inner man.[123]

The loving, believing man is the man who loves so utterly that the law takes its place simply as a pattern for loving, instead of functioning as a standard for judgment and condemnation. Those who condemned Jesus for violating some letter of the Sabbath law were chastised as having missed its essential humanity.

Finally, the Christian love-message diverges most sharply from the Jewish one in its apocalyptic-historic vision. To the Christian, but not to the Jew, history really stopped and started again with Jesus. It now moves toward its end, and at that end we shall be judged according to whether we have loved as Jesus taught us to love. It is a complex problem of no present concern, to decide how eschatological Jesus' own teaching actually was, and how much of the eschatology accrued to his teaching from other sources. But there can be no question in any Christian's understanding and dedication, that Jesus' life not merely made a difference in the world—as any Jew or pagan would be glad to confess—but that his life made *the* difference, all the difference in the world.

We return to John and find, after the recruiting in Chapter 1 and the miracle of the wine at Cana, the famous pun on "temple" in 2:14-22. Jesus drove the money-changers out of the temple of the Lord, rebuked the Jews, and answered their challenge, "Destroy this temple, and in three days I will raise it up." They misunderstood, failing to see how a temple built over forty-six years could be raised up again in three days. His point was, as we are told, that he could and would raise up his own body three days after the Jews had destroyed it; we learn that, though our bodies be lost, we can, through Jesus' love, be quickly resurrected.

After the teaching of Nicodemus in the third chapter comes what Martin Luther was to call "the gospel in miniature" (3:16-21).

> For God so loved the world that he gave his only Son, that whoever believes in him should not perish but have eternal life. For God sent the Son into the world, not to condemn the world, but that the world might be saved through him. He who believes in him is not condemned; he who does not believe is condemned already, because he has not believed in the name of the only Son of God. And this is the judgment, that the light has come into the world, and men loved darkness rather than light, because their deeds were evil. For every one who does evil hates the light, and does not come to the light, lest his deeds should be exposed. But he who does what is true comes to the light, that it may be clearly seen that his deeds have been wrought in God.

Here, most clearly of all, is Jesus the loving savior, not Jesus the judge. The "condemnation" of which the text speaks is self-condemnation; it is, once again, the renunciation or willful refusal to accept the truth God offers us; it is sin; it is isolation from God and therefore from each other, from any really human community.

The man who believes is really the man who accepts the infinite gift of grace God offers him through his Son. Through that gift, even sinful man is empowered to "do what is true," and thus to love aright.

The wrath of God, as we learned in our consideration of the Old Testament, is an expression of his love, no less than his giving, and we combine this Old Testament teaching with the father-son metaphor in the closing of the third chapter:

> the Father loves the Son, and has given all things into his hand. He who believes in the Son has eternal life; but he who does not obey the Son shall not see life, but the wrath of God rests upon him (35-36).

The Samaritan water and food are made symbols of love and life by Jesus, as are the miraculous cures in 4:50-54 and 5:3-9.

The sermon of Chapter five, together with the concluding words in Chapters fourteen, fifteen, and sixteen, contains Jesus' clearest claim to sonship and descent from Moses through the prophecies to their messianic fulfillment; once again, belief is identified with good and disbelief with evil. It is not that the Jews with whom Jesus speaks here have committed some explicit public sin; literally, they have committed no criminal act, and this is crucial. For they are even more sinful for having, deep within themselves, refused to open their hearts to the truth now revealed through Jesus.

> You have not the love of God within you. I have come in my Father's name, and you do not receive me; if another comes in his own name, him you will receive (5:42-43).

Plainly this Biblical teaching is that love must radiate back toward God from men, just as it has come down toward men from God. The only condition is our open-hearted willingness to accept—remember the circumcised heart of the earlier prophetic writings—and be saved.

Belief, then, is far more than intellectual assent. To believe is to incorporate into one's self a new way of living, to rededicate one's most intimate personality morally, in the light Jesus brings us. "This is the work of God, that you believe in him whom he has sent" (6:29).

The mystical identity of *truth*—and, since truth means belief, or love, of love as well—with *freedom* becomes clear in 8:31-34.

> Jesus then said to the Jews who had believed in him, "If you continue in my word, you are truly my disciples, and you will know the truth, and the truth will make you free." They answered him, "We are descendants of Abraham, and have never been in bondage to anyone. How is it that you say, You will be made free?" Jesus answered them, "Truly, truly, I say to you, every one who commits sin is a slave to sin."

Once again, the inconsistently Christian Jews will to misunderstand, taking "freedom" in a political rather than in Jesus' profounder moral-psychological meaning. There is sense in speaking of "slavery" to one's passions, or to a habit; Spinoza's freedom, for example, results from rising above the limitations of narrow concerns. So too with John's Jesus: he here condemns, as Paul did, those who are enslaved by sin, and he offers them instead the higher, firmer ground of freedom in righteousness.

One Platonic interpretation distinguishes sharply between this world of temporality and that "other" ideal world of eternity. This Hellenic notion, however Platonic it may be, had by the first century become a philosophical commonplace. Certainly some of the New Testament authors, including Paul and, in all likelihood, the author of the fourth gospel, knew some Greek philosophy. With a limited number of critical changes, the Greek dialectic of morality could be put to the service of the new Jewish heresy, and so it was. Platonic and quasi-Platonic insights are found in the Bible, most evidently in the Pauline epistles, but in John also, as in 3:6, already quoted, and here in 12:25:

> He who loves his life loses it, and he who hates his life in this world will keep it for eternal life.

Now, if this is Platonic at all, it is so in terms of the *Phaedo,* and hardly at all in terms of the *Symposium.* But it is by no means clear that Plato ever taught us to set aside the things of this life and to turn our backs upon them, in favor of the other, higher realm; I have already proposed a reading of much of Plato's text, in terms of which the loving continuity is stressed, rather than the discontinuity. Correspondingly and

in similar manner, the Biblical Christian message of love is frankly ambiguous. Sometimes life in this world is to be loved, these things about
us are to be cherished, in the older Hebraic sense; at other times, we
are warned not to love this life, but to hate it, in order that we may be
preserved for the eternal life with God.

As man, Jesus loved those whom he knew during his life here on earth,
and his love for his disciples is limitless:

> Now before the feast of the Passover, when Jesus knew that his hour
> had come to depart out of this world to the Father, having loved his own
> who were in the world, he loved them to the end (13:1).

—the "end," of course, being the imminent crucifixion. Beginning with
the new commandment, already cited:

> . . . that you love one another; even as I have loved you, that you
> also love one another. By this all men will know that you are my disciples,
> if you have love for one another (13:34-35)[124]

—and continuing through Chapter 17, we have Jesus' final message to
his disciples. This message is, as it must be, a message of loving faith.[125]

The love he preaches is, first of all, a human-communal love. The
pagan Romans were later to cry in amazement during the gladiatorial
entertainments, "See how these Christians love one another!" And in
loving one another, they were simply fulfilling their master's commandment.

At the same time, their love is a positive, outgoing dedication to the
Father, and this dedication, we are promised, will be reflected in moral
living. We know by how a man lives whether he truly loves the Lord,
and whether the Lord will live with him.

> He who has my commandments and keeps them, he it is who loves me;
> and he who loves me will be loved by my Father, and I will love him and
> manifest myself to him . . . if a man loves me, he will keep my word,
> and my Father will love him, and we will come to him and make our
> home with him (14:21, 23).

Once again foreshadowing the end of his life with us, Jesus uses the
language of love:

> You heard me say to you, "I go away, and I will come to you." If
> you loved me, you would have rejoiced, because I go to the Father; for
> the Father is greater than I . . . I do as the Father has commanded me,
> so that the world may know that I love the Father (14:28, 31).

Aristotle had said [126] that friendship lies in the loving rather than in
the being loved, and Jesus foregoes the language of servitude, addressing
his disciples as friends rather than as servants:

This is my commandment, that you love one another as I have loved you. Greater love has no man than this, that a man lay down his life for his friends. You are my friends if you do what I command you (15:12-14).

Here, as in the Old Testament, the faithful have been chosen by the Lord, and are, in consequence, hated by "the world":

If the world hates you, know that it has hated me before it hated you. If you were of the world, the world would love its own; but because you are not of the world, but I chose you out of the world, therefore the world hates you (15:18-19).

Chapter 17 is Jesus' own sublime, simple, and magnificent prayer. It sets forth beautifully the father-son-mankind relation, and closes with these lines (22-26):

The glory which thou hast given me I have given to them, that they may be one even as we are one, I in them and thou in me, that they may become perfectly one, so that the world may know that thou hast sent me and hast loved them even as thou hast loved me. Father, I desire that they also, whom thou hast given me, may be with me where I am, to behold my glory which thou hast given me in thy love for me before the foundation of the world. O righteous Father, the world has not known thee, but I have known thee; and these know that thou hast sent me. I made known to them thy name, and I will make it known, that the love with which thou hast loved me may be in them, and I in them.

Here, at the evangelical climax, Jesus sings in prayer through John. Unless we remember the readers of this letter, we shall miss its peculiar, amazing, paradoxical brilliance. These readers are the men of reason, the gnostics who recognize nonsense when they meet it. And here, incredible though it must appear, is our own Lord uttering such foolishness as "we are one" and "that they may be one" and "I in them and thou in me." What ever can a sane man think? Why (a gnostic might plausibly infer), a man would, if he took this sort of thing seriously, be led to question his reason!

This, of course, is exactly what Jesus and John intended. Man should be shown, they thought, that there is a communal ground more ultimate than that of logic, just as there is a basis for unity more fundamental than that of physical contiguity. That ground and basis is an identity of commitment, of dedication. Its name is love.

. . . the unity is not that of place, but of will; . . . the bond of unity is not sight working through material presence in material light, but Love working through spiritual sight or the spirit of truth, independently of material presence.[127]

The First Letter of John. Jesus exemplified perfect love, and commanded it. Paul preached love as the essence of the Christian faith. It was left to John, "the mystical apostle of love," to identify God with love, in the first of the three letters attributed to him.

John's first letter seems to grow out of the direct warmth of his personal experience of Jesus; it is as if the author had himself known, seen, and touched our Lord "in the flesh," and wrote feelingly to dispel the gnostic doubts by giving the lie to every claim that Jesus had merely "appeared." [128]

> That which was from the beginning, which we have heard, which we have seen with our eyes, which we have looked upon and touched with our hands, concerning the word of life—the life was made manifest, and we saw it, and testify to it, and proclaim to you the eternal life which was with the Father and was made manifest to us—that which we have seen and heard we proclaim also to you, so that you may have fellowship with us; and our fellowship is with the Father and with his Son Jesus Christ (I John 1:1-3).

Although there is blindness in every sinful soul—to be removed by faith in Jesus, as in John 9—we are told that "God is light and in him there is no darkness at all." This light, as John testifies, is the light of love:

> He who says he is in the light and hates his brother is in the darkness still. He who loves his brother abides in the light, and in it there is no cause for stumbling (2:9-11).

It shines in us as we honestly confess our sins and proclaim our genuine fellowship with each other and with Jesus.

These two fellowships are interdependent in human action: the condition of the Christian community-fellowship is common love for the Lord. We who are in fellowship with the Lord, and accept Jesus as redeemer of our sins, naturally enjoy fellowship with each other. We "keep our word." Here is an interesting and quite possibly deliberate ambiguity. The text reads:

> Whoever keeps his word, in him truly love for God is perfected. By this we may be sure that we are in him: he who says he abides in him ought to walk in the same way in which he walked (2:5-6).

—and, of course, he walked in love. The "his" in "whoever keeps his word" plainly refers, at first reading, to the keeper of the word; "whoever keeps his word" means, straightforwardly, "whoever is honest" or "whoever is faithful." But we remember also that Jesus is the Word of God, the Logos. So the keeper of the word is also the keeper of the Word; he who is faithful to his promise is faithful to the Lord.

We cannot be certain whether John here is a Pauline Puritan:

> Do not love the world or the things in the world. If any one loves the world, love for the Father is not in him. For all that is in the world, the lust of the flesh and the lust of the eyes and the pride of life, is not of the Father but is of the world. And the world passes away, and the lust of it; but he who does the will of God abides for ever (2:15-17).

He does write as a philosophical dualist, and does draw a hyper-Platonic distinction between the "world" and the Father. For the Christian—certainly for the Hellenized Jew—"loving the things of this world" is precisely parallel with the Old Testament's "worship of idols." At least during the earliest days of the Hebrews, most of the immoral love-worship had presumably been of false gods, or supernatural entities other than *Yahweh*; during Christian times past and emphatically present, the immoral love-worship is rather a dedication to lesser, natural things. The difference is of some importance, because the Christian who cherishes his Jewish heritage, as Jesus of Nazareth unmistakably did, need not, in withholding his love from this world, hate it. After all, God made it. The Christian can, and I think should, read this Johannine text in a Jewish sense: Do not dedicate your heart totally to any non-divine objects, neglecting God. Realize instead that God is the loving source of all that is good. Love him first and last, for he alone endures.

Knowing that Jesus came to us "in the flesh" (4:2), the Christian will also do his best to distinguish, in John's phrase, "lusts of the flesh" the "lusts" from the "flesh." After issuing his apocalyptic warning ("Children, it is the last hour"), John adapts a gnostic turn of phrase,[129] twists it and turns it against them in an arresting passage:

> If you know that he is righteous, you may be sure that every one who does right is born of him. See what love the Father has given us, that we should be called children of God; and so we are. The reason why the world does not know us is that it did not know him. Beloved, we are God's children now; it does not yet appear what we shall be, but we know that when he appears we shall be like him, for we shall see him as he is (2:29;3:2).

We know that Jesus, himself perfectly righteous, is the only source of our righteousness. The world not having "known" him—and we may read this in the double sense of "know," as "not having become acquainted with him during his life on earth" and also as "not having understood him" or "having rejected him"—does not love us who do know him. Because Jesus has loved us and made himself "known" to us, we can love and know him.

By this transcendent identification of *knowledge* with *love,* John is whipping the gnostics at their own game. Those who seek only to "know" cannot love; we alone who seek to love can truly know. St. Augustine is, as it were, vindicated in advance.

Brotherly love, as an earthly reflection of heavenly love, is the heart of John's third chapter. He teaches not alone that we *should* love our brothers, but that insofar as we are good, we *shall* love them. It was because Cain was evil that the first fratricide occurred, and through that murder we are to understand how our own righteousness can incur the world's hatred. In Jesus' loving sacrifice for our sins, we have both a model and an inspiration for our own love.

> By this we know love, that he laid down his life for us; and we ought to lay down our lives for the brethren. But if any one has the world's goods and sees his brother in need, yet closes his heart against him, how does God's love abide in him? Little children, let us not love in word or speech but in deed and in truth (3:16-18).

We meet the Johannine "double commandment" at the end of this chapter. The Shema has disappeared at last. In its place we have a purely Christian call. And the "two commandments" have literally become one:

> And this is his commandment, that we should believe in the name of his Son Jesus Christ and love one another, just as he has commanded us (3:23).

The key words of John's fourth chapter are as concise and vivid as any ever penned on love. I cite them intact:

> Beloved, let us love one another; for love is of God, and he who loves is born of God and knows God. He who does not love does not know God; for God is love. In this the love of God was made manifest among us, that God sent his only Son into the world, so that we might live through him. In this is love, not that we loved God but that he loved us and sent his Son to be the expiation for our sins. Beloved, if God so loved us, we also ought to love one another. No man has ever seen God; if we love one another, God abides in us and his love is perfected in us.
>
> By this we know that we abide in him and he in us, because he has given us of his own Spirit. And we have seen and testify that the Father has sent his Son as the Savior of the world. Whoever confesses that Jesus is the Son of God, God abides in him, and he in God. So we know and believe the love God has for us. God is love, and he who abides in love abides in God, and God abides in him. In this is love perfected with us, that we may have confidence for the day of judgment, because as he is so are we in this world. There is no fear in love, but perfect love casts out fear. For fear has to do with punishment, and he who fears is not perfected in love. We love, because he first loved us. If any one says, "I love God," and hates his brother, he is a liar; for he who does not love his brother whom he has seen, cannot love God whom he has not

seen. And this commandment we have from him, that he who loves God should love his brother also (4:7-21).

Knowledge and love are no longer two, but one, as the God we know and love is one. A failure of love is a failure of knowledge for, in the culminating identification toward which the Biblical conception has, in a sense, been moving since Genesis, *God is love.*

This is the very heart of Christianity. And here in the heart is mystery. Even an unregenerate Platonic or Stoic gnostic can understand love as a relationship between man and man, and of man for good, and for God. He can, perhaps, even envisage God loving, perhaps even poor sinners like ourselves. But through all this, love is a relationship, a going out from one person toward another person, or toward a thing. *Love* seems to name the dynamic tendency or movement, the intermediate striving or concern between or among lovers.

Yet here we have the bold, simple claim, not that God loves us benevolently or that we are to love him and each other, but that God *is* love. Wilder is correct:

> This supreme affirmation is a hard saying even to "men of good will" today, and is one of those things that "the natural man does not receive" and "is not able to understand." [130]

And Wilder tries to help us by naming (but, alas, not explaining) a distinction between "philosophic" and "practical" definitions:

> Love here is not merely an attribute of God but defines his nature, though in a practical rather than philosophic sense. God's nature is not exhausted by the quality of love, but love governs all its aspects and expressions.[131]

Wilder's colleague, Paul W. Hoon, goes further and clarifies by way of contrast, indicating that this love-God or God-love is not a changeless, immovable being eternally contemplating himself, as in some Oriental religions. He is not a life-force or fertility principle, as in some pagan religions. He is not sheer mathematical perfection, or the ideal form of beauty, as in some Hellenic religions. He is not even "energy," in contemporary scientific terms. He is purely sustaining, creative, overflowing, active concern. He is the universal dynamic, love. All lesser lovers love objects, even if those objects be thought to be only themselves. God alone, being infinite and perfect, needs no object, for he *is* love itself.[132]

Love is radiant. In creating, God radiated his loving self. We live in his image as we reflect his radiation and share his inner nature, by loving.

Having created us, and while sustaining us, God has also redeemed us through Jesus' death, perfectly pointing our Christian way of love: toward our brothers in Christ.[133]

Jesus saves our souls. He also teaches us, and is for us the perfect evidence of the Father's *agape*. Its proper fruit is our fearlessly[134] confident love of our fellow men.

Each man among us, says Elder John profoundly and with marvelous concision, is both in and out of this historic-temporal world and at the same time beyond it, with Jesus in anticipation of our day of judgment. "As he is, so are we in this world."

Each human lover owes all of his power of loving, and thus of becoming fully human, to God. "We love because he first loved us."

And, finally, we owe life itself, eternal life, to God:

> And this is the testimony, that God gave us eternal life, and this life is in his Son. He who has the Son has life; he who has not the Son has not life (5:11-12).

The gospel and letter of John together present a prayerful, revelatory picture of the moral dynamic of love. The focus is on the father-son-mankind complex, and the whole meaning of that complex is presented in terms of love.

This human level of love in John is, as it was in Hebraic days, presented as a full-hearted dedication of the total personality. Far richer of course than any superficial, infatuated inclination, this love is richer than even any "attachment" we are likely to call "emotional." [135] It is warm and absorbing, and it colors all we do and say. It inspires, illuminates, and disciplines. It is, in the deepest sense, the love that makes life worth living.

Ultimately, in metaphysical and mystic-metaphorical terms, it does even more than make life worth living; love makes death worth dying, and meanwhile makes it possible for us to live our lives at all, for without love we are dead in our hearts. The obstinate human heart, unresponsive to Jesus' invitation, becomes inhuman. Its pulse loses meaning, and becomes a mechanical tick-tock. The choice here, once again as it was in the earlier prophetic writings, is presented as the most momentous one of all: that between being our most genuine, essential selves, and denying our inmost being; between being born again to live forever in the glory of God, and dying now and forever; between light and darkness; between intimate community and stark isolation; between being and nonbeing; between love and hate.

CHRISTIAN LOVE AND PLATONIC LOVE

The obvious parallels between Socrates the man and Jesus the man-God have long been belabored. Both were dedicated moral teachers, admired and deeply misunderstood by all but a few during their lifetimes, persecuted, prosecuted, tried, convicted, condemned, and executed for the crime of loving and seeking to "save" their fellow men. Neither, so far as we know, wrote a word. Both exemplified, in their lives, the morality they taught.

Moreover, some Biblical and most post-Biblical Christianity is deeply Platonic. Christianity has been called the "infusion of the Hellenic spirit into the Gospel soul." Without Platonism, Christian thought would be unrecognizable to us today.

A Platonist might well salute a Christian for his objective recognition of, and dependence upon, perfection, and for his forthright rejection of careless, subjective "relativism." The Christian can well return the salute with a genuine respect for the magnificence of Plato's metaphysical temporal-eternal framework, and for the undeniable earnestness of his total moral dedication. Both their heroes die for truth (though Socrates did not die to save Athenians' souls, in any mystical sense; he died because it was his duty as an Athenian to die), and both insist upon the necessity of transcending the lower levels of love in favor of its highest goal.

But the time has now come for lines to be drawn. Despite the proselytizing efforts of the Rev. Benjamin Jowett (who sought to baptize Plato by translating him into English), and despite more than a century of devoutly intentioned misreading, we must not permit Socratic-Platonic philosophy to be identified with any kind of Christianity at all. The geniuses of these two world-views are irreconcilable. One may be neither a Christian nor a Platonist. One may be either a Christian or a Platonist. But one cannot possibly be both, at pain of outright inconsistency.

In the two conceptions of love these contrasts become clear:

1. Platonic love looks forward toward the Good. A Platonist endeavors as clearly as he can to envisage the Good that is, in order that he may work to make this limited world approach it. Literally all of time happens in the shadow of eternity, not all but thirty-three years or so. Christian love, on the other hand, looks backward as well as forward, and is explained by its loving source-God as well as in terms of its beloved destiny-God.

2. Plato's Good is not a person. Jesus' God is a person. Plato could not possibly pray to the Good, or worship the Good, as Jesus could and did pray to and worship God.

3. Plato's "demiurge" is a metaphysical force, distinct from goodness. It did not really "create" us, and certainly never loved us. The demiurge is not inherently good; it becomes good only (as with men) according as it loves goodness.

4. Plato (as I have interpreted him) has no place for sin. Immorality is evil, and is not excused. Immorality is unreasonable, unreasoning, ig-

norant, childish, blind, lustful. To be immoral is to be less than fully human. But being immoral is not being naughty.

5. Platonic goodness could not possibly become incarnate, live, suffer, and die. It is essentially timeless and universal. To pretend that the timeless could enter time, the universal become particular, is to propose an absurdity to a Platonist.

In sum, a Platonist must straightforwardly reject the antirationality of Christianity. He must deny the emphasis on the merely temporal acts of Jesus' life, and consider Christian glorification of unreasoned faith to be irresponsible. Within the framework of his thought, he could of course explain the historical success of Christianity.

Christians, of course, find Platonists to be typical gnostics, puffed up with pride. Sinfully unwilling to confess their own dependence, they harden their hearts against divine love and truth, and vaunt their conceptual skills, not recognizing that these too gain all their moral use and value from God who gave them to us, and to whose service they are properly directed. As a result, Platonism is cold and inhuman, or rather impersonal; its God is dead, or has never come alive; and its life, for want of human moral meaning, is therefore death.

With their metaphysical meaning-frameworks radically, but not entirely, distinct; with the dynamisms of their loves fundamentally differing; and with the ultimate roles of reason assigned to different worlds, Platonic and Christian love, though they may be compared and can be confused, ought never to be confounded.

A NOTE FOR A "NATURAL MAN"

A man tells himself: Paul says (in I Cor. 2:14) that a "natural" man —meaning by this a man in a state of nature, rather than of grace, or an "unspiritual" man, one who has not yet been saved—is not able to understand the gifts of the spirit of God, and that they are folly to him. Christians seem almost unanimously to second this occult teaching: unless a man loves God, he cannot truly understand God's love.

In Edward Caswall's translation of a hymn attributed to Bernard of Clairvaux,

> But what to those who find? Ah, this
> Nor tongue nor pen can show:
> The love of Jesus, what it is
> None but his loved ones know.[136]

Consider the plight of a man who is, in Paul's sense, "natural." He stands outside the Christian communion. He is not saved. If what Paul says is literally correct, he cannot understand Christian love.

Why this man is not saved will at once be evident to a Christian: either God in his wisdom has not seen fit to endow him with the grace that will inspire him with faith, or he is callous and obdurate, willfully stopping his ears and closing his heart to God's call. Thus, Paul denies the possibility of understanding the truth to all except to those who are already convinced of it.

When a Marxist says that one cannot understand Marxism until he becomes a Marxist, whereupon all will presumably become clear, his statement is to be repudiated as absurd. We must insist upon a distinction between understanding and belief, between assertion and truth, between conviction and evidence. Unless some mystical sense is attached to "understand," it is nonsense to tell a man that he must believe Marxist doctrine in order to understand it. Many of us believe that we do understand Marxism in some degree, and that we can see clearly where and how it falls short. We could not reject it as we do, unless we first understood it.

Similarly, Freud sometimes seemed to refute his critics by claiming that they did not really understand his doctrines, not being themselves Freudian psychoanalysts, or not having been psychoanalyzed. The disqualification was built into the system: he who finds fault with the teaching shows that he has not understood it. This claim is as nonsensical as that of Marxism, and for the same reason. We cannot accept a prior state of conviction as a condition for understanding a doctrine of which we remain to be convinced. In science or philosophy, we cannot be asked to believe a hypothesis as a condition for making sense of it; else how could we ever put it to any kind of test?

So in Christianity. If it seriously carries with it this self-protective, built-in guarantee, so that understanding is made dependent upon faith, the case for rational persuasion is conceded at the outset. Worse yet, this epistemological gimmick places every heresy in principle beyond Christian attack, and renders ridiculous Jesus' reproaches of the Pharisees and Paul's and John's own preachments against the Docetic and Antinomian gnostics.

We ought never to exclude mysticism on principle. Nor need we deny that there are believing states of mind in which illuminations are possible, which are not possible in any other way. If I am in love with a girl and you are not, and I insist that she is a particularly wonderful person, while you think her quite ordinary, I may enthusiastically cry, "But if only you loved her as I do, you would *see* how wonderful she is!"

In this sense, and only in this sense, can we understand what Paul says. If only natural, unsaved men would love God as Paul does, they would see for themselves how infinitely lovable he is.

But this sense is notoriously untrustworthy. Men have loved the most

preposterous women, and worshipped the most evil of idols, with en-
thusiasms hardly less impressive than Paul's. Until we can find some
extra-fideistic, extra-enthusiastic ground for distinguishing hallucinations
and illusions from clear vision, men will continue to wallow in their
blind "naturalness."

The "natural man" replies to himself: . . . and that's all very well,
so long as you can cling resolutely to your nickel-plated, hard-boiled
notion of "understanding." You win. But it's a pretty thin victory, after
all, isn't it? Are you really willing to accept the unhappy consequences of
your petty resolution to use "understanding" so narrowly?

Among these consequences is the fact that you render impossible the
understanding of many of life's richest treasures. To take a Biblical example, consider the lilies of the field. The botanist may in your sense
understand them, in that he can describe their pollination cycles and
prescribe soil and humidity conditions for growth, without ever seeing
and knowing their loveliness as they wave in the wind.

Or consider a quartet for strings. To a musical boor, the music means
nothing. Wouldn't you want to say to him, "Of course you can't make
any sense out of this music. You haven't really heard it. You aren't 'in
tune' with it."

Or, finally and crucially, how about human beings? *Can* you really
understand a man or woman cold-bloodedly, in quite the same way in
which you can understand a beetle skewered on a pin? Or don't you
really have to enter into some kind of intimate, affective, responsive communion with him, seeing and sensing his world his way, in order that you
may have insight into his humanness? [137]

If this be true of a human person whom we can see and touch, how
much more true it must be of God! And here, after all, we may have
what St. Paul was teaching: openheartedness is the condition for understanding the person of God and therefore for admitting his love.

NOTES ON BIBLICAL LOVE

My scriptural citations, except as noted below, are all from the Revised Standard
Version (New York, Toronto, and Edinburgh: Thomas Nelson and Sons, 1946 and
1952); copyrighted 1946 and 1952 by the Division of Christian Education, National
Council of Churches, and used by permission. *The Interpreter's Bible* is the twelve-
volume edition published in New York and Nashville by Abingdon-Cokesbury Press,
1952 *et seq.* When both volume and page are cited, "12:579" means Volume XII, page
579.

[1] Gen. 1:31.
[2] The tacit assumption is that the boredom of loneliness ill becomes the supreme
being.

[3] In I John 4:8.

[4] See William Graham Cole, *Sex and Love in the Bible* (New York: Association Press, 1959), p. 119: ". . . biblical religion deals with events rather than ideas, with the concrete rather than the abstract, with the historical rather than the detached eternal . . . one might say that every major heresy in Christian history represents an attempt to transform event into idea. . . ."

[5] See A. Cohen, *Everyman's Talmud* (New York: Dutton, 1949; London: J. M. Dent & Sons, Ltd.), p. 286. (Semachoth II, 6.)

[6] See Newman and Spitz, *The Talmudic Anthology* (New York: Behrman, 1947), pp. 196, 256.

[7] See Deut. 7:6-8.

[8] From the Talmud. See Montefiore and Loewe, *A Rabbinic Anthology* (London: Macmillan, 1938), pp. 109-110, No. 286.

[9] From the Talmud, Azoth III. 18. See Cohen, *op. cit.*, p. 22. The passage continues (George Foot Moore, *Judaism in the First Centuries of the Christian Era* [Cambridge: Harvard, 1927], I, p. 397):

> Beloved are the Israelites, because they are called sons of God; still greater love that it was made known to them that they are called sons of God, as it is said, "Ye are sons of the Lord your God" [Deut. 14:1]. Beloved are the Israelites, because to them was given the precious instrument; still greater love that it was made known to them that to them was given the precious instrument with which the world was created [the Torah-revelation]. "For good doctrine have I given to you, do not forsake my Torah."

Of this, Moore says (I, p. 398):

> More pregnant expression of the Jewish conception of God's relation to men could hardly be given. God's love for mankind in making man alone of all creatures in the image of God; his peculiar love to Israel in calling them his sons; the immensity of his love in giving to them the religion which was both instrumental and final cause in the creation of the world; and all these proofs of his love known not by inference or reasoning but by revelation direct from God himself.

[10] See Newman and Spitz, *The Hasidic Anthology* (New York: Bloch, 1944), p. 18, No. 7:5. The joyous service of the Lord is of course a central song in Psalms; see esp. Pss. 16, 42, 43, 67, 105.

[11] In the words of the Radviller rabbi. See *ibid.*, p. 221, No. 92:4.

[12] But see Cohen, *op. cit.*, pp. 212-213 on the meaning of "neighbor." It is sometimes urged that Leviticus enjoins only the love of Jews, and that the "universalization" came only later with the prophetic writings. This dispute is not in question here, since our concern is with the Jewish tradition as a whole, and there can be no possible doubt about a fully universalized love in developed Judaism.

[13] *Goyim* means both "nations" and "Gentiles."

[14] From the Talmud. See Morris Joseph, *Judaism as Creed and Life* (London: Routledge, 1925), p. 394. Joseph argues, consistently with the tradition, that if one truly loves his neighbor, he will necessarily love his enemy. See also Exod. 23:4-5.

[15] See Cohen, *op. cit.*, p. 65, and Montefiore and Loewe, *op. cit.*, No. 1326: "God said to Israel, 'My sons have I made you lack aught? What is it that I seek of you? Only that you love each other, honour each other and respect each other.' " And

again, from Newman and Spitz, *The Talmudic Anthology*, p. 256, No. 196: "A man should not say: 'I will love the learned and hate the unlearned,' but rather shall he say: 'I love them all.' "

Or, again (innumerable examples might be cited) from the medieval Maimonides (Moore, *op. cit.*, II, p. 87): "Thou shalt love thy neighbor as thyself. All the things that you wish that others should do to you, do you to your brother."

[16] See Newman and Spitz, *The Talmudic Anthology*, p. 256, No. 196. But see Freud's corrosive analysis of this central teaching.

[17] Cohen, *op. cit.*, p. 82.

[18] This question of the uniqueness of Christianity will be considered in the two succeeding sections, "Eros, Agape, and the Dimensions of Biblical Love" and "Matthew, Mark, and Luke."

[19] See Moore, *op. cit.*, II, p. 99. The twelfth century Bahya Ibn Pakuda's *Duties of the Hearts* seems to be an extended, popular analysis of the problem of motivation and duty within the conscience. See Isaac Husik, *A History of Medieval Jewish Philosophy* (Philadelphia: The Jewish Publication Society, 1946), Chap. VI. Our duty, according to Bahya (as Husik explains it) is to love sincerely in all acts. See also the Talmudic "Heaven regards the intentions," quoted from *Sanhedrin* 106b by Husik, p. 83.

[20] See J. H. Hertz, ed., *A Book of Jewish Thoughts* (London, New York: H. Milford, Oxford University Press, 1920), p. 25.

[21] Moore, *op. cit.*, I, pp. 263 ff. cites many additional sources in support of this.

[22] II Sam. 12:24.

[23] Dan. 9:23.

[24] See Moore, *op. cit.*, II, pp. 253 ff. That the chastisements are loving is scripturally evidenced by Lamentations 3.27-33; Job 5:17 ("Happy is the man whom God reproves"), and elsewhere.

[25] *The Interpreter's Bible*, 5:141.

[26] "Judah has been faithless and abomination has been committed in Israel and in Jerusalem; for Judah has profaned the sanctuary of the Lord, which he loves, and has married the daughter of a foreign god" (Mal. 2:11).

[27] *The Interpreter's Bible*, 5:111.

[28] See Harold Cooke Phillips, *The Interpreter's Bible*, 6:596.

[29] See Newman and Spitz, *The Hasidic Anthology*, p. 116, No. 49:1.

[30] See Cole, *op. cit.*, p. 55.

[31] See Bruce M. Metzger, *The Interpreter's Bible*, 7:58, and Amos N. Wilder, *ibid.*, 12:280: "Greek-speaking Judaism took over the commonplace pagan term to translate Hebrew words expressive of the love of God and the love of neighbor, and the church then filled it with the meanings implicit in the Christian experience."

In a personal letter, my colleague Dr. William Arrowsmith (to whom I am especially indebted) offers this delightful and plausible suggestion to explain why Paul so rarely used *philostorgein* for "love":

> [*Philostorgein*] is a frequent Hellenistic usage—Marcus Aurelius, Plato, Philodemus, inscriptions (Isiac), Polybius, Xenophon, even Aristotle, Aelian, and the New Testament (Ep. ad Romanos, 12.10—and what's more, as a gloss on *agape*). Now I can't be sure about this, but I suspect that *philostorgein*, if not a philosopher's word, is basically a literary word, probably a little highfalutin' for a bird like Paul: good enough for a gloss, but perhaps too polysyllabic or

too attached to philosophical—particularly Stoic—doctrines to carry the desired meaning.

In any case [Arrowsmith continues], Paul would have had trouble with *stergein* precisely because it too lacks a noun. The only available *stergein*-based noun would have been *philostorgia*, which is a mouthful and maybe a Stoic mouthful at that. Not the thing for a slave's religion in the slightly Hellenized East.

Paul's gloss is particularly interesting, and reveals something of the philosophical complexity. The passage in Romans reads "love one another with brotherly affection"; where one might have expected *philein*, one finds *agapan*, with *philostorgein* glossed over it.

[32] Anders Nygren, *Agape and Eros* (originally published in 1932 and 1938, revised, in part retranslated, and published in one volume at Philadelphia: Westminster Press, 1953, in the Watson translation), *passim*. For one among many more recent examples, see Paul Tillich, *Dynamics of Faith* (New York: Harper, 1957), pp. 114-115: "*Eros* is described as the desire for self-fulfillment by the other being, *agape* as the will to self-surrender for the sake of the other being. . . . No love is real without a unity of *eros* and *agape*. *Agape* without *eros* is obedience to moral law, without warmth, without longing, without reunion. *Eros* without *agape* is chaotic desire, denying the validity of the claim of the other one to be acknowledged as an independent self, able to love and be loved. Love as the unity of *eros* and *agape* is an implication of faith."

[33] Reinhold Niebuhr, *The Nature and Destiny of Man* (New York: Scribner's, 1949), 2:82. Excerpts used by permission of Charles Scribner's Sons.

[34] See, in point, *ibid.*, 2:88. ". . . it is not even right to insist that every action of the Christian must conform to *agape*, rather than to the norms of relative justice and mutual love by which life is maintained and conflicting interests are arbitrated in history. For as soon as the life and interest of others than the agent are involved in an action or policy, the sacrifice of those interests ceases to be 'self-sacrifice.' It may actually become an unjust betrayal of their interests."

[35] Niebuhr (*ibid.*, 2:186) quotes Martin Luther's *On Christian Liberty*, p. 260: "Thus from faith flow forth love and joy in the Lord, and from love a cheerful willing free spirit, disposed to serve our neighbour voluntarily, without taking into account any gratitude or ingratitude, praise or blame, gain or loss. Its object is not to lay men under obligation, nor does it distinguish between friends or enemies . . . but most freely spends its goods, whether it loses them through ingratitude or gains goodwill. . . ." and Niebuhr says of this passage: "Here Luther comprehends the whole beauty and power of Christian *agape*, particularly the transcendent freedom over all the prudential considerations of natural ethical attitudes."

[36] As Niebuhr notes, *op. cit.*, 2:84.

[37] Almost the standard reference here, and one to which we shall soon return, is Nygren, *op. cit.* See pp. 78-80.

[38] *Ibid.*, pp. 75-80.

[39] *Ibid.*, pp. 175 ff.

[40] As, for example, *ibid.*, p. 81.

[41] But only so, for since *agape* is defined as independent, spontaneous, and underived, and since man's love for God is none of these, it cannot be strictly *agape*. See Nygren, *op. cit.*, p. 126.

[42] John Short, *The Interpreter's Bible*, 10:166.

⁴³ *Op. cit.,* p. 32.

⁴⁴ See, for only one example, Niebuhr, *op. cit.*

⁴⁵ See Nygren, *op. cit.,* pp. 124-126. At I Corinthians 2:9, Paul cites Isaiah and translates man's love for God as *agape.* Speaking for himself, Paul does so at Romans 8:28 and I Corinthians 8:3, and also (if it be Pauline) at the end of Ephesians.

Is it not curious to claim (as Nygren does) that *agape* is almost uniquely Christian, and then to base this claim on Paul's usage (which is not consistent anyway)? While it is true that Paul sometimes calls the man-loving-God relationship *pistis,* "faith," as well as *agape,* one might consider the synoptic gospels even sounder ground for deciding what is "Christian" and what isn't. And the synoptists typically use *agapan,* not *pisteuein,* in their crucial passages (as at Matt. 22:37-40; Mark 12:28-34; and Luke 19:25-28). It is, I think, an anachronistic absurdity to impose standards of definitional rigor upon these texts, and to try to derive important conclusions from an author's use of *agapan* in one place, *philein* in another, and *pistein* or *pisteuein* in a third. The Holy Bible is not a system of deductive rigor, with each term having one clear meaning consistently adhered to. The writers were relating facts and preaching the gospel. They were more concerned with serving souls than with chopping logic.

⁴⁶ *Ibid.,* pp. 44-45.

⁴⁷ *Ibid.*

⁴⁸ *Ibid.,* p. 46. It is surprising that Nygren should have misread the Old Testament. It is even more surprising that he, in company with so many Christian theologians, should search the gospels for meticulous distinctions between Christianity and Judaism, when the answer to the question is so clear. What distinguishes Christianity from Judaism and all other religions is Jesus Christ, nothing more and nothing less. We return to this later, in our consideration of the synoptic gospels.

⁴⁹ *Ibid.,* p. 45.

⁵⁰ *Ibid.,* pp. 61-62. As Nygren points out, at Luke 10:25 it is a Jewish lawyer who follows the tradition in combining the teachings, and at Mark 12:25, when Jesus combines them, the scribes endorse him.

⁵¹ *Ibid.,* p. 66.

⁵² *Ibid.,* p. 71, n.2.

⁵³ *Ibid.,* p. 201.

⁵⁴ *Ibid.,* p. 250.

⁵⁵ Niebuhr, *op. cit.,* 2:68, 70.

⁵⁶ *Ibid.,* p. 87.

⁵⁷ "Magic" is here used to indicate events brought to pass by means inexplicable in human terms.

⁵⁸ Nygren, *op. cit.,* pp. 83-84.

⁵⁹ The parallel, for example, is logically wobbly. The debtor who was forgiven the larger debt loves more, because he was forgiven more. The woman seems to be forgiven more because she had loved more. And verse 47 is classically unhelpful: ". . . her sins, which are many, are forgiven, for she loved much; but he who is forgiven little, loves little." I offer no solution to this well-known dilemma. I simply resign it, following John Knox (*The Interpreter's Bible,* 8:141-42) and saying simply that the woman loves as she is being forgiven.

⁶⁰ Interpolated into John 8.

⁶¹ Never with more pungent vigor than by Friedrich Nietzsche.

[62] To the contrary Ethelbert Stauffer and Gottfried Quell, *s.v.* "love" in J. R. Coates, translator, *Bible Key Words from Gerhard Kittel's Theologisches Worterbuch zum Neuen Testament* (New York: Harper, 1951; W. Kohlhammer, Verlag, Stuttgart, Germany), p. 28: "Eros is promiscuous and finds its satisfaction here, there and everywhere, but Agape is the love that makes distinction, choosing its object and holding to it."

[63] For of course they are not. See Nygren, *op. cit.*, pp. 75-80. But even as finitely valuable, every Christian must sympathize, or feel-with, it.

[64] Alias the Sermon down "on the level," Luke 6:17 ff.

[65] *The Interpreter's Bible*, 8:218.

[66] The old "Hate the sin but love the sinner" formula comes to mind. But Walter Russell Bowie (*The Interpreter's Bible*, 8:121) ingeniously points out that loving need not imply liking, inferring that even God himself cannot like everything he sees down here, and interprets the text as urging us to love our enemies and neighbors without even pretending to like them.

[67] See also Luke 10:25-28 and Mark 12:28-34. As already indicated, in these instances, the man-loving-God relation is called *agapan* rather than *philein*. But the synoptists could have used *philein* as well, and I base no argument on the distinction. See note 45 above.

[68] Such as George A. Buttrick, *The Interpreter's Bible,* 7:524.

[69] Like Nygren, *op. cit.*, p. 98.

[70] But, as earlier noted, Nygren does not find the uniqueness of Christianity exactly here, but rather in the "love for sinners." Nonetheless, this is a familiar Protestant ground for claiming uniqueness.

[71] The texts, from Genesis to Revelation, are manifold and, collectively, ambiguous. This is a question of judgment, to be decided by a consideration not alone of isolated snippets of scripture, but by a sense of the whole. Perhaps partly because I believe that Jesus of Nazareth, born, living, and dying in love for man, sufficiently distinguishes Christianity from Judaism, I do not read the Hebrew texts as ungenerously (or so it appears to me) as do some Christian theologians, though I gladly admit that alternate readings can be rendered plausible.

[72] It is a fair presumption that the synoptists and Jesus himself so understood it, as does Anders Nygren today (*op. cit.*, pp. 100-101: "Self love is man's natural condition, and also the reason for the perversity of his will"). This is the basic, historic sense, I believe, and my ensuing discussion is not intended to impute latter-day sophistication to the ancient authors.

[73] See the distinctions among *self-acceptance, self-affirmation,* and *selfishness* in Paul Tillich's *Love, Power and Justice* (New York: Oxford, 1954), p. 34. The idea is of course commonplace in contemporary psychology. I know of no contemporary analysis of self-love more enlightening than that of Aristotle. See his *Nichomachean Ethics* IX, viii.

[74] See John Knox, *The Interpreter's Bible*, 8:196. Note that the Samaritan in Jesus' story was not doing theology. He never stopped to think that God was "in" his "neighbor," and that his love should be directed to God. He simply saw a man in distress and reached out lovingly to help him. So Nygren, in an excellent discussion of the point, urges that "love your neighbor" means "love this man here and now," not something artificial and abstract like "love God as God is in this man" or "love mankind, of which this man is part." See *op. cit.*, p. 98.

[75] John 13:34, not explicitly found in the synoptic gospels, but considered here for expository convenience.

[76] So called, in ingenious parallel with the "Sermon on the Mount," by Canon Brooke Foss Westcott in his *Introduction to St. John's Gospel* and elsewhere. See his *The Gospel According to St. John* (London: James Clarke, 1958 ed.), p. xliii.

[77] Rev. Edwin A. Abbott, D. D. *s.v.* "Gospels" in *Encyclopædia Britannica* (New Werner edition of 1903), 10:839.

[78] *Ibid.*

[79] Hugh Thompson Kerr, Jr., in *The Interpreter's Bible,* 5:123.

[80] In this section I use the phrase "Pauline love" in a deliberately broad sense, to cover all those canonical writings attributed to Paul; unraveling competitive author-ship claims is an interesting and important task I leave to the scholars. Approximately, Romans and both Corinthians are now deemed to be unquestionably authentic; Ephesians, Colossians, Philippians, Galatians and both Thessalonians less certainly so; and the pastoral letters (both Timothys, Titus and Philemon) almost certainly in-authentic. Except in one or two instances, noted below, authorship is irrelevant to my purpose, and for convenience I even include under this very general heading oc-casional notice of the (non-Pauline) "catholic" letters that fall between Philemon and the letters of John: Hebrews, James, and the two Peters.

[81] Such attempts as that of Nygren (*op. cit.,* p. 83) to prove by citations from the Old Testament that, for the Jews, salvation was to be earned by works rather than by faith are anachronisms.

[82] In his *Dynamic of Faith, op. cit., passim.*

[83] Gerald R. Cragg, *The Interpreter's Bible,* 9:435.

[84] See Robert R. Wicks, *The Interpreter's Bible,* 11:58, commenting on Phil. 2:12-13: "Unselfish love is not a strategy."

[85] Paul Tillich, *op. cit.,* pp. 115-16.

[86] For instance, the reading I propose frankly cannot be reconciled with I Corinthians 13, except under the assumption (which I am happy to make) that Paul was here using "faith" in a very different sense. "If I have all faith, so as to move mountains, but have not love, I am nothing," as well as the distinction (in verse 13) among faith, hope, and love, becomes nonsense if love is part of the meaning of faith. My belief is that any alternative reading will, here or elsewhere, require similar rein-terpretations. We must remember that, as the Bible itself tells us, "There are some things in (the letters of Paul) hard to understand, which the ignorant and unstable twist to their own destruction, as they do the other scriptures" (2 Pet. 3:16).

[87] See also Gal. 3:6 and Heb. 11:8-12 and 17-20.

[88] The reader may want to try this reading on Rom. 9:30-32.

[89] As at Rom. 3:24; 5:15; and 6:23.

[90] Rom. 6:5-11; Gal. 2:20 and elsewhere.

[91] See II Pet. 2:19: "Whatever overcomes a man, to that he is enslaved."

[92] And in the Gospel of John as well: "Truly, truly, I say to you, everyone who commits sin is a slave to sin" (8:34).

[93] Gerald R. Cragg, *The Interpreter's Bible,* 9:374.

[94] *The Interpreter's Bible,* 7:58.

[95] The qualifier "almost" is important: the traditional "healthy-mindedness" can go only so far in twentieth century culture.

[96] This is not the place to trace the whole bleak history of Christian asceticism. It is worth noting, however, if only to correct a widespread misapprehension, that the Roman Catholic policy of a celibate clergy is not to be understood as a condem-nation of sexuality as such.

[97] William Graham Cole, in his *Sex in Christianity and Psychoanalysis* (New York: Oxford University Press, 1955) and his *Sex and Love in the Bible* (New York: Association Press, 1959) makes a strong contemporary case for the Hebraic–liberal–anti-Pauline interpretation.

[98] For still further examples, see Gal. 5:25 and Col. 3:15.

[99] See also Gal. 5:14.

[100] See Bruce M. Metzger, *The Interpreter's Bible*, 7:58, for relevant grammatical considerations.

[101] See II Cor. 10:10.

[102] And, for that matter, with circumcision and uncircumcision. See Gal. 6:15.

[103] James Moffatt, *Love in the New Testament* (London: Hodder and Stoughton, 1929), pp. 180 ff.

[104] *Donne's Sermons*, selected passages by Logan Pearsall Smith (Oxford: The Clarendon Press, 1919), p. 134; cited in *The Interpreter's Bible*, 8:690.

[105] Cf. the "love undying" of Eph. 6:24.

[106] John Short makes this distinction (*The Interpreter's Bible*, 10:189-90), citing as synoptic analogues Mark 10:13-16; Luke 18:15-17; and Matthew 18:2-3 and 19:13-15.

[107] As Nygren persuasively argues against other scholars; see *Agape and Eros*, p. 141. G. Preston MacLeod, *The Interpreter's Bible*, 11:151-52, analyzes the faith-hope-love relationship.

[108] Both in and out of Paul, as we have already discovered, Platonism flows recurrently through the New Testament, perhaps most plainly in Hebrews, as at 8:1-5 and 12:22-23.

[109] The Old Testament figure, especially from Jeremiah, Isaiah, and Hosea, is found in Mark 2:19-20; Matthew 22:2; John 3:29; Ephesians 5:22-23; and probably in chapters 19-22 of Revelation.

[110] The classic text on this point, undisputed among Christians, but mystifying to all unbelievers, is I Corinthians 2:14: "The unspiritual [or "natural"] man does not receive the gifts of the Spirit of God, for they are folly to him, and he is not able to understand them because they are spiritually discerned." The mystery of course (and it is inseparable from Christianity or Marxism or any other mystery-teaching) is that a set of beliefs and dedications and acts is claimed as "true" and even obligatory when it is admittedly absurd to him who does not accept them. Only Pierre Bayle could do this important issue justice. I have appended to this text a brief "Note for a Natural Man."

[111] See also I Thessalonians 3:12-13 and II Thessalonians 1:3.

[112] Following what I take to be the main trend of Paul's teaching, I have in the text made him out to be a dualist, not consistently condemning the flesh, to be sure, but on the whole ascetically inclined. What, then, am I to do with the open rejection of asceticism in I Timothy? Here we find condemnations of

> deceitful spirits and doctrines of demons, through the pretensions of liars whose consciences are seared, who forbid marriage and enjoin abstinence from foods which God created to be received with thanksgiving by those who believe and know the truth. For everything created by God is good, and nothing is to be rejected if it is received with thanksgiving; for then it is consecrated by the word of God and prayer (4:1-5).

Verses 1-4 here may of course simply be one more attack upon the "Judaizing" preachers, who were trying to reintroduce the ancient dietary laws, and quite justified under the circumstances. But how can the same Paul who wrote Romans say in verse 5 that "Everything created by God is good"? My answer is easy: if there were not already abundant historical, philological, and other doctrinal reasons for doubting the authenticity of the pastoral letters, this alone would be strongly suggestive. It remains barely possible that Paul changed his mind, or that the specific circumstances of the writing of this letter required so radically different an "emphasis." I myself do not believe that there is any change of mind, or any contradiction either. Paul in I Timothy does not contradict Paul in Romans because Paul wrote Romans and Paul simply did not write the letters to Timothy.

[113] I do not mean to suggest that this idea is "new" in the Bible, as late as this, for of course it is not, but only that we have not yet met it in the present discussion. The earliest occurrence I can find is in Proverbs 10:12 ("Hatred stirs up strife, but love covers all offences") though this is perhaps a slightly different idea. Closer to the I Peter notion is Jesus' description of the woman who kissed his feet (Luke 7:47): ". . . her sins, which are many, are forgiven, for she loved much"; and without using the word love, James 5:20 expresses it also: "whoever brings back a sinner from the error of his way will save his soul from death and will cover a multitude of sins."

[114] Nygren, for example. See op. cit., p. 248.

[115] As with "Pauline Love," I do not enter the lists to dispute scholarship. I set Revelation aside (partly because I do not understand it) and take the fourth gospel and the letters of John to be, broadly, "Johannine."

[116] See, inter alia, for this hoary anecdote, Amos N. Wilder, The Interpreter's Bible, 12:209, citing Jerome's Commentary on Galatians.

[117] "Heresy" is quoted because it seems odd to speak outright of a heresy before there was any established dogma.

[118] By this I mean only that, following Frank Moore Cross, Jr. (The Interpreter's Bible, 12:662), I take John's gospel to be more Jewish than Hellenic or Hellenistic.

[119] The rebirth notion, common enough even before Christianity, runs fairly frequently through our canon. See, for only a few instances, I Peter 1:23 and I John 3:9. To the more typically Pauline flesh-spirit dichotomy of John 3:6, I return anon in the text.

[120] See his Love, Power and Justice, especially Chapter VII, 107 ff.

[121] Remember Romans 5:10: "For if while we were enemies we were reconciled to God by the death of his Son, much more, now that we are reconciled, shall we be saved by his life."

[122] See, for an apparent exception, John 14:21-23.

[123] William Graham Cole's discussion in Chapter I of his Sex in Christianity and Psychoanalysis is relevant. See especially p. 12.

[124] See the earlier discussion of the "new commandment" in "Matthew, Mark, and Luke."

[125] ". . . in the Fourth Gospel," says Dr. Abbott (op. cit., p. 834), "faith implies even more than in Paul's Epistles; it is a faculty that tests, transmutes, and develops the recipient soul; it means a trust in Christ, not only as a sacrifice, nor as propitiation, nor as miracle-worker, nor as Son of God, but as source and object of all love, and the be-all and end-all of every human life. It is a remarkable fact [he continues] that this evangelist never uses the term pistis, which is frequently used by the synoptists, while he uses the verb pisteuein about twice as often as it is used by all the synoptists put together. He prefers to contemplate faith, not as in itself a virtue, but rather as a mental act or state taking its quality from its object."

[126] *Nicomachean Ethics* VIII, 8:3.

[127] Edward A. Abbott, *op. cit.*, p. 840.

[128] Very likely, however, the "we" should be taken to mean "we Christians collectively," rather than as an editorial "we." Otherwise we must suppose that the apostle John was well above ninety years old when he wrote this beautiful letter.

[129] The phrase is "born of him," not earlier used in the Bible.

[130] Amos N. Wilder, *The Interpreter's Bible*, 5:279. See also my "Note for a Natural Man."

[131] *Ibid.*, 5:280.

[132] *Ibid.*, 5:259. See also Nygren, *Agape and Eros*, pp. 151-152.

[133] It is perhaps possible subtly to distinguish the identification of God with love in I John 4:8 from that in 4:16, claiming that the latter is closer to the teaching of Jesus. See the relevant exegesis and exposition by Amos N. Wilder and Paul W. Hoon respectively, *The Interpreter's Bible*, 12:278 ff.

[134] See Paul W. Hoon, *The Interpreter's Bible*, 12:287: "[John] never appeals to fear in order to persuade men to love. On the contrary, he appeals to love in order to dispel fear."

[135] See Tillich, *Love, Power and Justice*, p. 26.

[136] *The Interpreter's Bible*, 5:108. An even odder oddity is found in I John 5:9-10: "If we receive the testimony of men, the testimony of God is greater; for this is the testimony of God that he has borne witness to his Son. He who believes in the Son of God has the testimony in himself. He who does not believe God has made him a liar, because he has not believed in the testimony that God has borne to his son." Given the context, it is at least possible (though, perhaps, improbable; I do not insist upon the point) that by "believe God" the Elder means "believe in God." With this reading, we have a very strange situation indeed: a man who disbelieves that God exists must therefore believe that God is a liar, because God testified through Jesus to his own existence!

[137] After writing these words late one night, I found these sentences in John Short (*The Interpreter's Bible*, 10:183): "Really to understand literature, one must love it. The same is true of music or any other art. Above all, it is true of men and women in their mutual relationships. . . . Love sees beneath the surface because love is in harmony with reality. To love men in this way is to believe in their best. To believe in the best is to help to arouse and evoke it." See also Asher Moore, "Psychoanalysis, Man, and Value," *Inquiry*, Vol. 1, 1961, pp. 53-65.

III

F R E U D I A N   L O V E

Just as there is no single concept of Platonic love, but rather a range of metaphysical and moral meanings; and just as there is no single concept of Biblical love, but rather a similarly rich range of meanings, religious and philosophical; so also there is no single concept of Freudian or psychoanalytic love.

Sigmund Freud, by consent now almost common, was a genius. His mind combined toughness, subtlety, industry, insight, ingenuity, courage, and an astonishing candor. In a sense of "science" almost lost now, concerned as we are with statistics and methods, Freud can be called a scientist of love. Yet, Freud was more than a scientist and less than one. He purchased psychological scope, insight, and suggestiveness at the price of consistent clarity.

No single coherent theory of the human personality can be called "Freudian." Freud's insights grew deeper and broader and were constantly modified as he worked through his materials. He is the most unsystematic system-builder in the history of human thought, and among the most intriguing to read. His work is a labyrinth, maddening to a reader who seeks to follow any direct and clearly charted course. Finding in some patient a peculiarly intriguing, unsuspected symptom, he pursues it down a dozen unrewarding avenues, and despite our best scientific intentions, we too often find these side-roads fascinating and lend them our attention as he did his.

We must read Freud not only as a descriptive psychological scientist, patiently unraveling the complexities of the human personality. We must also read him as a creative, imaginative artist.

It will by now be plain that I take the Freudian teaching seriously, and believe it to be a monumental contribution to man's understanding of himself. That Freud is at present out of fashion among American experimental psychologists may better attest their myopia and their disinterest in human beings than his confusion. Nonetheless, we shall not understand Freud if our reading of his work becomes an act of hero-worship.

Freud was philosophically naïve, as many geniuses have been.[1] Metaphysically, he was a nineteenth century materialist, with no epistemological sophistication at all, and it is ludicrous to read speculative psychoanalytic refutations of the work of traditional philosophers. Methodologically, Freud was (as I have already noted) prodigal; he genially invented new concepts and categories, or adapted old ones, whenever the current problem refused to yield to the devices at hand, without worrying about any comprehensive consistency.[2]

Our problem here is to glean, from the wealth of Freud's writings, a picture of love consistent with at least some main teachings, so that we can understand still another distinctive metaphysic and morality of love.

THE METAPHYSICAL FRAMEWORK

"Leben, lieben, arbeiten," Freud said when asked for criteria of mental health. To live, to love, to work: these are his marks of what passes in our puzzling world for sanity.

Yet, as Freud knew and insisted, the value of each of these is relative. The range within which one man may live, love, and work differs profoundly from that of another man. And a fatal therapeutic error is to impose any one man's life-plan, love-plan, or work-plan upon any other man. A key to Freud's rich humanity is his insistence upon the value of the personality—hence, his reluctance to condemn and his deep, sympathetic respect for individuals' different ways of solving their problems.

At root, Freud conceived the world as a mechanical-dynamic system. Mass-energy units are the building blocks of his universe. What happens, happens because it is pushed from behind, not because it is attracted beyond itself by any ideal force. We must abandon all teleology if we would enter Freud's world; though within that world we shall every moment be concerned with desires and needs that press us beyond the present into an unknown future.[3]

Freudian materialism finds its metaphysical genesis in the full flush of nineteenth century German voluntaristic romanticism. The organic dynamism of Freud is of a piece with the World-Will of Artur Schopenhauer; his affirmation is Nietzsche's yea-saying.[4]

Schopenhauer's noumenal world-force is blind, irresistible, indescribable, irreducible, and ultimately uncontrollable. Every act, event, or thing that we objectify in the world is but a partial, transient manifestation of the Will, become mere idea. We live in total dependence upon and subjection to World-Will; and we suffer so long as we frantically posit our individual wills as if they (and we) were real. The more we seek satisfaction, the more surely it eludes us. The fate of Fate is agony, and we share that fate so long as we seek . . . even if we seek only not to share it. The Schopenhauerian (and Oriental) secret is to cease the search itself, to suspend the very struggle, without ever having struggled to attain the suspension.

Freud's orientation is not wholly Schopenhauerian, and not at all Oriental. But his conception of "libido" surely shares with Schopenhauer's World-Will its dynamic, blind, imperious character. What World-Will is metaphysically, in Schopenhauer's universe, libido is psychologically, in Freud's.

Nietzsche's river flows as powerfully as Schopenhauer's, though perhaps less deeply. Nietzsche's *act* of defiance of the world's values is a self-assertive transcendence over every external claim upon the self; the energies ordinary men invest in the petty, prefabricated ideals they accept from the world are by extraordinary men thrown fully into the world's teeth. One does not choose not to obey the claims of the world's values; one totally gives them the lie, denying that they can ever make any rightful claim at all. What *I* want and need defines value, and alone deserves my total dedication. Every worldly value is thus "transvaluated," being derived wholly from within my ego. The analogy with Freudian "displacement" was evident to Freud himself:

> What I have called dream-displacement might equally be described [in Nietzsche's phrase] as a "transvaluation of psychical values." [5]

Freud's first model is the machine, fed by fuel, internally ignited, pushing and pulling its parts in strictest accordance with the laws of mechanics. Mental activity, so far as Freud concerned himself with it at all during this very early stage of his career, when he was doing traditional neurological research, was mechanical through and through.

But this model is almost at once outgrown, because Freud was too sensible to dream that any very precise Newtonian laws could be contrived that would do even the remotest justice to the internal dynamics of the human personality, let alone to the complex relations among persons, or between persons and the social institutions that surround, sustain and threaten them.

So Freud adopted, and largely maintained, the organism as his basic model. At its simplest, the cell is born, ingests, excretes, grows, multiplies, dies. It comes from its parent or parents as an autonomous but dependent biological system. Its needs inhere, and demand fulfillment. Given a favorable environment, these needs are met and the cell thrives. Given unfavorable surroundings, the cell withers to death. It is nonsense to ask the purpose of the cell's life or being. It simply is, because of what came before it. It acts as it does because of what it is and what it meets. It is as if it sought to reproduce itself; more simply, it behaves in a self-re-productive manner. But all of its behavior is made to make sense in terms of some present or prior state of the cell and its community; the imputation of meaning in terms of any future ideal-to-be-achieved is condemned a priori.

Freud does not pronounce this condemnation after deliberate judg-ment; he nowhere cites reasons for it. Instead, he assumes—correctly, in terms of the scientific temper of the age—that a Platonic pattern of telic explanation is somehow inappropriate. A Plato reborn would appear not so much mistaken as quaint, out of place and time; his judgments would seem not exactly false, but rather somehow beside the point.

At its simplest, any biological or psychological explanation is typically genetic. We explain a man's behavior by tracing it back to its roots, as we explain the discoloration of a flower's petal by finding some chemical deficiency in the soil from which it grows. We adduce inherent tendencies within the human organism, strictly analogous to such tendencies within the flower as phototropism. The flower copes with flood or drought, or it dies; and so does the man. The specific *ways* in which the individual flower copes reflect both its own nature and its environment; and so, again, with the man.

But within these limitations, the kinds and directions of coping will be explained—and it is assumed by Freud that everything can in princi-ple be explained in scientific terms—according to regular principles ap-plicable to all similar circumstances, in complete generality. Individual desires are admitted as explanatory categories only after these desires are reduced to general instinctive principles shared with all other indi-viduals of the same species. Idiosyncrasies, like miracles, are defined out of genuine possibility. Whatever happens, with no exceptions, is ex-plicable; and we are not to admit in explanation the possibility that the personality freely chooses any course of action, unless we can in turn translate the "free choice" into regular patterns of responses to stimuli. Freud believed that the concept of free will is a curious, relatively un-important self-delusion; at best, it is but an obstacle impeding scientific curiosity, and if taken seriously it could undermine the conditions under which alone research into the mind's operations could be carried on.

Many people, as is well known, contest the assumption of complete psychical determinism by appealing to a special feeling of conviction that there is a free will. This feeling of conviction exists; and it does not give way before a belief in determinism. Like every normal feeling it must have something to warrant it. But so far as I can observe, it does not manifest itself in the great and important decisions of the will: on these occasions the feeling that we have is rather one of psychical compulsion, and we are glad to invoke it on our behalf. ("Here I stand: I can do no other.") On the other hand, it is precisely with regard to the unimportant, indifferent decisions that we would like to claim that we could just as well have acted otherwise: that we have acted of our free—and unmotivated—will. According to our analyses it is not necessary to dispute the right to the feeling of conviction of having a free will. If the distinction between conscious and unconscious motivation is taken into account, our feeling of conviction informs us that conscious motivation does not extend to all our motor decisions. *De minimis non curat lex.* But what is thus left free by the one side receives its motivation from the other side, from the unconscious; and in this way determination in the psychical sphere is still carried out without any gap.[6]

Traditional materialism prescribes a corresponding resolution of the traditional mind-body problem. If mental activity is consistently construed after the model of machine or organism—and if these models themselves are construed materialistically—then plainly there will be no difficulty in commensurating a "mental" language with a "physical" language, and this commensuration has historically been the crux of the mind-body problem. All "mental" language will in principle be translatable without loss into "physical" language. Whenever challenged, Freud can typically claim that somatic characterizations are primary, while psychical ones are derivative and theoretically reducible to somatic languages.

Nonetheless, there remains in Freud an interesting version of the mind-body problem. When, during the late Eighties and early Nineties, Freud was a research physiological neurologist, he might well have considered hysteria and neurosis to be simply complex, public manifestations of more fundamental physical pathology. Throughout Freud's life—and to a surprising degree, even today—medical men have consistently inclined to understand mental illness as no more than symptomatic of chemical-physical disbalance. Until very recently, with the overwhelming but still mysterious symptomatic success of synthetic chemicals, and with intriguing results in neuroelectronic physiology, physicians' skepticism about depth psychology had been an almost universal, free act of metaphysical faith. Even the chemicals have by no means elevated (or depressed) this act of faith to the status of rational conviction.

At first, Freud had to fight the battle almost alone. He found in his clinical work patients whose physical findings were completely negative, yet who suffered hysterical tics and coughs. A strict materialist could perhaps reassure such patients that there must be some organic disorder, too subtle for present diagnostic procedures, underlying his problems.

Freud was not so strict. Without ever denying the ultimate importance of physiology, he empirically realized that these patients needed help that physiologists could not give. With Breuer, Freud found that men and women can sometimes talk-think-feel their way from helplessness toward normal living. By using his model-analogies, Freud could help his patients relate their present behavior to past behavior in ways that sometimes relieved some intolerable symptoms. In the theory that grew from his therapy, Freud tried to spell out his analogies, and to provide guidelines for helping other patients achieve the self-understanding, self-release, and self-respect that relieve some psychical torments.

The language of Freudian analogies is frankly mental. It contains such terms as "instinct," "inhibition," "ego," and "repression," none of which is translatable, *tout court,* into any equivalent anatomical or physiological terms. Those unlearned drives that are constant (or regularly recurrent) and intra-organically stimulated, like drives for food and for reduction of sexual tension, Freud calls "instincts." In a later, more sophisticated language, Freud's "sex instinct" is a variable intervening between antecedent gonadal tensions and consequent coital (and, of course, pre-coital) behavior. Until the antecedent conditions can be specified and more directly connected for control to consequent behavior, "instincts" or some equivalent concept must serve—so Freud believed—to make sense out of how men live and suffer.[7] Freud has been much criticized for irresponsibility in his use of terms; it is claimed that he set psychology back toward a "pre-scientific" stage. But Freud's solution to the mind-body problem is eminently practical. It is true that these conceptual categories are not, at the outset, fully defined, but remain subject to subsequent theoretical refinement in the light of later evidence. Freud recognized that everyone who seeks empirical accuracy ought to expect to use concepts as tools for explaining facts, and not to worship them as rigid idols.

> . . . a science erected on empirical interpretation . . . will not envy speculation its privilege of having a smooth, logically unassailable foundation, but will gladly content itself with nebulous, scarcely imaginable basic concepts, which it hopes to apprehend more clearly in the course of its development, or which it is even prepared to replace by others. For these ideas are not the foundation of science, upon which everything rests: that foundation is observation alone. They are not the bottom but the top of the whole structure, and they can be replaced and discarded without damaging it. The same thing is happening in our day in the science of physics, the basic notions of which as regards matter, centres of force, attraction, etc., are scarcely less debatable than the corresponding notions in psycho-analysis.[8]

Or again, both sensibly and humanely,

> We have often heard it maintained that sciences should be built up on clear and sharply defined basic concepts. In actual fact no science, not even the most exact, begins with such definitions. The true beginning of scientific activity consists rather in describing phenomena and then in proceeding to group, classify and correlate them. Even at the stage of description it is not possible to avoid applying certain abstract ideas to the material in hand, ideas derived from somewhere or other but certainly not from the new observations alone. Such ideas—which will later become the basic concepts of the science—are still more indispensable as the material is further worked over. They must at first necessarily possess some degree of indefiniteness; there can be no question of any clear delimitation of their content.[9]

Our human universe, then, consists of organisms naturally evolved, containing surging, outpressing needs. These needs are blind. We, as babies, push outward incoherently. We demand. The world denies what we demand of it, which is that our every demand be instantly gratified. We learn. We grow.

But we remain organisms responding to pressures from within us, and to obligations imposed upon us by our societies. We behave regularly, and no mythical homunculi are invoked as agents of free will to conceal our scientific ignorance. We do feel free: consciously, our decisions are uncontrolled. We do decide, but we decide within a framework of explanation. Science admits no myth. Traditional free will remains the easy recourse of the scientifically timid . . . and timidity is not the word for Dr. Freud.

Placing man, then, wholeheartedly and unqualifiedly within a natural framework of cause and effect, stimulus and response, Freud sees every value as human. Our highest ideals are but projections of our all too human selves. We are moved to fulfill ourselves—and, perhaps, to destroy ourselves—by what we inherently are, and by how we respond to and react against the world in which we are condemned to live and die. Our every aspiration is a movement out from "here" toward a "there" envisaged only as a progressive development out of "here." No God-given essence guides us; no Platonically subsisting ideal inspires us.

The paths we follow in our search are the ways of love. Their map is Freud's conception of love's genesis.

THE DEVELOPMENT OF THE THEORY OF LOVE

Love begins with life itself. To live at all is to love, and to live healthily implies, throughout life, at least some love for life.

The love of a man for a maid is a complex and wondrous thing. Its history, seen from Freud's vantage point, is so tortuous that its occasional success is astonishing. Ideally, and therefore rarely, an earlier affectionate, "anaclitic" love blends with the later "sensual"-sexual love and, for the first few years of marriage, may provide a full and healthy outlet to the human adult.

In lay language, Freudian love is identified with sexuality. This identification both is and is not justified in Freud's writings. The layman who supposes that Freudian psychoanalysis makes of genital sexuality a universal motivation is mistaken. But the layman who views psychoanalysis as having extended and deepened our understanding of sexuality, and as having placed our love relationships within a creative-sexual context, is essentially correct.

> We call [by the name "libido"] the energy, regarded as a quantitative magnitude (though not at present actually measurable), of those instincts which have to do with all that may be comprised under the word "love." The nucleus of what we mean by love naturally consists (and this is commonly called love, and what the poets sing of) in sexual love with sexual union as its aim. But we do not separate from this—what in any case has a share in the name "love"—on the one hand, self-love, and on the other, love for parents and children, friendship and love for humanity in general, and also devotion to concrete objects and to abstract ideas. Our justification lies in the fact that psycho-analytic research has taught us that all these tendencies are an expression of the same instinctual impulses; in relations between the sexes these impulses force their way towards sexual union, but in other circumstances they are diverted from this aim or are prevented from reaching it, though always preserving enough of their original nature to keep their identity recognizable (as in such features as the longing for proximity, and self-sacrifice).
>
> We are of opinion, then, that language has carried out an entirely justifiable piece of unification in creating the word "love" with its numerous uses, and that we cannot do better than take it as the basis of our scientific discussions and expositions as well.[10]

In the light of this explanation, the familiar charge of "pansexuality" loses much of its force. Again, Freud tells a friend:

> . . . our word "erotic" includes what in religion is called "love" and is not at all restricted to gross sensual pleasure.[11]

> We use the word "sexuality" in the same comprehensive sense as that in which the German language uses the word *lieben*.[12]

—and this is a sense not far distant from that of "desire," and is used fully as broadly as "love." If, then, "sexuality" is equally broad, the sting is removed from the familiar accusation that Freud "sexualizes" all human needs. To say of an infant that it needs milk and desires its mother's presence is notably less shocking than to speak of a baby as sexual; yet, if "need" and "want" are included within the meaning of "sexuality," the difference in meaning is hardly impressive.

The slight difference is meaningful, however, and Freud's recognition of infantile sexuality[13] is historically important. It is not easy, sixty or more years later, to imagine the Victorian horror with which our grandparents must have greeted the suggestion that babies are sexual creatures; sex, as every decent person thought he knew, begins with puberty in boys and with marriage (if even then) in girls. Even more difficult for us to achieve is sympathetic understanding of our grandparents' puzzlement. Surely parents long before Freud found their babies exploring their genital organs with evident joy. It must have required an extraordinary feat of self-deception to pretend that sexual (and even genital) response awaits the onset of adolescence.

Our grandparents would not have been so shocked if Freud's allegation that infants are sexual had been only verbal. However, it was not only verbal, and redefining the term "sexual" will not, therefore, relieve quite all the shock.

Freud meant quite clearly that infants have desires out of which will develop (among others) all their later, explicitly sexual desires, and that the psychical problems they will later face, whether obviously sexual or not, will be traceable back to childhood states and events. Between the tendencies of children and their subsequent adult needs lie acute redirections and refocusings, intensifications and relaxations, but not sharp breaks.

Freud was repeatedly urged by his friends not to choose the word "sexuality" in talking about infantile sexuality. He consistently refused, on the grounds that sexuality is nothing to be ashamed of, and that a scientist should be both candid and courageous.

> Psycho-analysis gives these love instincts the name of sexual instincts, *a priori* and by reason of their origin. The majority of "educated" people have regarded this nomenclature as an insult, and have taken their revenge by retorting upon psycho-analysis with the reproach of "pansexualism." Anyone who considers sex as something mortifying and humiliating to human nature is at liberty to make use of the more genteel expressions "Eros" and "erotic." I might have done so myself from the first and thus have spared myself much opposition. But I did not want to, for I like to avoid concessions to faintheartedness. One can never tell where that road may lead one; one gives way first in words, and then little by little in substance too. I cannot see any merit in being ashamed of sex. . . .[14]

Freud has been interpreted as practicing verbal legerdemain, by redefining "sexuality." Ernest Jones argues that this interpretation disserves the master. It is not that Freud uses the word "sexuality" in any new, broader sense, Jones suggests;[15] it is rather that he continues to mean by "sexuality" what we have always meant by it; but he finds facts that demonstrate the existence of sexuality in infants, and he reports the facts as he finds them. He "widened the popular conception of what things *are* sexual."

Even more clearly, if we consider only the early Freudian formulations, sexual instincts cannot be considered universal in their scope, for they are said to conflict with other instincts:

> [Opponents of psycho-analysis] accused it of "pansexualism," though the psycho-analytic theory of the instincts had always been strictly dualistic and had at no time failed to recognize, alongside the sexual instincts, others to which it actually ascribed force enough to suppress the sexual instincts. (These mutually opposing forces were described to begin with as the sexual instincts and the ego instincts. A later theoretical development changed them into Eros and the instinct of death or destruction.)[16]

Postponing consideration of Freud's final (and least widely accepted) formulations of love, we find the infant born with two groups of instincts: those that direct energy toward the preservation of his organism, and those that after arduous and inevitably anxious transformations will become genitally sexual. The former are first manifested in the infant's dependence upon his mother for nourishment. His expression of hunger in sucking is every human's first act of love. The baby's nonsexual needs are gratified by the milk that sustains his life.

But his sexual needs demand gratification as well. The baby needs to love. No independent love object is at hand. So it is as if his sexual needs "leaned against" his ego-preservative needs.[17]

These leaning-against needs Freud calls "anaclitic." They are the genetic root of love. Far from being gross and passionate-possessive, they are affectionate and quiet-intimate. The suckling babe does not (yet) seek to overpower his nursing mother; he rather welcomes and responds to the embracing comfort she offers.

The self, then, is the one and only ultimate source of Freudian love. Out from the self flows love toward objects, and back from objects flows this love once again. The name Freud gave to this "self" in all his early works, and—unhappily, for the sake of consistent clarity, in many of his later works as well—is "ego."

> The ego is a great reservoir from which the libido that is destined for objects flows out and into which it flows back from those objects.[18]

But when Freud comes later to make distinction of the self into "ego" and "id" and "super-ego," he usually attributes motivational ultimacy to the "id," calling it the reservoir.

At the very beginning, all the libido is accumulated in the id, while the ego is still in process of formation or is still feeble. The id sends part of this libido out into erotic object-cathexes, whereupon the ego, now grown stronger, tries to get hold of this object-libido and to force itself on the id as a love-object. The narcissism of the ego is thus a secondary one, which has been withdrawn from objects.[19]

But the theory was growing and changing as Freud worked through his patients' problems. The first important change from the early ego-versus-sexual instinct explanation came with the introduction of the important conception called "narcissism." Here the motivating force of the ego-preservative instincts themselves, until now sharply distinguished from sexual "libido," is explained dynamically in terms of a return into the ego of love-energy first directed outward toward an object: "This object I love is good; how good I must be to need it!" The name for this psychic stage of self-love is "narcissism"; its energy is the "ego-libido" of the "ego-instincts."

We see . . . an antithesis between ego-libido and object-libido. The more of the one is employed, the more the other becomes depleted. The highest phase of development of which object-libido is capable is seen in the state of being in love, when the subject seems to give up his own personality in favour of an object-cathexis; while we have the opposite condition in the paranoic's phantasy (or self-perception) of the "end of the world." . . . not until there is object-cathexis is it possible to discriminate a sexual energy—the libido—from an energy of the ego-instincts.[20]

In pain and illness, as in sleep, we withdraw our interests—and all libidinal energies—from objects back into ourselves.[21] Even in health and awake we direct much of our energy inward, toward our selves. We "regard" our selves and "respect" our selves in preserving our selves against the threats of the world. To a point, we must do this, or die.

But only to a point. Tension builds within us. We cannot remain healthy if we care too little for our selves, but if this care becomes too exclusive—if too much of our energy is reflected back into the ego—illness is inevitable.

The resolution is love. We must go outward again toward objects, cherishing them as precious to us.[22]

What we call adult love is, always and everywhere, a function of these basic tendencies: taking one's self as a love-object ("narcissism"), and attaching one's self ("anaclitically") to another person, typically a person who feeds and protects us, or a substitute for that person. We may love what we are, or what we once were, or what we would like to become, or (as in a mother's love for her child) what was once a part of ourselves; or we may love our mothers and fathers and their successors.[23] Loving our children is typically narcissistic, and characterized (as is all narcissism) by "overvaluation" of the beloved object: we blind ourselves to the faults and weaknesses of our children, just as we idealize our sweethearts.[24]

Self-love cannot, with healthy children, be dangerously exaggerated, because every child discovers to his dismay that even his parents, for all their welcome idealization, find him less than perfect, and so does society, and so, in consequence, does the child himself. He remains self-lovable, to be sure, but he can no longer utterly worship himself. So he grows into a realization of the difference between what he is and what he believes that he ought to be. An "ego-ideal" is generated within him, and this ego-ideal drains off some love-energy. Our "conscience" keeps track of us, continually comparing our actual performance in life and our own ideal of performance.[25]

"Being in love," as an adult, involves forfeiting some of our narcissistic self-regard, and consequently lowering ourselves in our own estimation . . . in the natural hope (or neurotic fear) of becoming an object of the love of another person, and consequently restoring our self-regard. In genuinely happy adult love, as in the primal state, object-libido and ego-libido cannot be distinguished.[26]

> Being in love consists in a flowing-over of ego-libido on to the object. It has the power to remove repressions and re-instate perversions. It exalts the sexual object into a sexual ideal. Since, with the object type (or attachment type), being in love occurs in virtue of the fulfilment of infantile conditions for loving, we may say that whatever fulfils that condition is idealized.[27]

The oft-remarked Freudian dualism is abundantly evident here and elsewhere in the texts; its recurrence attests more Freud's own psychical inclinations than any underlying metaphysical discoveries.[28]

> Running through all [Freud's] work there is what Heinz Hartmann has called "a very characteristic kind of dialectical thinking that tends to base theories on the interaction of two opposite powers." This was of course most pronounced in his basic classifications: love-hunger; ego-sexuality; auto-erotism–hetero-erotism; Eros-Thanatos; life-death, and so on. I remember how alien this seemed to me, having been brought up in a biological school that thought of instincts in the plural. But the same fondness for pairs is found again and again: love-hate, exhibitionism-scopophilism, etc. It is as if Freud had a difficulty in contemplating any topic unless he could divide it into two opposites, and never more than two. That there was a conflict between two opposing forces in the mind was for him a basic fact . . . Someone once said facetiously that he had never learned to count beyond the number two.

All of this development is well summarized as Freud speaks of:

> . . . two currents whose union is necessary to ensure a completely nor-
> mal attitude in love. . . . The affectionate current is the older of the two.
> It springs from the earliest years of childhood; it is formed on the basis
> of the interests of the self-preservative instinct and is directed to the mem-
> bers of the family and those who look after the child. From the very
> beginning it carries along with it contributions from the sexual in-
> stincts—components of erotic interest—which can already be seen more
> or less clearly even in childhood . . . It corresponds to *the child's pri-*
> *mary object-choice.* We learn in this way that the sexual instincts find
> their first objects by attaching themselves to the valuations made by the
> ego-instincts, precisely in the way in which the first sexual satisfactions
> are experienced in attachment to the bodily functions necessary for the
> preservation of life. The "affection" shown by the child's parents and
> those who look after him, which seldom fails to betray its erotic nature
> ("the child is an erotic plaything"), does a very great deal to raise the
> contributions made by erotism to the cathexes of his ego-instincts . . .
> These affectionate fixations of the child persist throughout childhood,
> and continually carry along with them erotism, which is consequently di-
> verted from its sexual aims. Then at the age of puberty they are joined
> by the powerful "sensual" current which no longer mistakes its aims.[29]

We need not detail the successive erotic stages (anal, oral, homosexual,
genital). They are, in Freud's conception, simply growth plateaus, levels
in healthy development toward adult sexual love. The growth is neither
inevitable nor irreversible; there are, in the jargon, both "fixations" and
"repressions."

But when adulthood is achieved, even though insecurely, men and
women may be maturely "in love." Freud compares "being in love" with
hypnotism:[30]

> In one class of cases being in love is nothing more than object-cathexis
> on the part of the sexual instincts with a view to directly sexual satisfac-
> tion, a cathexis which expires, moreover, when this aim has been reached;
> this is what is called common, sensual love. But, as we know, the libidinal
> situation rarely remains so simple. It was possible to calculate with cer-
> tainty upon the revival of the need which had just expired; and this must
> no doubt have been the first motive for directing a lasting cathexis upon
> the sexual object and for "loving" it in the passionless intervals as well.
>   To this must be added another factor derived from the very remark-
> able course of development which is pursued by the erotic life of man. In
> its first phase, which has usually come to an end by the time a child is five
> years old, he has found the first object for his love in one or other of his
> parents, and all of his sexual instincts with their demand for satisfaction
> have been united upon this object. The repression which then sets in

compels him to renounce the greater number of these infantile sexual aims, and leaves behind a profound modification in his relation to his parents. The child still remains tied to his parents, but by instincts which must be described as being "inhibited in their aim." The emotions which he feels henceforward towards these objects of his love are characterized as "affectionate." It is well known that the earlier "sensual" tendencies remain more or less strongly preserved in the unconscious, so that in a certain sense the whole of the original current continues to exist.

[Usually] . . . the adolescent succeeds in bringing about a certain degree of synthesis between the unsensual, heavenly love and the sensual, earthly love, and his relation to his sexual object is characterized by the inter-action of uninhibited instincts and of instincts inhibited in their aim. The depth to which anyone is in love, as contrasted with his purely sensual desire, may be measured by the size of the share taken by the aim-inhibited instincts of affection.

Through this period of Freud's development, he was perplexed to maintain his precious dualism. For if the self-preservational instincts were narcissistically "ego-libidinal," they were nonetheless libidinal, and there-fore of a kind with sexual-libidinal instincts.

The eventual recovery came only with Freud's final theoretical move in his construction of love's life history. This move was the boldest of all, for it replaced the earliest dualism and the intermediate narcissism with the final emerging quasi-cosmic dichotomy between love-life and hate-death.

Typically, Freud thought his way toward this climactic conception through a series of intermediate dualisms or polarities.[31]

Love cannot be understood alone, since it so typically reflects its am-bivalent opposite, hate. Some of Freud's subtlest and most obscure analy-sis is found in his genetic derivations of these attitudes.

The basic antithesis, first found and longest controlling, is between the ego and the non-ego, the subject and the object. This distinction is thrust upon us at the outset, as soon as the child finds that external stimuli can (sometimes) be silenced by means of muscular action, but that these means are unavailing against internal, instinctual stimuli.[32]

Both pleasure and pain (or "unpleasure") can result from the gratifi-cation or frustration of these early demands, and pleasure-unpleasure thus form the second fundamental ("economic") polarity. When the sub-ject instinctively acts upon the external world (or even, narcissistically, upon his own inner self) he is only responding to the world; and here we have the ("biological") third of our polarities: active-passive.

Correspondingly, but not at all in parallel, three polarities arise when we try to construe the "opposites" of love.

The first is simply hate, the desire to destroy or consume that which we believe to threaten our being, or to cause us pain. The second is the movement already indicated, from narcissistic loving-oneself actively out toward loving another and being loved in return. The third polarity places love and hate together, as opposed to indifference.[33]

Now, when purely narcissistic libido gives way to object-libido, pleasure and unpleasure become realities to the self. Pleasure-sources attract us, and we love them. Unpleasure-sources repel us, and we hate them. But it is not our instincts that love and hate; we do.

> . . . the attitudes of love and hate cannot be made use of for the relations of *instincts* to their objects, but are reserved for the relations of the *total ego* to objects. But if we consider linguistic usage, which is certainly not without significance, we shall see that there is a further limitation to the meaning of love and hate. We do not say of objects which serve the interests or self-preservation that we *love* them; we emphasize the fact that we *need* them. . . .
>
> Thus the word "to love" moves further and further into the sphere of the pure pleasure-relation of the ego to the object and finally becomes fixed to sexual objects in the narrower sense and to those which satisfy the needs of sublimated sexual instincts.[34]

Reviewing the stages in love's development, Freud achieves his final explanations of the "ambivalent" relation between love and hate:

> Love is derived from the capacity of the ego to satisfy some of its instinctual impulses auto-erotically by obtaining organ-pleasure. It is originally narcissistic, then passes over on to objects, which have been incorporated into the extended ego, and expresses the motor efforts of the ego towards these objects as sources of pleasure. It becomes intimately linked with the activity of the later sexual instincts and, when these have been completely synthesized, coincides with the sexual impulsion as a whole. Preliminary stages of love emerge as provisional sexual aims while the sexual instincts are passing through their complicated development. As the first of these aims we recognize the phase of incorporating or devouring—a type of love which is consistent with abolishing the object's separate existence and which may therefore be described as ambivalent. At the higher stage of the pregenital sadistic-anal organization, the striving for the object appears in the form of an urge for mastery, to which injury or annihilation of the object is a matter of indifference. Love in this form and at this preliminary stage is hardly to be distinguished from hate in its attitude toward the object. Not until the genital organization is established does love become the opposite of hate.
>
> Hate, as a relation to objects, is older than love. It derives from the narcissistic ego's primordial repudiation of the external world with its outpouring of stimuli. As an expression of the reaction of unpleasure evoked by objects, it always remains in an intimate relation with the self-preservative instincts; so that sexual and ego-instincts can readily develop an antithesis which repeats that of love and hate. When the ego-instincts dominate the sexual function, as is the case at the stage of the sadistic-

anal organization, they impart the qualities of hate to the instinctual aim as well.

The history of the origins and relations of love makes us understand how it is that love so frequently manifests itself as "ambivalent"—i.e. as accompanied by impulses of hate against the same object.[35]

Freud was thus fascinated by the polarity between love and hate. Again and again he wove and raveled strands of thought, now seeming to derive the two from the same source, now treating them as genetically-instinctually contradictory.[36]

In the most fully developed position, Freud's basic dualism of instincts remains firm, though each of the two fundamental instincts—Eros and Thanatos—gives rise to numerous derivative "instincts." We inherently tend, so Freud thought, to die. We seek to reduce tensions, to relax, to descend, and lower the level of life itself. Fechner's so-called principle of constancy, or homeostasis, seemed undeniable, and life must be explained as a preparation for death. Seeking to die, we seek also to destroy.

Yet, curiously, the energy with which we destroy must itself come from our other basic tendency: to encourage, to live, and to love. Eros is the uniting and binding, the building up and blending, the increase-of-tension within us.

> . . . the death instincts are by their nature mute and . . . the clamour of life proceeds for the most part from Eros. And from the struggle against Eros![37]
>
> . . . the claims of Eros, of the sexual instincts, . . . in the form of instinctual needs, hold up the falling level and introduce fresh tensions. The id—guided by the pleasure principle—that is, by the perception of unpleasure—fends off these tensions in various ways. It does so in the first place by complying as swiftly as possible with the demands of the non-desexualized libido—by striving for the satisfaction of the directly sexual trends. But it does so in a far more comprehensive fashion in relation to one particular form of satisfaction in which all component demands converge—[38]

As Ernest Jones phrases it,[39]

> The ego hates all objects (in the outer world) that signify privation, whether of sexual or of ego satisfaction. So love and hate do not stand in a simple relation to one another; it is only through a rather complicated development that they come later to represent opposites. Hate emanates essentially from the ego group of instincts, but through the similarity in expression of hate and the sadistic component of the anal-sadistic phase of libidinal development hate may enter into a close association with love, leading to the familiar ambivalence in human relations.

It was, then, the very complexity of love that brought Freud deviously to his concept of hate, and it was hate that brought him to the concept of death. As these concepts grew in his mind, love-libido became Eros. Mature human love is described as a "synthesis of instincts" [40] and when transcendentalized into a binding or unifying movement is compared with the binding together of the cells of a metazoon.[41]

By necessary contrast, "instinctive" hate becomes, in the end, a primally polar death-destructive force inherent in every one of us.[42] This force is directed only in part toward the outer world; centrally and typically, it is directed back toward the self in a suicidal "death-wish."

Clearly, Freud's mind is now moving cosmically. As we shall soon see, it is love that makes society possible. And it is love's counterpart, hate-death, that ultimately makes civilization impossible. But neither alone can explain what needs explanation. As Freud put it in a letter to his theological friend, Oskar Pfister:[43]

> I have, as you agree, done much to show the importance of love. My experience, however, does not confirm your view that it is at the basis of everything unless you add hate to it; which is psychologically correct. But then that at once gives a gloomy look to the world.

LOVE AND MORALITY

As in Plato and the Bible, so also in Freud: love is inseparable from morality. From each point of view, to love well is to live well.

Here the parallel stops short. For in the Platonic and Biblical worlds, the values of loving lie beyond the act. In them, we love well as our love is well derived and well directed. But Freud's natural world knows no extra-mundane principle of derivation or direction. Its every value is encompassed within the nature of loving itself.

Scientists purport to describe, rather than to prescribe, and Freud was forever purporting to be scientific. He suffered every time his conscience impelled him to draw a moral consequence from any finding—and he could hardly write a dozen pages without doing so. Except from an astringently ascetic view of the nature of science, Freud is here less to be discredited as unscientific than to be credited as human.

Never confessed, there stands behind the entire Freudian ethic a silent Aristotelianism of "nature." Broadly speaking, Freud considered good that loving act, that man, and that society that is "natural," and Freud's honest, straightforward ethic contains most of the clear virtues and all of the muddled vices we have inherited from Aristotle. I do not of course suggest that Freud assigns to reason any role very like that which Aristotle assigns to it; nor do I forget the deep-rooted metaphysical differences between the two ways of thought. But, Aristotle, after all, more than anyone else framed our ways of understanding our proper roles in life in terms of our nature as men; Aristotle sought seriously to describe men as they fundamentally are, and to derive their obligations from their natures; Aristotle insistently and matter-of-factly studied the ugly, aberrant aspects of human behavior, as well as man's loftier aspirations. In all these respects, Freud is here within an ancient and honored tradition. That Freud developed a radically different conception of the nature of reason, which results in important changes in the ethical view, cannot be gainsaid. But he developed his new conception within a framework still essentially Aristotelian.

We are animals. We can no more deny our animal origins than can the horse of Schulda survive when fed less and less grain each day. No transcendent "good" could warrant any antiorganic morality. Every plausible criterion of moral judgment uncritically presupposes that individual and social survival are better than extinction.

We are human animals. Moral considerations arise only among animals that—like ourselves—plan, make decisions, accept responsibility; rattlesnakes cannot sin in striking mice or men, because we suppose them never to decide or knowingly to accept the consequences of their acts.

Our human morality is both personal and social, because we are at once individual and social. Freud, like his philosophical ancestor Aristotle, takes account of both.

Personal Morality

Because every person is socially conditioned, beginning at his mother's breast, there is no ultimate difference between individual and social morality, any more than any such difference obtains between individual and social psychology in general. But we can conveniently look at individual-social morality from each point of view.

Freud entertained few or no illusions about his fellow man, and—despite his deep personal concern for human welfare—was skeptical about ethical doctrines in general.

> I don't cudgel my brains much about good and evil, but I have not found much "good" in the average human being. Most of them are in my experience riff-raff, whether they loudly proclaim this or that ethical doctrine or none at all.[44]

Freud's approach is, of course, not traditionally philosophical, but typically psycho-genetic. He asks not "What do we mean by 'good' or 'right'?" but rather "How do we learn the uses of these terms? How do we grow into morally judging adults?"

His world begins with the baby, and infancy knows no law. "Approvals" and "disapprovals" are identical with immediate gratifications or their denials. Warmth, food, and cooing sounds are good; wet diapers, hunger pangs and colic cramps are evil.

As soon as objects become distinguished from each other and from the self, love begins to flow out from the self toward them. Looking back toward infancy, Freud dimly discerns the emergent differentiation of a nether unconscious-preconscious "id" from an active conscious "ego," and a recognition on the baby's part of others like and unlike him.

And as soon as the self begins to be a self at all, and to move out with love, that very self changes. It is as if the darkly glowing ego, only gradually developing awareness of itself as it reaches outward, already feels the loss of love from its own great "reservoir," the id. Starkly, it changes into the image of the newly posited love-object, as if to attract back to itself the newly lost love. "Look," it seems to say to its own id, "you can love me too—I am so like the object." [45]

Thereafter, a key unlikeness is the surprising discovery of genital distinctions. A boy, who has taken his mother as his first and deepest love-object (and Oedipally rejected his rival-father) may try to deny the threatening absence of a penis in girls, but must at last come to terms with it. He does so by concluding that girls' evident deficiencies must be a punishment—and that if he is naughty, he too may lose his precious penis. This "castration complex" has the economic function (in the ideal case, but never fully achieved) of demolishing the crucial "Oedipal" stage, and making possible subsequent advances toward adult, predominantly genital sexuality.

The girl grows along a different route. At first doubting or denying, then subsequently confessing, the boy's possession of a penis, she is shocked by her own deficiency. "Penis envy" is the correlate of the castration complex, but far from bringing her beyond the Oedipal level, she is only now ready to enter upon it, and to impute all desirability to her father. Most naturally, she wants his baby and all his love.[46]

Whatever the object of love, from mother's breast to parent to same-sex friend to sweetheart—and including even the self from whom all love-blessings flow—that toward which we dedicate love naturally appears lovable. In male adulthood, this disproportionate esteem will be called "sexual over-estimation."

Meanwhile, however, my love objects "come into" me, even as I "go out" toward them. I am learning; my attitudes of approval and disapproval are taking shape. Even a very young child is learning, through the conflicts of frustration and the delights of gratification, that some aspects of his inner self and some aspects of the world around him are to be admired, and others are not. Most puzzling of all, he is learning that his desires are not exactly congruent with his approvals. He is discovering, to his shocked horror, that he desires and really needs some things of which he does not approve.

Maturation, in important part, is precisely this process of moral growth in love. At first, those whom the child loves exhibit their approvals and disapprovals to him. When they approve what the child loves and disapprove what the child hates, all is well and good. But when—as must happen—the child's world of values is suddenly skewed by parental disapproval of delightful behavior, his dilemma is painful. He has two recourses, and typically adopts both.

He may withhold some love from the frustrating parent, trying as it were to force the world to come to terms with his self-centered needs. Or he may gradually find his self changing in response to the demands the world makes upon him. He comes to approve what his parents approve, to loathe (even in himself) what they have shown that they loathe.

Thus grows the "moral sense," by building into the self prohibitions and permissions painfully absorbed from the world, by learning to judge even one's most intimate inclinations, and by developing an internal ideal of the kind of person one could be proud of being.

This building, learning, developing, is at the heart of civilization and socialization. The infant is not antisocial, or uncivil; he is nonsocial, precivil. His loving energy knows neither boundary nor focus. Growing up is growing out into a world that channels and directs energetic overflow into socially permissible behavior. Becoming a mature part of that world is learning to find genuine fulfillment and self-respect in ways, at first foreign, which other human beings, as well as one's self, can approve. Becoming civilized is like becoming naturalized as a citizen of another land: it involves absorbing many foreign ways into the personality, identifying what must be and what ought to be with what the person wills to be.

But a person who surrenders all his needs to the incessant demands of his society is hardly a person at all, and surely not mature. The problem is rather to continue to exist, as differentiable, self-seeking, and other-seeking persons, while at the same time finding instinctual fulfillments in ways that do not too painfully frustrate the other people with whom we must live and work and upon whom we depend. What we imprecisely call "putting ourselves in another's place" involves both feeling-with another person and feeling-into him, both sym-pathy and em-pathy. It does not involve becoming sponges or blotters; it does require a really autonomous responsiveness by no means easy to achieve.

For certain limited social-scientific purposes, it is convenient to conceive men as players or takers of "roles." Every man must, of course, simultaneously fulfill many roles. Freud will not let us forget that this convenience ought never to obscure the fact that it is, after all, the same person who plays them all, and that his way of carrying out the roles assigned to him and undertaken by him—what we might call his "style" —is a function of all the loving he has ever done.

Each role has its special norms or criteria which also must be "internalized." Specific moral judgments will be visited upon individuals, individually or institutionally, in accordance with the norms learned by the judges.

Freud has repeatedly been accused of moralizing in all this complex characterization of learning-growth. It is worth sorting out some of these charges.

First and most radically, Freud has been charged with undermining all morality by proposing a genetic-economic-motivational account of ethical judgment. Careless readers, including a number of psychoanalysts, confuse genesis with validation.[47] The answer is simple, and Freud himself almost consistently understood it. To account for a child's learning of arithmetic is not to reduce arithmetic to psychology. As we noted in our account of Plato's thought, the square of four is sixteen, no matter how it is learned, or how many children make computational errors. Mathematics is no less valuable a discipline if some mathematicians enter it as a psychic escape from neurosis. Michelangelo's Moses and Leonardo's Madonnas are no less beautiful for the personal problems of their creators. And so with moral judgments: the fact that we socially learn standards of behavior does not in itself say anything about their validity. To accuse Freud of "nothing-but" reduction of morality to psychogenesis is to charge him with a logical blunder he did not commit.

Freud did not, to be sure, assign to moral values any supernatural status, origin, or sanction; but, for all his genetic account of moral learning, he could consistently have done so. Those who view every nontheistic moral interpretation as satanically "subjective" think whimsy is the only alternative to God, and unbridled license the inevitable consequence of natural psychology. Freud was by no means so silly. Whatever the extremes to which enthusiastic amateurs of psychoanalysis may have gone, Freud's own position is clear. The charge of moral "subjectivism," cannot be substantiated. Freud fully understood our moral judgments to be functions not of private vagaries, but of biological and social dynamics.

The distinction we need lies between the therapeutic dynamics of the psychoanalytic situation and the practical dynamics of social situations. Under careful technical controls the psychoanalytic patient is permitted expressions he could not permit himself, in the interests of his own self-enlightenment, toward the goal of a reintegration of his threatened personality structure. The analyst, as analyst, ideally never passes moral judgment; he tries only to understand, to help the patient to heal himself. The risk-free, no-commitment character of this very special world is radically different from the world beyond the door, where patient and analyst alike must take social risks and commit themselves. In therapy, the patient really can do no wrong. He may, and invariably does, do stupid, self-defeating, childish things; but during actual therapy he cannot behave immorally, any more than can an anesthetized patient on an operating table. The analyst, during therapy, may make professional-technical blunders; but if he as an individual human being ever enters into a same-level real-life moral praise and blame relationship with his patient, the therapy is at an end.

Within the situation, there is one pre-eminent value, and it is presumably identical in principle (though much less easy to define and to recognize) with that shared by a medical team in an operating room. The overriding aim is to restore this patient to health, and to this end all other values must presently be subordinated. In principle, physicians work as hard to preserve the life of a man condemned to die on the gallows as they do to save the life of a president or pope. Their moral judgments are professionally irrelevant. So with an analyst. But the analyst is of course not required to approve his patient's ways of life, any more than an internist approves a malignant growth.

It is occasionally supposed that this value of health becomes a moral ideal—or even the moral ideal—implicit in psychoanalysis. There is some plausibility in this supposition, if only because therapists must assume that, ceteris paribus, health is better than disease. But Freud realized perfectly clearly that the ceteris is never paribus, and he nowhere proposed to root out every psychic disbalance in the world; indeed, he recognized the impossibility of doing so.

The succinct solution is that while health is always a value, it is never the only human value, and only rarely a moral one. Freud did not sentimentally identify crime with ill health. Obsessed saints are more neurotic than are mild sinners, but are no less saintly for their neuroses. Some degree of health is a condition for effective moral behavior; but the successful analysis that restores health no more guarantees morality than it does happiness.[48] The physician of the body learns that health is never an unconditional value, and that some diseases are better left alone than cured, for the cure might kill. Freud sanely points out the psychological counterpart:[49]

> . . . our attitude to life ought not to be that of a fanatic for hygiene or therapy. We must admit that the ideal prevention of neurotic illnesses which we have in mind would not be of advantage to every individual. A good number of those who now take flight into illness would not, under the conditions we have assumed, support the conflict but would rapidly succumb or would cause a mischief greater than their own neurotic ill-

ness. Neuroses have their social justification: the "gain from illness" they provide is not always a purely subjective one.

"Maturity" is another pseudo-norm spawned by popular psychoanalysis. Everyone wants furiously to be "mature," and the more juvenile our entertainments become, the more bad faith we suffer for enjoying them. The baby's mind in the baby's body is a beautiful and charming thing, as someone has said; but it is terrifying to find a physically adult and powerful person responding with the mind of an infant.

"Maturity" is even less clearly defined than "health" in popular usage. Empirically, the only token of maturity is behavior and (as with "health") so many variant behavior patterns can, each in its own context, appear mature that no single, clearly definitive standard can be set. Nor need one be, except in the most general terms. Ideally, we must admit different standards of maturity for different people; behavior fully mature for one person could easily be childish for another.

In Freudian terms, a man is sexually mature if he has absorbed and transcended his Oedipal and narcissistic levels, has come to terms with his natural oral and anal tendencies, and genitally focused his needs. But plainly many people who have done this behave like babies in certain other areas of life, and some who are otherwise broadly and abundantly mature remain in some sexual respects childlike. And—to go beyond Freud—men and women who have altogether lost the magic of childhood are barely human husks.

A mature person is not simply someone who has made his peace. Such a man is resigned. If not quite yet a husk, he is at best a seed pod. Maturity does not exclude vigor. Mature intelligence goes to work instead of to seed. It need not mean resignation from the battle of life, or resignation to one's lot in it. The mature man distinguishes those battles worth fighting from those that are not; in these, he concludes an uneasy armistice with the world.

But maturity must never become a moral ideal, since one strives toward an ideal. One cannot simply strive to grow up, unless (again, as with health) one defines all morality as maturity.

There is, says Rieff,[50]

> . . . a fatal lack of commitment about Freud's ideal type. To be busy, spirited, and self-confident is a goal that will inspire only those who have resigned the ghosts of older and nobler inspirations. Freud never understood the ethic of self-sacrifice. The omission leaves his humane doctrine a little cold, and capable of the most sinister applications.

Later in his excellent book, Rieff understands, and argues correctly, that one cannot strictly speak of any "ideal type" in Freud at all. Freud does not construct any such type, because his moral concern is rather for the psychological conditions underlying any behavior that could be called moral, than for the delineation of any single model of morality.

The central condition Rieff defines as *honesty*, especially with one's self.[51] There is nothing immoral in illness, mental or physical. And Freud's counsel of honesty is advice to the lovelorn, not Sunday school preachment. We are all, he wisely understands, lovelorn. Most of us demand too much of ourselves and too little of others. We fragment ourselves, or passively suffer our fragmentation by others. We are sick from our ideals. The man who is desperately anxious and obsessively miserable is typically the man who aspires unrealistically. He remains a child, not yet having outgrown the infantile dream of happiness. Freud was, in important respects, a Stoic of the grand tradition. He taught (as Rieff puts it) that we must learn to replace misery with common unhappiness.

> According to the Freudian counsel, man must not strain too far the limitations of his instinctual nature. Therefore, knowing, becoming conscious of these limits, is itself a primary ethical act. Consciousness, self-knowledge, interpretative revelation and decision, candor, talking things through—all presume a necessary reduction of ethical aspiration. Without this imperative, Freud's conception of therapy is meaningless. "A little more truthfulness," Freud recommends, instead of the painful old passion for goodness. Psychoanalysis shares the paths of truthfulness common to rationalist doctrines. People ought to be forthright. If they express their true natures, goodness will take care of itself. The ethic of honesty does no more than establish the capacity to break the moral habits into which decisions, once made, tend to form themselves. Freud's is a penultimate ethic tooled to the criticism of ultimates. It regards the disposition of human potentiality as a matter beyond prescription.[52]

One final paradox, and we have done: Freud is sometimes taken today as the apotheosis of nineteenth century irrationalism, and there is some justice in the claim. Ever since David Hume's corrosive analysis of human behavior, reason as a moral governor had been under attack. Hume's "Reason is, and properly ought to be, the slave of the passions," became the Romantics' rallying cry. Freud, in exhibiting the extrarational roots of human behavior, turned rationalism into rationalization. To reason is to rationalize: to think is not to justify, but to give excuses. So Freud has too often been interpreted as an apologist and apostle for a life beyond reason, a life of obedience to emotive-affective instinct.

We should now be able to see that this picture of Freud is a caricature. Insofar as Freud is a consistent thinker, it could not be otherwise. There is nothing in the least irrational about claiming that reason is a limited faculty or set of skills, or that our basic instinctive needs must find some kinds of gratification, else we become desperately ill. The use of reason need not imply its worship. Indeed, if reason is not to govern our lives morally, it is unreasonable to pretend that it should.

We can without doing any violence proclaim that Freud, far from minimizing the uses of reason, or underestimating its importance, is urging it upon us. He says that the power of the intellect makes itself felt not immediately, but all the more certainly in the end. Freud is asking that we act reasonably, humbly, realistically, modestly—foregoing Platonic perfections and resisting seductive infantile utopias, making our way patiently through life toward death: living, working and loving.

In a Freudian framework, love can tell, and love alone, which man is mature. That man who can wholeheartedly love a woman of about his own age, without disesteeming either her or himself, who can give and take in love openly and honestly, with neither fetishistic pride nor anxious guilt, is relatively mature. Such a man is likely to be able to live and work. What more can a modest man ask?

Love, Society and Civilization

Love has one more mission to fulfill. It must explain how and why men come together to form social groups. And, with its hateful-instinctive partner, it must betray the fateful, inherent weakness of every attempt at civilization.

We naturally think of Freud as an "individual" rather than as a "social" psychologist. Therapeutically, we are of course correct; Freud was not given (as have been some of his successors) to speculations about "neurotic" or "hysterical" societies. Men and women are psychoanalyzed, one at a time, each in terms of his own unique background, each working through his own love-conflicts, each coming to know himself and his world.

But these men and women are all social products. Their biological inheritances have been shaped into human personalities through interaction with one another. Freud could claim that, theoretically, his is a social psychology through and through. From Oedipus to Thanatos, every subjective conflict and every personal predicament is intersubjectively, interpersonally conditioned.

Freud recognized, as everyone must and as many of his contemporaries were showing, that men in groups behave differently from the ways in which the same men behave when alone. Freud considered and rejected explanations proposed to account for these differences. He dug more deeply, asking not "Why do the behaviors differ?" but rather "Why do men join together in social and political groups?"

The key lies in the most profound human-instinctual paradox of all:

our deepest erotic needs, impossible of private fulfillment, must be aborted or redirected once they come into the light of the very other people we most deeply need. And if—*per impossibile* in any civilization—our erotic needs were to find full satisfaction, we should suffer disappointment and frustration on that very account.

> . . . the psychical value of erotic needs is reduced as soon as their satisfaction becomes easy. An obstacle is required in order to heighten libido; and where natural resistances to satisfaction have not been sufficient men have at all times erected conventional ones so as to be able to enjoy love. This is true of both individuals and of nations. In times in which there were no difficulties standing in the way of sexual satisfaction, such as perhaps during the decline of the ancient civilizations, love became worthless and life empty, and strong reaction-formations were required to restore indispensable affective values . . . the ascetic current in Christianity created psychical values for love which pagan antiquity was never able to confer on it.[53]

If by freedom we mean lack of frustration, only a rare infant, and no child, let alone any adult, is free, for the very reason that the process of socialization inevitably harnesses and channels energies within expressive patterns approved by some group. The infant learns that he is not the world, and that he must give up as well as take in.

The developing ego draws itself away from its socially environing world, and builds a protective-defensive barrier about itself, preserving this barrier imperfectly and desperately.

> There is only one state—admittedly an unusual state, but not one that can be stigmatized as pathological—in which it does not do this. At the height of being in love the boundary between ego and object threatens to melt away. Against all the evidence of his senses, a man who is in love declares that "I" and "you" are one, and is prepared to behave as if it were a fact.[54]

Not all of what must be learned is love-direction. The child must also learn to work, else his very social fabric will ravel, and he will starve.

> The communal life of human beings had, therefore, a twofold foundation: the compulsion to work, which was created by external necessity, and the power of love, which made the man unwilling to be deprived of his sexual object—the woman—and made the woman unwilling to be deprived of the part of herself that had been separated off from her—her child. Eros and Ananke [love and necessity] have become the parents of human civilization too.[55]

In all the subsequent development of civilization, love remains important.

The love which founded the family continues to operate in civilization both in its original form, in which it does not renounce direct sexual satisfaction, and in its modified form as aim-inhibited affection. In each, it continues to carry on its function of binding together considerable numbers of people, and it does so in a more intensive fashion than can be effected through the interest of work in common. The careless way in which language uses the word "love" has its genetic justification. People give the name "love" to the relation between a man and a woman whose genital needs have led them to found a family; but they also give the name "love" to the positive feelings between parents and children, and between the brothers and sisters of a family, although *we* are obliged to describe this as "aim-inhibited love" or "affection." Love with an inhibited aim was in fact originally fully sensual love, and it is so still in man's unconscious. Both—fully sensual love and aim-inhibited love—extend outside the family and create new bonds with people who before were strangers. Genital love leads to the formation of new families, and aim-inhibited love to "friendships" which become valuable from a cultural standpoint because they escape some of the limitations of genital love, as, for instance, its exclusiveness. But in the course of development the relation of love to civilization loses its unambiguity. On the one hand love comes into opposition to the interests of civilization; on the other, civilization threatens love with substantial restrictions.

This rift between them seems unavoidable. The reason for it is not immediately recognizable. It expresses itself at first as a conflict between the family and the larger community to which the individual belongs. We have already perceived that one of the main endeavours of civilization is to bring people together into large unities. But the family will not give the individual up. The more closely the members of a family are attached to one another, the more often do they tend to cut themselves off from others, and the more difficult is it for them to enter into the wider circle of life. The mode of life in common which is phylogenetically the older, and which is the only one that exists in childhood, will not let itself be superseded by the cultural mode of life which has been acquired later. Detaching himself from his family becomes a task that faces every young person, and society often helps him in the solution of it by means of puberty and initiation rites. We get the impression that these are difficulties which are inherent in all psychical—and, indeed, at bottom, in all organic—development.[56]

His family, however psychoanalytically sophisticated, warps every baby in dethroning him. The growth of the baby's mind is guided as is the growth of a garden. The wildest weeds must resolutely be pulled so that the precious flowers can be protected and encouraged. In some over-formal gardens, boxwoods may be pruned into wholly artificial shapes, and trees dwarfed or stimulated, for the amusement of the gardeners. In other, less formal ones, some rich and random growths may be encouraged—up to a point. But no garden can be permitted to become a jungle-thicket.

In raising our children, we are cultivating our gardens. Or overcultivating them, forcing them to reflect our own images, as we in turn dimly reflect those of our own parents. Or undercultivating them, as we lament the rankness of the delinquent weeds.

Our analogy fails at last, because these children we once were are jungle beasts, not jungle plants. But they are beasts of burden, as well as of prey. We want to submit ourselves, no less than to demand the submission of others to us. We want to absorb, consume, and master our worlds; but we want also to be absorbed, consumed, and mastered by it. And both of these wants are, in Freud's sense, erotic. Both are Eros in action.

> From Freud's individual psychology, his image of love takes on a darker coloring than can be conveyed by comfortable terms like "sociability" or "affection" or, for that matter, "love." Eros is greedy and sadistic or abjectly submissive. It is this second, masochistic possibility that Freud ascribes to the feelings of the crowd. The love through which we become sociable signifies a willful self-defeat: the "I" submerges itself in the group.[57]

Freud's picture of the genesis of the social group has been compared with that of Hobbes, and some Freudian texts permit this interpretation.[58] But Hobbes's men in a state of nature are vastly more rational and intellectual than are Freud's. They seem self-consciously to calculate their prospective advantage from contracting a commonwealth, deliberately to balance it against the "inconveniences" of the natural war of all against all, and judiciously to opt for the former.

Not so with infants, who are the Freudian primitives. Though his state of nature (had he ever explicitly described one) would not have differed notably from Hobbes's, Freud's conception of the formation of the state is profoundly different. *De facto,* children grow into societies; they do not choose to form them. *De jure* (or rather *de amore*) men enter societies masochistically.

Every man is a breathing paradox. He erotically wants and needs to dominate—and thus remains forever a rebel, resenting the strait jacket he inherits. But he also erotically wants and needs to be dominated— and thus willingly bows to the yoke, finding himself in losing himself. Thus in religion, and thus also in civilization. The price of paradox is pain. To gain some satisfactions, we learn to forego our demands for all. We learn to find erotic satisfaction in acts of love that our fellow masters and servants can tolerate. We become surgeons, or compose sonnets or sonatas. Or we write books about love.

Freud summarizes the relevant dynamics of this change in terms of love:

> . . . the pre-existence of strong "bad" impulses in infancy is often the actual condition for an unmistakable inclination towards "good" in the adult. Those who as children have been the most pronounced egoists may well become the most helpful and self-sacrificing members of the community; most of our sentimentalists, friends of humanity and protectors of animals have been evolved from little sadists and animal-tormentors.
>
> The transformation of "bad" instincts is brought about by two factors working in the same direction, an internal and an external one. The internal factor consists in the influence exercised on the bad (let us say, the egoistic) instincts by erotism—that is, by the human need for love, taken in its widest sense. By the admixture of *erotic* components the egoistic instincts are transformed into *social* ones. We learn to value being loved as an advantage for which we are willing to sacrifice other advantages. The external factor is the force exercised by upbringing, which represents the claims of our cultural environment, and this is continued later by the direct pressure of that environment. Civilization has been attained through the renunciation of instinctual satisfaction, and it demands the same renunciation from each newcomer in turn. Throughout an individual's life there is a constant replacement of external by internal compulsion. The influences of civilization cause an ever-increasing transformation of egoistic trends into altruistic and social ones by an admixture of erotic elements.[59]

Freud nowhere nihilistically exalts individuals over societies, as Nietzsche did. He nowhere condemns civilizations *in toto;* he recognized Rousseau's savage for the silly romantic myth he is. Inhibition, repression, sublimation, frustration, and pain are inevitable in civilization. So, alas, is neurosis.

> . . . we may perhaps be forced to become reconciled to the idea that it is quite impossible to adjust the claims of the sexual instinct to the demands of civilization; that in consequence of its cultural development renunciation and suffering, as well as the danger of extinction in the remotest future, cannot be avoided by the human race. This gloomy prognosis rests, it is true, on the single conjecture that the non-satisfaction that goes with civilization is the necessary consequence of certain peculiarities which the sexual instinct has assumed under the pressure of culture. The very incapacity of the sexual instinct to yield complete satisfaction as soon as it submits to the first demands of civilization becomes the source, however, of the noblest cultural achievements which are brought into being by ever more extensive sublimation of its instinctual components. . . . It seems . . . that the irreconcilable difference between the demands of the two instincts—the sexual and the egoistic—has made men capable of ever higher achievements, though subject, it is true, to a constant danger, to which, in the form of neurosis, the weaker are succumbing today.[60]

The "discontents" of civilization are with us, unavoidably, late and soon. No Frommesque "art of loving," no calisthenic healthy-mindedness, no liberal-utilitarian technology, no Marxist revolution will ever conceivably bring peace on earth, good will toward men. The reason is blunt and basic: We humans carry within us the seeds of our own destruction, and we nourish them continuously. We must hate as well as love. We will to destroy ourselves and our fellow men, as well as to create and protect them.

> . . . when the mental counter-forces which ordinarily inhibit (our aggressiveness) are out of action, it also manifests itself spontaneously and reveals man as a savage beast to whom consideration towards his own kind is something alien. Anyone who calls to mind the atrocities committed during the racial migrations or the invasions of the Huns, or by the people known as Mongols under Jenghiz Khan and Tamerlane, or at the capture of Jerusalem by the pious Crusaders, or even, indeed, the horrors of the recent World War [of 1914-18]—anyone who calls these things to mind will have to bow humbly before the truth of this view.
>
> The existence of this inclination to aggression, which we can detect in ourselves and justly assume to be present in others, is the factor which disturbs our relations with our neighbour and which forces civilization into such a high expenditure [of energy]. In consequence of this primary mutual hostility of human beings, civilized society is perpetually threatened with disintegration. The interest of work in common would not hold it together; instinctual passions are stronger than reasonable interests.[61]

Deriving the obscure death instinct from sadistic tendencies, Freud relates hate to love once again:

> It is in sadism, where the death instinct twists the erotic aim in its own sense and yet at the same time fully satisfies the erotic urge, that we succeed in obtaining the clearest insight into its nature and its relation to Eros. But even where it emerges without any sexual purpose, in the blindest fury of destructiveness, we cannot fail to recognize that the satisfaction of the instinct is accompanied by an extraordinarily high degree of narcissistic enjoyment, owing to its presenting the ego with a fulfilment of the latter's old wishes for omnipotence.[62]

This embarrassing, much-debated, speculative hypothesis of "hate-instincts" and "death-wishes" is not susceptible of any A-B-C proof. Freud freely admitted this.[63] He believed it consistent with his profoundest researches into the human mind, as well as with every candid observation of collective human behavior. I do not pretend to decide the issue here, but only remind the reader that Freud was not a sentimental, muddled fool during the final twenty years of his long and painful life, but a still vigorous, creative intelligence, and that he—almost alone—seriously, repeatedly defended this view. Had he lived only six more years, Freud would have found cold, ugly, barren confirmation in the confirming holocausts of Dachau and Hiroshima.

FREUDIAN LOVE AND RELIGIOUS LOVE

Culturally, Freud was a Jew. Religiously, he was an atheistic hermit. Philosophically, he was a scientific materialist of the nineteenth century, in some respects curiously naïve. The fascination religion held for him moved Freud to some of his most acute analyses, as well as to some of his least persuasive dichotomies.

Totem and Tabu, Moses and Monotheism, and *The Future of an Illusion* are the principal works in which Freud entertained and criticized traditional Hebrew-Christian beliefs. It is surprising to find a mind so subtle as his, so flexible and sensible-sensitive and ingenious, appearing almost clumsy in its consideration of certain religious claims.

It is refreshing, too, for Freud is nothing if not forthright. By comparison with their master, his epigonoi occasionally appear to be panders for shopworn gods.

Considered as a set of truth claims, our entire religious tradition (and every other one as well) is to Freud an illusion, founded upon flimsy ragtags of evidence, hand-me-downs from ancient men even more ignorant than we are, and upon psychologically suspicious peremptory refusals to offer any evidence at all. Compared with the patient, modest claims of scientific worshippers of *Logos* (so Freud suggests) religious claims are too ridiculous to credit. Yet they purport to answer the most profoundly important questions of all. Science, in claiming only tentatively to answer less profound questions, stands on solid ground, and alone deserves our credence.[64] There cannot be any real competition between religion and science, because religion is illusory and science is true. It is as simple as that.

So it seemed to Freud, if we ask only the easy question, "What ought we to believe?" We ought to confess our ignorance on the issues science cannot answer, and live humbly as best we can without illusions. But there are more interesting questions to ask. For example, "How can we explain the universality of religious illusions? Why should men have lived and died for illusions?"

Freud's full answers to these questions would take us unnecessarily deep into his speculative anthropology, and if we are to see something of the role of Freudian love in religion, we need only a general characterization. The resolution lies, of course, in the childhoods of men and of tribes.

That child who emulates and loves his earthly father, even as he is

jealous of and hates him, endows him worshipfully with all virtues—
with many more virtues, indeed, than any mortal could lightly bear. The
child nurtures his own "ego-ideal" in his father's image. Failing, as he
matures, to find in his own father the perfection he must (to preserve
his own identity) posit as "objective," man makes God in his father's
image. Our religious *Weltanschauung*, says Freud, is thus determined by
the situation that subsisted in our childhood.[65]

To what degree we must credit as historical Freud's gruesome pictures
of cannibalistic brethren is of no crucial account; the psychic residuum
is plain. Religion came into being and survives only as it fills a deep
mental need for an ideal, unchanging focus for human love. Religion
is thus an attempt to get control over the sensory world by means of the
wish-world [66] and in this way may protect men against neurosis.

> The protection against neurotic illness, which religion vouchsafes to
> those who believe in it, is easily explained: it removes their parental com-
> plex, on which the sense of guilt in individuals as well as in the whole
> human race depends, and disposes of it, while the unbeliever has to
> grapple with the problem on his own.[67]

Freud's interpretation is thus not a philosophy, but a natural history
of religion. Religious dogmas and dedications, though fictive-illusory,
are not condemned by Freud, and cast out like devils. They do serve
critically important functions in many personality-structures. They supply frameworks within which dissolving identities can sometimes be pre-
cipitated once again, and brought toward coherence. In this sense, even
Freudian psychoanalysis is not anti-religious. With a broad hint of Vien-
nese irony, Freud says:

> In itself psychoanalysis is neither religious nor the opposite, but an im-
> partial instrument which can serve the clergy as well as the laity when it
> is used only to free suffering people. I have been very struck at realizing
> how I had never thought of the extraordinary help the psychoanalytic
> method can be in pastoral work, probably because wicked heretics like
> us are so far away from that circle.[68]

Our religious tradition posits as inherently valuable an ultimate love-
object, God, and denies the possibility, even in principle, of reducing
that object to finite, mortal dimensions. Far from explaining the infinite
in terms of the finite (as Freud must do), the Christian will typically find
in the infinite the only meaning the finite world could have.

The telic character of Hebrew-Christian love betrays to Freud its
"unscientific" (and therefore merely psychological-palliative) character.
Religious love is directed toward God. But, in Freudian terms, all "directions-toward" manifest psychic states. Directions-toward invisible, un-
realizable ideals are, at best, neurotic defenses.

But God, in our tradition, is not alone the ultimate goal of love; he is also love's ultimate source. And here also the Freudian explanation fundamentally diverges. For it is psychoanalytically no less absurd to cite a supernatural source for love than to cite a supernatural goal. Love's wellsprings, psychoanalytically, remain wholly natural: they are the instinctual energies we biologically evolved men are born with, nothing more and nothing less. Rieff's pungent summary is well justified:

> . . . there is scant justification for Freud's having invoked for his conception of love the most ancient and respectable lineage. To declare amiably that when the apostle Paul . . . praises love above all else, he certainly understands it in the same "wider" sense as the psychoanalyst, does not help reconcile the Freudian meaning to the Pauline. In the relevant Pauline text, I Corinthians 13, love (translated in the King James version as "charity") has an authoritative, compelling quality which is in Freud's conception as well. But the Christian compulsion of love is different in both origin and effect. *Agape* is a sentiment that limits the self to a respectful relation with the not-self; it projects a spontaneous and unmotivated regard for others which excludes the Freudian connection of love and the aggrandizement of the self. In the Christian sense, too, love is authoritarian; but the two senses of authority differ. Freud traced love back to the parental fact of domination. Power is the father of love, and in love one follows the paternal example of power, in a relation that must include a superior and a subordinate. Christian theology refers love forward, to the ever-present example of Jesus, who, in a series of unique demonstrations, taught the figure of divine love. Jesus revealed the authority of love. Examining ostensibly the same emotion, Freud discovered the love of authority.[69]

Sometimes religious-neurotic defenses grow out of an illegitimate extension of genital delight. They take the form of a vaguely universalized, non-specific love. In loving God, we are supposed somehow to love everything in general and therefore nothing in particular. Freud cites St. Francis of Assisi as his model.

> A small minority are enabled by their constitution to find happiness, in spite of everything, along the path of love. But far-reaching mental changes in the function of love are necessary before this can happen. These people make themselves independent of their object's acquiescence by displacing what they mainly value from being loved on to loving; they protect themselves against the loss of the object by directing their love, not to single objects but to all men alike; and they avoid the uncertainties and disappointments of genital love by turning away from its sexual aims and transforming the instinct into an impulse with an *inhibited aim*. What they bring about in themselves in this way is a state of evenly suspended, steadfast affectionate feeling, which has little external resemblance any more to the stormy agitations of genital love, from which it is nevertheless

derived. Perhaps St. Francis of Assisi went furthest in thus exploiting love for the benefit of an inner feeling of happiness . . . according to one ethical view . . . this readiness for a universal love of mankind and the world represents the highest standpoint which man can reach. Even at this early stage of the discussion I should like to bring forward my two main objections to this view. A love that does not discriminate seems to me to forfeit a part of its own value, by doing an injustice to its object; and secondly, not all men are worthy of love.[70]

An even bitterer attack is directed at the late-Jewish, Stoic, and typically Christian injunction "Thou shalt love thy neighbor as thyself." Freud's cutting, sobering, anti-Schweitzerian analysis of this moral homily deserves extended citation:

Let us adopt a naïve attitude towards it, as though we were hearing it for the first time; we shall be unable then to suppress a feeling of surprise and bewilderment. Why should we do it? What good will it do us? But, above all, how shall we achieve it? How can it be possible? My love is something valuable to me which I ought not to throw away without reflection. It imposes duties on me for whose fulfilment I must be ready to make sacrifices. If I love someone, he must deserve it in some way. (I leave out of account the use he may be to me, and also his possible significance for me as a sexual object, for neither of these two kinds of relationship comes into question where the precept to love my neighbour is concerned.) He deserves it if he is so like me in important ways that I can love myself in him; and he deserves it if he is so much more perfect than myself that I can love my ideal of my own self in him. Again, I have to love him if he is my friend's son, since the pain my friend would feel if any harm came to him would be my pain too—I should have to share it. But if he is a stranger to me and if he cannot attract me by any worth of his own or any significance that he may already have acquired for my emotional life, it will be hard for me to love him. Indeed, I should be wrong to do so, for my love is valued by all my own people as a sign of my preferring them, and it is an injustice to them if I put a stranger on a par with them. But if I am to love him (with this universal love) merely because he, too, is an inhabitant of this earth, like an insect, an earthworm or a grass-snake, then I fear that only a small modicum of my love will fall to his share—not by any possibility as much as, by the judgement of my reason, I am entitled to retain for myself. What is the point of a precept enunciated with so much solemnity if its fulfilment cannot be recommended as reasonable?

On closer inspection, I find still further difficulties. Not merely is this stranger in general unworthy of my love; I must honestly confess that he has more claim to my hostility and even my hatred. He seems not to have the least trace of love for me and shows me not the slightest consideration. If it will do him any good he has no hesitation in injuring me, nor does he ask himself whether the amount of advantage he gains bears any proportion to the extent of the harm he does to me. Indeed, he need not even obtain an advantage; if he can satisfy any sort of desire by it, he thinks nothing of jeering at me, insulting me, slandering me and showing his superior power; and the more secure he feels and the more helpless I am, the more certainly I can expect him to behave like this to me. If he behaves differently, if he shows me consideration and forbearance as a stranger, I am ready to treat him in the same way, in any case and quite apart from any precept. Indeed, if this grandiose commandment had run "Love thy neighbour as thy neighbour loves thee," I should not take exception to it. And there is a second commandment, which seems to me even more incomprehensible and arouses still stronger opposition in me. It is "Love thine enemies." If I think it over, however, I see that I am wrong in treating it as a greater imposition. At bottom it is the same thing.[71]

It is evident that a Christian should and presumably would be grateful to Freud for psychoanalytic therapy; there can be nothing anti-Christian or anti-Jewish in attempts to help people to live decent lives. Freud and many of his followers, for all their weaknesses, were dedicated men, genuinely loving many of their fellow human beings. The theory of psychoanalysis, in distinction from the therapy, possesses only one central insight, from a Christian point of view, but that one insight is the most profound one of all. In psychoanalysis, as in Judaism and in Christianity, love is absolutely central in the human personality, the one category without which no meaning is possible.

The Jewish-Christian regret would of course be that Freud, granted insight by God, and granted a great mind, so totally misdirected it, by painting an impossibly inadequate cartoon of religious meaning, and of the entire higher side of man's nature. No one in our religious tradition need (so I have earlier argued) deny the pervasiveness of human sexual needs, or the diversity of their expressions. No one need question the desirability of enlightened social reforms. But (so the religious man would protest) to stop short here, as Freud does, and to trace our love needs back only to our instinctual natures, is to misrepresent them, just as they are misrepresented when their genuinely cosmic goals are shriveled to the status of psychological "projections."

Freud's estimate of the devout Jew or Christian would surely be both genial and undeceived. He would and did respectfully admire the fertility of man's myth-building imagination. He loved poetry, and well knew that religion has inspired many of the most beautiful poems ever written. And he found a therapeutic place for religious sublimation as a necessary neurotic defense. But Freud the serious scientist would boldly have given the lie to every supernatural truth claim. Judaism and Christianity, he would have said, are (as descriptions of the way the world is) obviously unscientific and therefore beyond consideration. There is no substantial evidence to indicate that any important supernatural-religious claim contains any truth at all. We ought therefore (Freud would have concluded) to enjoy our religious illusions without surrendering to them, for we must live and die in the real world.

I conclude that attempts to reconcile Freudian psychoanalysis with Judaism and/or Christianity, however fashionable, heroic, and earnest, are misguided and invariably represent a failure of nerve. The Jew and the Christian betray their historic genius by naturalizing Jehovah into a surrogate father-image. The analyst betrays his if he admits supernatural hypotheses as candidates for true-false belief.

The underlying muddle is categorical. The sense in which a devout Jew or Christian claims his religious faith to be true cannot be the same in which an analyst claims his psychological hypotheses to be true, unless the two positions are confessed to be candidly competitive, and at least one is forthrightly denied. Logically, they are contraries: both may be false, but both cannot be true in the same sense of the word.

Of course, Freud has taught us to beware of seductively logical models for the human mind. But Freud was no more a mystic than he was a sentimentalist. Even his generosity would have been strained had he lived to find psychoanalysis put to the service of pastoral counseling not to salvage sick minds but to steer them along the path to God. Jewish-Christian loves have some characters in common with Freudian love, but the hearts of the world-views are and will remain universes apart.

FREUDIAN LOVE AND PLATONIC LOVE

As he sought, without justification, to invoke St. Paul and the Christian tradition in support of his interpretation of love, so Freud also sought, and equally without justification, to invoke the still older authority of Plato. His error here is at least equally egregious.

Let the parallels first be set forth. Both Freudian and Platonic loves are rich, broad, and deep. Within the meaning of "Eros," in both, are encompassed genital-sexual love, fraternal and civic love, the loves of science and art and perfection. Dualities and triads can be compared: Freud's id-ego-superego can, for example, be forced into some kind of parallel with the tripartite self and state in *Republic,* the civilians corresponding to the id, the auxiliary-protectors to the ego, and the guardians to the superego; or again, the irrational horse in the *Phaedo*'s chariot-myth may be compared with the id, the modest horse with the ego, and the driver with the superego (or should the latter two be reversed? No matter, as we shall see).

Socrates followed Athens' ancient tradition in proclaiming that we should "know ourselves," and who could today find a clearer epitome for psychoanalysis? It is even fair to say that Plato was the first to recognize infantile sexuality, and to hint broadly at unconscious mental processes. Surely Plato would have welcomed the Freudian claim of the pervasiveness of human love, of its universal motivating power, and, in consequence, of the internal dynamic analogy between lower loves and higher ones.

Attracted by such superficial parallels as these, Freud's disciples enthusiastically published articles on them, which were proudly read by Freud, and enthusiastically and uncritically entered into the corpus of future writings.[72]

The truth is that Freudian love is very nearly the obverse of Platonic love. In their metaphysical bases, and in their dynamic directions, they not merely differ, but in effect contradict one another. So far are the two interpretations from being (as Freud thought) coincident, that neither could be true if the other were even meaningful.

The basic loving difference is evident: Plato's love is wholly telic, goal-directed. In his world, the merely natural makes sense only as it yearns and moves toward the more-than-nature, the ideals themselves. Loves that stop short of perfection, as all earthly loves do, are good only as they exemplify something of the beyond. Somatic-sexual gratification, even when condoned and not condemned, is but a way station along the high road to truth. He who stops here is but a beast, a less-than-man; in Freudian jargon, he has "fixated" at a preliminary stage of development, and even if he later passes beyond, he may possibly "regress."

Freudian love, on the contrary, moves out from a chaotic, undifferentiated, instinctive energy-source along predictable and prescribable paths toward mature life and only partially, painfully civilized love. Every love that a Platonist would call "beyond" adult, fully somatic sexuality Freud would describe as "aim-inhibited." The love of knowledge, the love of beauty in art, the love of God: all these are "sublimated" redirections of nether urges incapable of finding any more direct gratification . . . just as, in turn, sexual intercourse would be, for a Platonist, an inverse kind of "sublimation."

> I suspect that, had Plato lived today, he would have been profoundly interested in the new depth-psychology, but appalled by the tendency to reduce the human reason to an instrument for rationalising unconscious impulses.

. . . says E. R. Dodds.[73]

> . . . the psychoanalytic Eros is basically unlike the Platonic. Indeed Freud's idea of sexuality serves as a critique of the Platonic idea, in which the emotion takes on the merit of its object, so that "higher" love (i.e.,

love for "higher" objects) is, according to the *Symposium*, more valuable than the "lower." In Freud's view, however generously he invested Eros with meaning, there remains a bankruptcy clause; his doctrine amounts to an unremitting chastisement of the "sacred" on behalf of the "profane (or animal) love." Thus his earliest, dualistic construction of Eros was concerned to sift what is genuinely sexual from the sublimated versions of it, those in which culture tames sexual energy and diverts it to its own purposes. Of course sexuality can be attached to the most noble objects. But these are the guises of Caliban, molded into a thousand acceptable shapes by a succession of Prosperos. Unfortunately Caliban remains Caliban—underneath; in Freud's conception, sexuality remains bound by its original instinctual character.[74]

As Plato brings animal life and love up toward human levels in the pursuit of perfection, so Freud reverses the interpretation:

> The present development of human beings requires, as it seems to me, no different explanation from that of animals. What appears in a minority of human individuals as an untiring impulsion towards further perfection can easily be understood as a result of the instinctual repression upon which is based all that is most precious in human civilization.[75]

One could dream of some easy decision-pattern in terms of which we might decide the "issue" between Plato and Freud, some "experimental design" which, if carefully enacted, might crucially reveal whether our loves are to be explained Platonically in terms of goals or psychoanalytically in terms of sources, and whether, in consequence, "meanings" are to be construed prospectively or retrospectively.

There is no such test. There never will be any such test. The "issue" between Plato and Freud is not scientific at all, and scientific tests apply only to scientific issues.

The issue is philosophical. Philosophical issues, to be sure, are not scientific ones; their challenge may be more puzzling or less, their range of difficulty more or less extreme. But they have, as scientific issues have not, the peculiar character of being in principle unavoidable. One can, without making up his mind on any chemical or physical problem (and thus begging the question), judge that chemistry and physics are unworthy of one's attention; however foolish such a decision might be, it contains no internal inconsistency. A perplexing character of philosophical questions is that they cannot be rejected except from the vantage point of some philosophical position.

Whether consciously or not, philosophical decisions are made. Most of them, alas, are made all too automatically, out of personal and cultural roots that run so deep we remain for the most part unaware even that we are committing ourselves at all, let alone what we are committing ourselves to, and why.

The absence of a formulable "decision-procedure" is sometimes taken as evidence that no decision can significantly be preferred over any other —that all are equally subjective. To suppose this is to pretend, on utterly inadequate evidence, that formulability defines the significance of decision-procedures. I submit that this is preposterous. Every day we decide issues, including all our most important personal and social issues, without being able to formulate the procedures that guide us in arriving at our decisions. And we effectively distinguish relatively wise, well-founded decisions from relatively foolish, ill-grounded ones; even though, if challenged, we should be embarrassed to produce the grounds of our distinction.

Deciding such a fundamental philosophical issue as that between Plato and Freud is of this sort; we must first try sympathetically to identify with each plausible manner of construing experience. We must imaginatively test alternative explanations, extending explanatory patterns more and more broadly as we go. We must ask ourselves some questions of a peculiarly complex and unclear sort: "What if I knew very much more than I do know? What if I knew my every motivation and everybody else's as well, every antecedent and consequent of every act ever performed or even contemplated, and could totally transcend the battlefield on which outrageous fortune casts its slings and arrows? Would the world then look to me Platonic or Freudian? Or neither? How *would* the world make sense?"

"In each way," one might try to reply, "but each in its own time and terms." Doesn't it depend on what kind of sense one wants to make? We do sometimes need to help men to discover or construct sense in their shattered lives; an antecedent-causal psychology may help us to do so. We also sometimes want and need to place modes and models of behavior in value-ordered sequence; a frankly moral metaphysic may fit our need. *Must* our "yeas" and "nays" forever be either all-inclusive or all-exclusive?

A Concluding Estimate

What, then, shall we say of Freudian psychoanalysis in the end? Is it true or is it false? The answer to this question is that it cannot even be asked.

Of only the simplest scientific claims can one directly ask, "Is this true or false?" Of theories complex enough to be interesting and important, confirmations and disconfirmations may be exceedingly indirect, and may take years of work even to plan.

Surely Freudian psychoanalysis is not a simple scientific claim; it is rather a labyrinth of mutually implicative insights. No single direct confirmation can ever be hoped for. Extended, and occasionally almost desperate, attempts have been made to reduce Freudianism to systematic clarity, and to determine the validity of psychoanalytic claims. Small wonder that Freud's teachings have been resistant to such testing, and that post-Freudian analysts have felt that the precious core of Freud is untouched by allegedly "disconfirmatory" evidence.

The nearest analogue is with the "pragmatic prayer" pattern: William James seriously proposed, following another pragmatist, that we test the efficacy of prayer by arranging a sensibly controlled experiment, so many people praying for a certain boon, so many others not praying for it. *Prima facie,* this makes perfectly good sense: How else—pragmatically— could one determine whether prayer is really efficacious?

But *secunda facie,* James's proposal is preposterous. Why? Precisely because prayer is not so simply a get-things-done enterprise. A religious man ought not to bank his faith on any simple matter of true-or-false historical fact, to be confirmed today or disconfirmed tomorrow. His orientation is rather "get-meaning-from" than "test-truth-of." And when we are in a "get-meaning-from" frame of mind we properly concern ourselves less with "But is it (merely) true?" than with "How do these meanings help me to feel at home in the world, and to make sense out of it?"

Freudianism is like our Biblical orientation, in that its scope precludes the possibility of precision. Its message makes meaning rather than mere truth. In consequence, it cannot simply be true—nor can it simply be false, either. Or, to put it another way about, Freudianism as a whole (like Christianity as a whole) is—if "true" at all—so universally true and defensible that it cannot be considered a theory.

It might be supposed that a system of ideas true under any possible empirical circumstances would have an advantage over one that could be disproved, depending upon the situation. Ought we not, if we can, invest our faith in a bank whose credit, no matter what the demands upon it, cannot be overdrawn?

We might invest our "faith," perhaps, whatever exactly that means, but we most certainly ought not thus to invest our scientific trust. The only bank of which we could know in advance that it could meet *any* financial emergency would be a bank that printed its own money—that is, a play bank, unworthy of competing with any real repository of scientifically funded beliefs.

So it is with Freudianism. No one can prove it false, because however the facts turn out in a given case, there is always a Freudian explanation. If Brown sends his mother a present on her birthday, he is concealing his Oedipally grounded passion; but if he forgets to send her even a birthday card, he is revealing an Oedipally grounded aggression toward his mother. He's analyzed if he does, and analyzed if he doesn't. No possible behavior could convince the Freudian that Freudian categories were inappropriate or irrelevant, or that Freudian claims are in any way dubitable; "It is merely," the devout can always reply, "that you have adduced the wrong categories, or adduced the correct categories only to misapply them, or that you have neglected the context."

Yet we do not congratulate ourselves that we have at last come upon the psychic panacea. We recognize that for a theory to be totally free from the possibility of falsehood, far from making it pristine and perfect, rather removes it from the world of descriptive fact. And we interpret the implausibility of some Freudian interpretations not as evidence of their falsity (which, in principle, could no more be demonstrated than their truth), but rather as indicating the need, in the particular case, for even more ingenuity.

A dream analysis by Freud himself, or by another of the early acknowledged masters, may itself become a subject for discussion or even debate. But the outcome of the discussion ought never naïvely to be "He's right" or "He's wrong," any more than we use these phrases to describe a brilliant cadenza by Casadesus. Truth and falsity do not enter the picture in quite the same way as they do in more traditional sciences, and the analyses are none the worse for that; the real issue, one might plausibly propose, is whether the analyst, like the pianist, has performed beautifully, given his materials. Has he skillfully exploited every subtle hint in the manifest content, adverted just persuasively enough to the dreamer's immediate symbol-sources, creatively displayed the crucial cathetic displacement, dramatically exposed layer after layer of verbal and imagic condensation, climactically recapitulated the patient's early childhood, and brought off with brio the repression-releasing coda? [76]

Professor Freud himself would of course have been mortified to meet an esthetic reading of his dream interpretations, and so are his devout descendants. "We are dealing with human suffering; we are healing desperately ill patients. How dare you entertain esthetic criteria as if they were even relevant?" My reply is direct: Casadesus is no less serious when he plays the piano. His creative intelligence is as fully engaged as is Freud's. And, as Freud well knew, art is of profoundly human—and even therapeutic—importance to mankind.

The present analogy is not therefore to be taken as in any degree condemnatory. My suggestion is that Freud truly enriched science with art —as too few psychologists have had the taste and genius to dare.

NOTES ON FREUDIAN LOVE

The standard edition of Freud is now *The Standard Edition of the Complete Psychological Works of Sigmund Freud,* in 24 volumes, not all of which have yet been published. The general editor is James Strachey, in collaboration with Anna Freud and assisted by Alix Strachey and Alan Tyson. The Standard Edition is published in London by the Hogarth Press and the Institute of Psycho-Analysis, 1957 *et seq.* In the references below I give in brief the name of the Freudian text cited, "*SE*" for "Standard Edition," the volume number in arabic, and the page or pages. Thus " 'Five Lectures,' 11:39" means "See 'Five Lectures on Psycho-Analysis,' Standard Edition, Volume XI, page 39." Those Freudian works not yet included in the Standard Edition I have cited in full, except for the *New Introductory Lectures on Psycho-Analysis*, translated by W. J. H. Sproth (New York: W. H. Norton & Co., 1933). Ernest Jones's masterful biography, *The Life and Work of Sigmund Freud* (New York: Basic Books, 1957) is already everyone's Freudian vademecum. I refer to it simply as "Jones, 2:335," meaning "See Volume II of Jones's biography, p. 335."

[1] Freud was a classically educated humanist, sophisticated, subtle, and far more literate than his contemporary critics. He usually spoke of philosophy with respect, except that he did consider it "merely intellectual"! Freud sometimes wistfully regretted that he could not free his thought (as he thought philosophers could do) from "scientific responsibility to the facts." The fullest Freudian discussion of psychoanalytic "philosophy" is his denial that there is any such thing. He claimed that psychoanalysis neither presupposes nor implies any *Weltanschauung*. See the last of the *New Introductory Lectures*.

[2] As a compound instance of Freud's conceptual fecundity, consider this: We know that children like to look at the naked bodies of other people, especially of members of the opposite sex. This is, in usual Freudian language, evidence of the "scopophilic instinct." But in one, and so far as I can discover, only one, place Freud actually invents a concept to cover what he usually calls "infantile sexual curiosity," or the desire to know about sexual matters. This desire he christens (in the Rat-Man Case, *SE* 10:245) "the epistemophilic instinct!"

[3] Yet, curiously, Freud felt compelled to talk in telic terms again and again. In *Three Essays, SE,* 7:184 n.2, he says:

> In biological discussions it is scarcely possible to avoid a teleological way of thinking, even though one is aware that in any particular instance one is not secure against error.

In an earlier discussion Freud had apologetically interpolated, "if such a teleological form of statement is permissible . . ." (*Ibid.,* p. 156). From time to time Freud would be chastised by his colleagues for such "lapses."

[4] Schopenhauer's explicit recognition of the basic, widespread power of sexuality was of course gladly acknowledged by Freud:

> There are famous philosophers who may be cited as forerunners—above all the great thinker Schopenhauer, whose unconscious "Will" is equivalent to the mental instincts of psycho-analysis. It was this same thinker, moreover, who in words of unforgettable impressiveness admonished mankind of the importance, still so greatly under-estimated by it, of its sexual craving. Psycho-analysis has this advantage only, that it has not affirmed these two propositions which are so distressing to narcissism—the psychical importance of sexuality and the un-consciousness of mental life—on an *abstract* basis, but has demonstrated them in matters that touch every individual personally and force him to take up some attitude towards these problems. ("A Difficulty in Psychoanalysis," *SE,* 17:143-44.) See also the numerous references cited by the editor at *SE,* 19:223-24.

[5] *On Dreams, SE,* 5:654-55. Compare: ". . . the dream has above all to evade the censorship, and with that end in view the dream-work makes use of a *displacement*

of psychical intensities to the point of a transvaluation of all psychical values." (*The Interpretation of Dreams*, SE, 5:507.) Freud was interested also in Nietzsche's discussions of dreams. Consider: "We can guess how much to the point is Nietzsche's assertion that in dreams 'some primaeval relic of humanity is at work which we can now scarcely reach any longer by a direct path.'" *Ibid.*, SE, 5:548-49. See also SE, 4:330. (Vol. V is copyright 1952 by W. W. Norton & Co., Inc.)

[6] *Psychopathology of Everyday Life*, SE, 6:253-54. See also SE, 17:236, and the third and fifth *Introductory Lectures*.

[7] Freud's own admirable discussion of this methodological problem is to be found in "Instincts and their Vicissitudes," SE, 14:117-40. He there says of instincts that they are stimuli arising within the organism, and that no flight can avail against them. "Instinctual stimuli," he says at SE, 14:120-22, "oblige the nervous system to renounce its ideal intention of keeping off stimuli, for they maintain an incessant and unavoidable afflux of stimulation. We may therefore well conclude that instincts and not external stimuli are the true motive forces that have led the nervous system, with its unlimited capacities, to its present high level of development. There is naturally nothing to prevent our supposing that the instincts themselves are, at least in part, precipitates of the effects of external stimulation, which in the course of phylogenesis have brought about modifications in the living substance. . . . If we now apply ourselves to considering mental life from a *biological* point of view, an 'instinct' appears to us as a concept on the frontier between the mental and the somatic, as the psychical representative of the stimuli originating from within the organism and reaching the mind, as a measure of the demand made upon the mind for work in consequence of its connection with the body." See also *New Introductory Lectures*, 132-133.

[8] "On Narcissism," SE, 14:77.

[9] "Instincts and their Vicissitudes," SE, 14:117.

[10] *Group Psychology and the Analysis of the Ego*, SE, 18:90-91.

[11] In a letter to Oskar Pfister, February 9, 1909. See Jones, 2:440.

[12] "Wild Psycho-Analysis," SE, 11:223.

[13] Classically, but by no means exclusively, in the second of the *Three Essays*, SE, 7:173-206.

[14] *Group Psychology and the Analysis of the Ego*, SE, 18:91.

[15] Jones, 2:283.

[16] "The Resistances to Psycho-Analysis," SE, 19:218.

[17] Strictly, our conception of the baby as a sexual being here depends upon ("leans against") our conception of him as a self-preserving organism. The best discussion will be found in *Three Essays*, SE, 7:222.

[18] "A Difficulty in the Path of Psycho-Analysis," SE, 17:139.

[19] *The Ego and the Id*, SE, 19:46. The editor, in Appendix B, 19:63-66, cites several apparently contradictory passages, and plausibly proposes that the "reservoir" is best described as a primal, pre-differentiated ego-id. (Vol. XIX is copyright © 1960 by James Strachey.)

[20] "On Narcissism," SE, 14:76. Note that Freud expressly rejects (p. 79) the notion that ego-libido and object-libido can be derived from any more primitive Urlibido.

[21] "On Narcissism," SE, 14:82-3.

[22] *Ibid.*, p. 85. See also "Instincts and their Vicissitudes," SE, 14:117-140.

[23] "On Narcissism," SE, 14:90.

[24] *Ibid.*, p. 91. "Sexual overestimation" is the usual jargon.

[25] *SE*'s editor points out that "conscience" and "ego-ideal" will in Freud's later thought be combined into "super-ego." See *ibid.*, p. 95, n.2.

[26] *Ibid.*, pp. 98-100.

[27] *Ibid.*, pp. 100-101.

[28] Jones, 2:320, 422. See, in instance, *SE*, 14:124, 132-3, and especially Jones, 3:266-7.

[29] "On the Universal Tendency to Debasement in the Sphere of Love," *SE*, 11:180-1.

[30] *Group Psychology and the Analysis of the Ego, SE,* 18:111-112.

[31] It will here be especially evident to any student of Freud's work that there is no single "Freudian" pattern of analysis. Sometimes "sexual" or "sexual-libidinal" instincts are distinguished from others; sometimes all instinctive cathexis is interpreted in terms of tension-reduction; sometimes organ-pleasure is posited as an instinctive goal; sometimes "self-preservation" becomes almost exclusive; at last love-life-creation and hate-death-destruction are assigned primal functions. See the editor's introduction to "Instincts and their Vicissitudes," *SE*, 14:113-16.

[32] "Instincts and their Vicissitudes," *SE*, 14:134.

[33] *Ibid.*, p. 133.

[34] *Ibid.*, p. 137.

[35] *Ibid.*, pp. 138-39.

[36] The entire vexed question is considered in the editor's introduction to "Instincts and their Vicissitudes," *SE*, 14:111-116, esp. 115-116, with references to relevant passages in other Freudian texts.

[37] *The Ego and the Id, SE,* 19:46.

[38] *Ibid.*, p. 47.

[39] Jones, 2:319. See also Freud's "Rat-man" analysis, *SE*, 10:238 ff.

[40] "Instincts and their Vicissitudes," *SE*, 14:138.

[41] Jones, 3:275, citing esp. *SE*, 7:134. See also Jones 3:283.

[42] Jones (at 3:276-7) sharply criticizes Freud's introduction of the "death-instinct" concept, arguing that it has neither a physical nor a biological basis, and claiming that those few post-Freudian analysts who today speak of "death-instincts" do so only clinically.

[43] March 17, 1910. See Jones, 2:448.

[44] In a letter to Oskar Pfister, October 9, 1918. See Jones, 2:457.

[45] *The Ego and the Id, SE,* 19:30.

[46] On these admittedly dubious distinctions, see especially *The Ego and the Id, SE,* 19:13-66; "The Dissolution of the Oedipus Complex," *SE*, 19:173-79; and "Some Psychical Consequences of the Anatomical Distinction Between the Sexes," *SE*, 19:248-58.

[47] I have argued this case in "Is Justification Scientifically Impossible?" *Ethics* LXIX, 1958, 19-47. See especially pp. 24-31.

[48] See Heinz Hartmann, *Psychoanalysis and Moral Values* (New York: International Universities Press, Inc., 1960), pp. 64-75.

[49] "The Future Prospects of Psychoanalysis," *SE*, 11:150.

[50] Philip Rieff, *Freud the Mind of the Moralist* (New York: The Viking Press, 1959), pp. 55-6.

[51] *Op. cit.*, Chapter IX, especially pp. 315-328.

[52] *Ibid.*, pp. 322-3.

[53] "On the Universal Tendency to Debasement in the Sphere of Love," *SE*, 11:187-8.

[54] *Civilization and Its Discontents*, *SE*, 21:66. (Vol. XXI is copyright © 1961 by James Strachey.)

[55] *Ibid.*, 21:101.

[56] *Ibid.*, 21:102-3.

[57] Rieff, p. 234.

[58] For example, *Civilization and Its Discontents*, *SE*, 21:95-6.

[59] "The Disillusionment of the War," *SE*, 14:282.

[60] "On the Universal Tendency to Debasement in the Sphere of Love," *SE*, 11:190.

[61] *Civilization and Its Discontents*, *SE*, 21:112.

[62] *Ibid.*, 21:121.

[63] *Op. cit.*, *SE*, 118-121.

[64] The most concise argument will be found in *The Future of an Illusion*, *SE*, 21, especially Chapter V, 25-29.

[65] In the last of the *New Introductory Lectures*.

[66] *Ibid.*

[67] *Leonardo da Vinci and a Memory of His Childhood*, *SE*, 11:123.

[68] In a letter to Oskar Pfister, February 9, 1909. See Jones, 2:440.

[69] Rieff, *op. cit.*, pp. 152-3. Rieff cites *SE*, 18:91, from *Group Psychology and the Analysis of the Ego*.

[70] *Civilization and Its Discontents*, *SE*, 21:101-2.

[71] *Ibid.*, 21:109-110.

[72] The psychoanalytic literature contains a genuinely remarkable confusion. Far from recognizing the really basic divergence between the interpretations of love presented by Plato and by Freud, Freudian disciples (and, later, even the master himself) have the astonishing audacity to claim Plato for their own. The first example is M. Nachmansohn ("Freud's Libidotheorie verglichen mit der Eroslehre Platos," *Internationale Zeitschrift für Psychoanalyse*, 1915, 3:65 ff.) who says that all the amplifications of the usual conception of the sexual instinct that Freud has made, much to the disgust of so many academicians, are to be found already in the works of the founder of the Academy. Oskar Pfister ("Plato: a Fore-Runner of Psycho-Analysis," *International Journal of Psycho-Analysis*, 1922, 3:169-74) iterates Nachmansohn's errors: "Of all the thinkers of the western world Plato was the first to observe our subject deeply and to describe it plainly. According to him, Eros, Love, is above all the instinct of sex or propagation" (169). Freud, in the 1920 Preface to the Fourth Edition of *Three Essays* (*SE*, 7:134) endorses Nachmansohn's view:

> ". . . anyone who looks down with contempt upon psycho-analysis from a superior vantage-point should remember how closely the enlarged sexuality of psycho-analysis coincides with the Eros of the divine Plato.

Or again,

> . . . what psycho-analysis called sexuality was by no means identical with the impulsion towards a union of the two sexes or towards producing a pleasurable sensation in the genitals; it had far more resemblance to the all-inclusive and all-preserving Eros of Plato's *Symposium*. ("The Resistances to Psycho-Analysis," *SE*, 19:218.)

Still again, in *Group Psychology and the Analysis of the Ego*, *SE*, 18:91, Freud says:

By coming to this decision, psycho-analysis has let loose a storm of indignation, as though it had been guilty of an act of outrageous innovation. Yet it has done nothing original in taking love in this "wider" sense. In its origin, function, and relation to sexual love, the *Eros* of the philosopher Plato coincides exactly with the love-force, the libido, of psycho-analysis, as has been shown in detail by Nachmansohn (1915) and Pfister (1921).

In his *Three Essays on Sexuality,* Freud commits still another remarkable error, betraying an almost uncanny misconception of Athenian love:

The most striking distinction between the erotic life of antiquity and our own no doubt lies in the fact that the ancients laid the stress upon the instinct itself whereas we emphasize its object. The ancients glorified the instinct and were prepared on its account to honour even an inferior object; while we despise the instinctual activity in itself, and find excuses for it only in the merits of the object. (*SE,* 7:149 n.1)

If by "ancients" here we are to read Plato, it is difficult to discredit Freud with so extraordinary a misreading. For Plato the dynamism of love derives all its value from its ultimate object; "inferior objects" were honored not because of love but rather because they revealed in a limited manner the ultimately and properly beloved object. And Freud appears here to be as mistaken about psychoanalysis as he is about Plato!

[73] E. R. Dodds, *The Greeks and the Irrational* (Berkeley and Los Angeles: The University of California Press, 1954), p. 218.

[74] Rieff, *op. cit.,* 153. There ensues (158-68) a good general discussion of Freudian love.

[75] Jones, 3:307, citing *SE,* 18.

[76] Cleanth Brooks (in *The Well Wrought Urn* [New York: A Harvest Book; Harcourt, Brace & World, Inc., 1947], p. 127) says, "Freud's brilliant accounts of dreams resemble science less than they do poems—Odes on the Intimations of all too human humanity from the unconscious recollections of early childhood."

And Thomas Mann (*Freud, Goethe, Wagner* [New York: Alfred A. Knopf, 1939], p. 17) calls Freud "an artist of thought, like Schopenhauer."

SOME OTHER  SPECTRUM BOOKS

A SPECTRUM BOOK

PHILOSOPHY

* Also available in limited clothbound edition.

RELIGION

PSYCHOTHERAPY

* Also available in limited clothbound edition.

TWENTIETH CENTURY VIEWS

Also available in limited clothbound edition.

Also available in limited clothbound edition.